BORN TO WANDER

AUTOBIOGRAPHY OF

John Ball

1794-1884

Compiled by His Daughters

Kate Ball Powers

Flora Ball Hopkins

Lucy Ball

Annotated and with a new introduction by Gary Burbridge
Index by Anne D. Slade

ISBN 0-9617708-4-8

Library of Congress Catalog Card Number: 94-077965

Designed and printed by **West Michigan Printing, Inc.**
840 Ottawa NW, Grand Rapids. Michigan 49503

Edited by **Editorial Consultants**
2215 Oak Industrial Drive NE, Grand Rapids, Michigan 49505

Bound by **John H. Dekker & Sons**
2941 Clydon SW, Grand Rapids, Michigan 49509

PREFACE

To read the words of John Ball is to learn about the life of an American pioneer whose quest for knowledge and zest for adventure have seldom been matched in American history. An explorer and an adventurer, John Ball was also an entrepreneur, a civic leader, and a devoted family man whose contributions to the growth and development of Grand Rapids and the state of Michigan deserve to be remembered along with his travels and adventures.

John Ball lived until his 90th year, and had begun writing his autobiography. The work was unfinished when he died, and his daughters, Kate, Flora and Lucy, gathered additional information from his letters, diaries, and other personal papers and published the book in 1925. Long out of print, this work, along with the John Ball papers in the Grand Rapids Public Library and the Clarke Historical Library at Central Michigan University, is an important reference source for those seeking to understand early Grand Rapids and the people who shaped its history.

The year 1994 marks the 200th anniversary of John Ball's birth. To commemorate the occasion, many of his descendants have planned to gather in Grand Rapids to honor his memory and celebrate his illustrious past. At the same time, the Grand Rapids Historical Commission has chosen to pay tribute to John Ball with this reprint of his autobiography, augmented by many new illustrations and by footnotes explaining obscure references in the text.

I would like to dedicate my effort in preparing this book to my wife, Mary Jo Pesano, and to my children, Geoffrey and Julia Burbridge.

I also wish to extend thanks to many others whose help and support have been essential: Gordon Olson, Grand Rapids City Historian, encouraged me throughout the project. Michael Hoffman of the Local History Collections Department at the Grand Rapids Public Library provided efficient reference service and found the illustrations needed to enhance this reprint. Chris Gray of the City Planning Department prepared the maps found throughout the text. Ellen Arlinsky of Editorial Consultants carefully edited the entire manuscript. At West Michigan Printing, Lynn Gort designed the reprint, Sharla Obetts shot each photograph to obtain the highest possible quality, and the printing crew did their usual good job. The same can be said of the staff at Dekker Bindery who completed the bookmaking process. A special thank-you goes to Anne Slade, who compiled the index, and to the members of the Grand Rapids Historical Commission, whose support and suggestions made this a better book.

Gary Burbridge
Grand Rapids Community College
June, 1994

TABLE OF CONTENTS

INTRODUCTION

BOOK THE FIRST
Early Life, 1794-1831

BOOK THE SECOND
Across the Plains to Oregon and the Return Home by Cape Horn, 1832-1835

INTRODUCTION

John Ball was a seasoned explorer by the time his search for Michigan timber lands led him to Grand Rapids in 1836. Born in Hebron, New Hampshire, on November 12, 1794, he graduated from Dartmouth College in 1820, spent the next two years studying law, and embarked on his first travel adventure in 1822. Booking passage on a schooner bound for Darien, Georgia, because "that was about as far south as I could sail on the Atlantic side of the United States...," he nearly lost his life when the ship foundered on a sandbar just short of its destination and was wrecked in a sudden storm.

In its early days, John Ball Park was characterized by floral gardens, picnic areas, and a grotto (far left) with a fresh flowing spring. [Grand Rapids Public Library, Photograph Collection, #54-16-2]

Despite the near disaster of his first sea voyage, Ball never lost his desire for travel. He was able to indulge that taste throughout his life with occasional journeys to the eastern and southern United States and a two-year stay in Europe that ended in June 1873, only months before he celebrated his 80th birthday. His greatest adventure, however, began in 1832 when, at the age of 38, he succumbed to wanderlust by joining Nathaniel Wyeth's party bound for Oregon. Following in the footsteps of Lewis and Clark, he traveled across the North American continent, leaving for posterity not only the memories recounted in his autobiography but also two papers on the natural history of the West (Appendix) that were published in 1834 and 1835 in *Silliman's Scientific Journal.*

Trained at Dartmouth as a scientist, Ball proved to be a keen observer throughout his western voyage, diligently keeping daily records of the weather, geology, wildlife and the distance traveled. Blessed with boundless curiosity and an immense store of charm, Ball was "gladly received as a guest" wherever he went, according to his contemporary, George S. White, "because of his intelligence, attainments and information."

As delightful a guest as he must have been, Ball never overstayed his welcome. Unwilling, for example, to take undue advantage of the hospitality he received at Oregon's Fort Vancouver in the fall of 1832, Ball, who had been a school teacher in his younger days in New Hampshire, accepted an offer to teach at the first school ever opened in Oregon. Not long afterwards, he took up farming and raised the first wheat in Oregon. But that "rather primitive and lonely life" did not suit a man of his gregarious nature, and in the fall of 1833 he traveled on a

Hudson Bay Company ship to San Francisco and then to Hawaii. There, after seeing the sights and meeting the king, he secured passage on a whaling vessel which took him first to Tahiti, then around Cape Horn, and finally to Rio de Janeiro. In Brazil, after meeting and favorably impressing Lieutenant (one day to be commodore) David Farragut, he managed to secure a clerk's position and berth aboard the U.S. schooner *Boxer* bound for Norfolk, Virginia, where he finally landed in the summer of 1835.

The following year, "discontented, half disheartened [and] little inclined or fitted after my wild wanderings to sit down to any business," Ball was off on a land-looking jaunt to Michigan Territory. Originally interested in land for development in the Detroit area, he pushed farther west when he decided that prices for the state's eastern lands were too high. Reaching Grand Rapids in November 1836, he found a noisy, wide-open town that was still nearly two years away from being granted its village charter by the Michigan legislature, and a lot further than that from its modern position as Michigan's second city.

At the time of Ball's arrival in the little Michigan settlement, land speculators seeking to make their fortunes and New England farmers eager for a fresh start comprised a population that barely totaled 600 individuals. By the time Ball died in 1884, however, the population had grown to 41,000; several thousand new residents were arriving each year; and the city was in the first stages of establishing its reputation as the nation's furniture capital.

More important than the land Ball found in Michigan Territory to purchase for friends, relatives and investors back east was the opportunity that Grand Rapids represented for a man of his abilities to achieve financial success and attain civic prominence. After spending the winter of 1836 looking at land throughout western Michigan, Ball hung out his lawyer's shingle and became a Grand Rapids resident the following spring.

Quickly establishing himself as a pillar of the community, he was elected in 1838 to a term in the state legislature, representing the "Grand River District," consisting of Kent, Ottawa, Ionia and Clinton counties. In 1845, by virtue of his appointment as special commissioner by the governor, he was responsible for letting contracts and disbursing money for the building of a state road from Hastings through Middleville to Grand Rapids. He was also the resident agent for a society to promote emigration from Europe to western Michigan, and he is particularly remembered for encouraging Scandinavian settlement in this region.

One of his most compelling interests during the 48 years he lived in Grand Rapids was the local school system. He served as a member of the Grand Rapids Board of Education for 21 years, and for three years — 1856, 1860 and 1862 — he was a school inspector. Committed to the need for quality public education, Ball helped raise funds for an elementary school building in 1848 and contributed $100, a substantial sum back then, of his own funds toward the effort.

Ball was also an entrepreneur whose business ventures included gypsum quarrying, salt-well drilling, and the manufacture of stucco. Late in the 1840s, he became president of the Grand Rapids and Northern Railroad, which won approval to construct

When he gave it to the city in his will, John Ball's "40" was still separated from residential areas by large sections of open land. [Grand Rapids Public Library, Postcard Collection, #78-1-89]

BOOK THE FIRST
Early Life, 1794-1831

FIRST YEARS
CHAPTER I

Birth in 1794

This twelfth day of November, 1874, is my birthday, and I enter my eightieth year, having been born in 1794.

Now going back to the time of my birth, let me look at the state and condition of the world in general, and my own country in particular.

It was only eighteen years from our Declaration of Independence and but five after the first inauguration of our government, the commencement of Washington's second term as President.

Franklin was dead, but most of the actors in our Revolution and the formation of our government were still living and acting their part in carrying out the provisions of the Government they had so patriotically achieved and put in operation.

Old blind George the Third was King of England still, and the French Revolution had just been achieved. The first Napoleon had lately been promoted from Colonel to Brigadier General for having driven the British out of Toulon. He was then twenty-five years old.

The United States then numbered fifteen, Vermont and Kentucky having been added to the original thirteen, and it was bounded south by Florida and Louisiana and west by the Mississippi River. And the vast country northwest of the Ohio River was not even organized into a territory. For in that same year, 1794, General Wayne fought his last battle with the Indians in what is now Ohio and Indiana.

There were then in the United States about 4,000,000 inhabitants, one-tenth of the present population, not probably more than 200,000 west of the Alleghanies, and Western New York and Pennsylvania but little settled.

World at That Date

This same year, 1794, Poland was severed, having been defended to the last with pike and scythe by the brave Kosciuszko of our Revolution and his followers. Prussia under William the Second was till then of limited extent, and Germany more divided into provinces and free towns than now.

Portugal claimed Brazil, and Spain all the rest of not only South America but of North America, except the United States as above, and the North which was claimed by the British and Russians. To be sure, after the purchase of Louisiana, the United States set up that it should extend to the Pacific, because one, Captain Grey, in his ship *Columbia*, discovered in 1793 or 94 the Columbia River.

The wars between the English and the French at that time much influenced the politics of this country. The French having aided us in our Revolution claimed our friendship, and the British claimed at least neutrality. Our parties were then called Federalists and Republicans, but by each other in the way of stigma, Tories and Jacobins. And the celebrated Jay treaty this year, 1794, ratified by us with the British, was much complained of by the French as being to them unjust.

Not only in national matters but in the arts and sciences in the abstract, and still more in their practical application, what a change has indeed come over this world of ours within this eighty years of my life. Then, no steam to propel vessels on rivers and oceans and to share the labor of millions of laboring hands, nor telegraph to enable us to converse with our friends on the other side of the earth, nor gas to turn night into day, nor a thousand other things new and too numerous, if known to me, to mention.

I do not propose to give any general history of the world or its doings, but thought, suggested by this my eightieth birthday, to say something of myself and incidentally of my connections. And in doing so, though I have always been deemed a very modest man, I shall now, of course, be egotistical.

Ancestors

To show how narrow the settlement of the states was at the commencement of the Revolution, about that time my father, my mother's father, and a few others emigrated from Hollis, New Hampshire to Cockermouth, now Hebron, in said state, and my wife's ancestor, Webster, with others to the adjoining town of Plymouth. And in doing so they went thirty miles beyond the last house, which was that of Daniel Webster's father, at what is now Franklin, and still Plymouth and Hebron are but about one hundred miles from Boston.

Most of the Balls of New England and the west trace their origin back to Worcester County, Massachusetts, where it is claimed the first of the name from England settled at an early period of the settlement of those parts, and my grandfather was a native of that county. It is said to be a common name in Virginia, and I was once claimed, when traveling there to be of that state from my name; but the only evidence of the New England and the Virginian Balls being of the same stock is the alleged resemblance of myself to General Washington, whose mother's name was Mary Ball.

Of my immediate ancestors, they were honest and honorable but never acquired any special renown. My grandfather's name on my mother's side was Nevins, the only grandparent I ever saw. He was of Scotch descent and said to have been born on his mother's passage to this country. They called him Deacon. He was of the Scotch Presbyterian order, and I remember he chided us children severely for any levity on Sunday.

My father and a few neighbors were ordered out to join the Revolutionary army at Saratoga. But after a few days' march they were directed to return and guard their own back settlements against the Indians residing between them and Canada, and they, the Indians, did sack the little settlement at Royalton, Vermont. So my father did not become a hero of the Revolution. He first settled on the plain on the river that falls into Newfound pond, in Hebron, but soon moved two miles north onto a part called Tenney's Hill, on to the very top of the hill. The land on this farm of two hundred acres descending in every direction except to the north, which rose into forest and naked mountain rocks. On this hill, detached from all the rest of the world, having steep sides and rising up to 1,000 feet in height, there settled at first three or four families and it never exceeded eight or ten.

Hebron, New Hampshire, as it looked at mid-19th century. John Ball was born in 1794 on a hillside farm just to the right of the site in this photograph. [Clarke Memorial Library, Central Michigan University, #1588]

New Hampshire Farm

From my native hill home there was a grand look out over a wonderfully beautiful and varied lake, valley, and mountain country. To the southeasterly direction is the pond as all such bodies of water are called in that country, seven miles long by four wide, and diversified shore. To the northwest from this extended a valley in which was the meeting house and the one store and a few shops and houses. At the southwest of the pond rises abruptly from the water a conical mountain called the Sugar Loaf. Looking just to the right of this, at the distance of forty miles, is Kearsarge Mountain, our noon mark. A little west of the Sugar Loaf rises abruptly the end of a range that extends to the northwest, over which glistens in the sun the gray, granite mountain Cardigan. And over the valleys west and east are other ranges of rocky and wooded mountains.

Here on this bleak, high hill was I born, the tenth child of my parents, the oldest, Sarah, nearly twenty years my senior. Then Hannah, Bridget Snow, named for a grandmother, Lucy, Nathaniel, Ebenezer, Willie, as he was always called who died in childhood, Deborah and William, all reared in comparative indigence but entire and absolute independence. My parents being quite as well off as their townsmen and neighbors, with their economy and indomitable industry, each and all sustained themselves on those granite hills in comfort and competency — circumstances that have given the New Englander his character. Every child worked, doing what his age and capacity best fitted him to perform.

We were all born in log cabins. One cabin was burned, from which an infant child was saved. My earliest recollection, when about three years old, is the blasting of some big granite boulders for the building of the chimney of the new frame house my father was then building. I had gone out with the other children to be witness at a distance. Big stones formed each jamb and back of the fireplace, and a long mica slate piece from a quarry on the farm, made the mantle tree above. But some way was procured brick enough to make an oven, the oven in which my good mother baked that splendid rye and Indian bread, in big loaves; pork and beans, apples to eat with our bread and milk, and mince, pumpkin and apple pies.

She fed us well, but almost entirely from the products from the farm, the fields and the dairy. But we were taught by her and father, too, to eat what was prepared for us, asking no questions. For breakfast and dinner my father always had his mug of cider; mother and older children tea or coffee, sometimes, the latter often made from brown bread or peas, and for supper bread and milk was the almost universal dish for all.

Work of some kind was the business of my earliest years, to pick up chips, draw the cider, drive the cows to and from pasture, bring the water from the spring, a short distance off, those splendid springs of pure soft water, for it does not dissolve the granite as the lime rock. There were the upper and the lower springs near the house, Jobe's Spring, named from the man who once lived near it, and numerous others. And there were the West Brook and the East Brook, little rippling springs from the mountains north of the farm. In these we bathed in the warm summer days, but never learned to swim, to my after regret, for there was no water to float a boy nearer then the lake two miles away.

In the spring and summer I dropped the corn, rode the horse to plow it, shook out the hay or grain to dry as my older brothers mowed it, and raked after them as they pitched and loaded the hay, and when older played my due part with the scythe. At that I could beat my brother William, though he was older and much stronger than myself. But at mowing I never saw the man who could mow with the ease and rapidity of my brother Nathaniel. Then I picked up the stones in the plow fields and assisted in drawing and laying stones into walls or fences. I took my due part in hoeing the corn and potatoes and gathering and digging the same. I now well recollect where I was hoeing corn in the east field with my brother when that celebrated eclipse of the sun of 1806 happened. It was to us a very interesting sight, and then so dark the cocks crowed.

With me it was all work and no play. The only holidays of the year were the fourth of July and Thanksgiving. Few amusements indoors or out. And Sunday, with its rigid requirement for its observances, was the dullest day of all. We usually went to a meeting, a walk of two miles down and up a steep hill, after a hard week's work. In winter there was little time to play and that was mostly occupied in sliding down the hills on the snow, on sleds made by ourselves. A bent sapling, or small ash tree split, small posts and slats, made a light, but strong vehicle. And there was the care of the cattle at the barns, the feeding and milking the cows; and in the spring the care of the calves and lambs.

Early Education

Our opportunity for an education was very limited. New Hampshire had no public fund for that purpose, and their laws provided that each town should annually vote such an amount as should be needed for the purpose of schools, to be divided between the districts, according to the number of children in each, of a certain age. The number of children in our district was so small that our part of the money would support a school but six or seven weeks in the year. And there was no remedy, for as small as the number of scholars was, being only from ten to fifteen, we were so detached from any other inhabited territory we could not be attached to any other district.

My father's education being very limited, he did not seem to think any further education than an ability to read, write and cipher in the simple rules to be needful. And at home we had no book instruction, for we had no other than the Bible, Watts' Hymns and Psalms, an annual almanac, and a few school books, consisting of Webster's Spelling Book with its fables and accompanying pictures, Morse's Geography, the author, the father of the telegraph man; Adam's Arithmetic, and some school reading book.

My mother had never been to school at all, but she could read and was very fond of reading, when she could obtain a book and had the time. She had naturally a fine mind, and was ever curious to learn all that could be, within her very limited means. With her aspirations her life was truly hard. Our parents observed quite strictly, the then, more than now, universal custom of family prayers, morning and evening, and the asking a blessing and returning thanks at table. When my father was absent, whose prayers were rather formal, my mother performed the duty, and with wonderful ability. The petitions were varied and appropriate to the occasion, and the language correct and beautiful as was ever uttered by the most highly educated person.

I must say something more of our school and its attendant matters. The old schoolhouse was of one room and an entryway, with a big fireplace for warming, and fixed benches and desks, a movable table for the master. How well I remember the good, kind man, Master Nevins, who taught there winters. The house stood on the meeting of two roads, on a side hill, and near by was a gushing spring of pure water, to quench the thirst.

The few weeks of school time were almost the only time we children had for each others' society, for the close work at home at all other times kept us apart. There at the school we met and had our chats. Boys and at times girls too, joined in the slides and snowballing. The original families on said high hill, who made a permanent stay, were the Lovejoy, Crosby and Ball families whose children and grandchildren, and a few others, composed the school. We

were in freedom and attachment as one family. And the remembrance and attachment, has to a great extent, continued with me through life.

Still in our childhood they so mated off as to leave me much alone, caused perhaps in part by my retiring ways. So in summer if I could catch a leisure time from work, my choice would usually be to retire alone to some shady nook of the woods, or wander along the rushing brooks, climb the trees or the rocky crags.

One summer's afternoon, my brother Ebenezer, who though some eight years my elder, seemed much attached to me and sympathized more with me than most of the others of my family, proposed that we should take a jaunt off northeast from the farm through the woods, then quite dense for some distance, to a conspicuous rock or ledge called the pulpit, for from it one overlooked not only the deep valley below, but the ponds, with others Winnipesaukee and hills, and mountains beyond. We reached it with some hard climbing and enjoyed the splendid prospect but proposed to return by a higher and, as we thought, a more easy route. We traveled on and on all the time in a dense forest, wondering why we did not come out in sight of the farm and buildings, when finally, just before dark, we emerged into the extreme north clearing of our next neighbor's farm some two miles northwest of home.

Home Life

I have said that the family subsisted almost entirely on the products of the farm. Still once in the year, in winter, my father would take some butter, cheese and perhaps other products and go below, as it was called, to his old home, Hollis, and sometimes Boston, and exchange the same for the year's supply of groceries and other needed things. His return was a time of quite a sensation in the family.

But little was brought home in the way of clothing, for that was almost entirely made for the men, and women too, from the wool and flax produced on the farm, manufactured by my mother and sisters. There were the big spinning wheels for the wool and the little foot wheel for the linen, the twirling of which, by my industrious mother, I have often heard from my bed. And they, too, wove on the hand loom the yarn they spun. I remember when even the crading machines first came into use in that part of the country. For men's use the woolen cloth was dyed and dressed at the mill. This fulled and dressed cloth for men's garments was sometimes made up by professed tailors, men and women, who went from house to house to do such jobs. But the women made all of the thin clothes, and bleached the linen cloth after woven, and made the same into sheets, shirts, table-cloths and towels.

Religious Life

My parents were attached to the Congregational Church, as most of the people were, in my childhood, in that part of the country. They had erected a church in Hebron about the year 1800, and the minister was a Mr. Page, who was generally well liked and all he said, according to the times, was implicitly received, till at the time of the election of Jefferson for President, he preached a political sermon, and as a Mr. Bartlet said, "Mr. Page, we employ you to preach Jesus Christ and him crucified, but you preach Thomas Jefferson and him justified." His people, though agreed in their religion, were not in their politics; so, of course, it gave great offense to Mr. Jefferson's political opponents, and the church being about equally divided politically, they became so in their fellowship. Their differences and difficulties soon became unreconcilable, even so far as to seriously interfere with kind, neighborly feeling.

One reason for thus speaking of it is its sad effect upon my mother's happiness, and on my own mind, although so young, being but seven or eight years old, so young that my parents, not supposing I should notice it, carried on their sad conversation on the subject in my hearing. They were of the opposing side to the minister and were much dissatisfied with him and his adherents. Hard things were said on both sides. My father would say, "They lie," but my mother, out of her charity, would answer, "They do not mean to," and father would answer, "They do, they know they lie." Young as I was I better understood the purport of all this than they or anyone would think. In spite of my prior instruction, the thought would arise in my mind, as to the utility of churches, ministers and all those things, and it probably has had its influence on my life.

A few years after a wild religious reformation took place in our town.[1] It commenced in the east part of the same among the Methodists, then a new sect in those parts, and it soon spread through the whole community. They held frequent day and night and all-night meetings, where all took part in exhorting, singing, weeping and groaning, and even the falling power, as it was called, when persons would fall down apparently in a trance. To all this I was a spectator, still being but little moved, though I supposed others experienced all they showed, even most of my own family, though all my elders, seemed deeply

moved. I felt an uneasiness that I was not also affected and secretly prayed that I might share and also be converted. For it was claimed that all in the whole place had been, but four, and I was one of that number.

Still all the while I watched every movement. When a young man had fallen at one of these night meetings and others said he was cold; though extremely diffident, I must see for myself, and on feeling of him he seemed warmer than myself, and I wondered that they would say that he was cold, and doubts began to arise as to the matter, induced probably by my being quiet and attentive. My sister Lucy once asked me if I had felt no change in my mind during the reformation. I answered her, "No." Well, had I not sometime before? I answered her the same. Then she said, "Perhaps this change took place before you can recollect." It surprised me and I said to her, "If there is no more than this in the conversion you talk about, there is not as much to it as you pretend there is." And from that time commenced serious doubts, whether the whole of it was not a matter of emotion, sympathy, and delusion.

Members of the Family

While I was still a child my four older sisters married, Sarah to Mr. Colby, Hannah to Mr. Ladd, Bridget to Mr. Brooks, and Lucy to Mr. Ferrin, all townsmen, except Ladd, who resided in the adjoining town of Alexander. Each had his farm and lived, like their neighbors, by their industry. The first of my leaving home was occasionally to go and live with some of them for a time. Of course, I became attached to their children, a number of them being near my own age.

As for the boys, my father claimed their time till they were twenty-one, and they continued to work at home, until of that age. My oldest brother, Nathaniel, continued to work there until he procured an adjoining farm and set up for himself, and few men worked with more ease and to better effect. He was little given to reading in his boyhood, but finally became a great reader, and having a good, strong mind, his acquisitions were unusually great for his opportunity. He had a good comprehension of all public matters, but could never be induced to accept public office. His wife's name was Blood, in youth a joyous one, a great singer, and in every way a true helpmate. They had two children, a son and a daughter. The son when a young man went to sea and neither he nor the ship were ever again heard from. His daughter, Mrs. Dean, with her mother are

---

[1] *The "Second Great Awakening" swept the northeastern and western parts of the United States in the late 18th and early 19th centuries.*

now residing at Wentworth, New Hampshire. The daughter is an esteemed correspondent of mine.

My next brother, Ebenezer, was in his boyhood a greater reader and more of a thinker. I well recollect that sometimes he expressed doubts as to the opinion and ways of those around us, and considering his limited opportunity, showed talent by his acquisitions. He waited, not quite patiently, for his twenty-first birthday, that he might be his own man and leave home, which he did on the very day, and went first to Sterling, Massachusetts and there learned the business of chair-making. He afterwards worked in Boston, and was there at the coming of the war of 1812 and when the Militia was called out for service, he was stationed on one of the islands in the Harbor, where he took cold, sickened, and in the attempt to get him home, he died before reaching there, but his body was brought there for burial. Severely did I feel his loss. We had always corresponded and he had encouraged me in my efforts for an education by words and proposed aid.

My sister, Deborah, possessed a vigorous body and mind, quite self-reliant and early sought to carry it out, so went away from home and learned the tailor's trade, and worked at the same. She married William Powers. I knew his grandfather Willie and father William, of the neighboring town of Groton, and they, William the third and my sister, went to Lansingburgh, where he had been before, to reside. But of them I shall have occasion to speak more.

My brother William, who was but two years my senior, and with whom I always worked on the farm when boys, was strong, but rather slow in his movements. Still he would work on till the whole day's work was done, if it took to a late hour. Being the older he claimed the right to direct the work in a way that to me was not always entirely satisfactory. It seemed hard to work all day and part of the night in the long autumn days. At school he rather excelled in arithmetic, but had little taste for other studies, and never became much of a reader. He once made quite a sensible remark, which he applied to his son E. Morris, that he thought more conversation and less reading would be more profitable.

As I had determined to leave home if I could, I gave him to understand if he would stay and provide well for our parents I would set up no claim from that source, and he did stay and worked the old mountain farm while our parents lived. He married and had two sons and a daughter, but she died in childhood. The older son named E. Morris, stayed with his father during his boyhood, except when absent for the purpose of education.

When leaving home after journeying for a time, he came to Grand Rapids, where he still resides, and his father followed him there. The other son Jasper N., named for a classmate of mine, received a collegiate education at Dartmouth, and studied divinity in the city of New York, married a New Jersey woman and went as a missionary to Turkey. After residing there in that capacity some years, his wife's health failing, they came home with their two children and the mother died. A time after he returned to Turkey, had two other children, his own health failing they came home and he too soon died. His wife and children live in Grand Rapids, but the brother, I am sorry to say, has never married, has an abundance and lives quietly with his mother, his father having died here a few years since.

More Education

As for myself I early became quite dissatisfied at having so limited an opportunity for an education, so as soon as I deemed it safe to do so I broached the subject to my father. I knew he adhered strictly to the opinion that work and implicit obedience were the things most useful and needful in the education of boys, but after much importunity, he consented that I might go into the next town of Groton to a clergyman by the name of Rolph, who kept a kind of private school. It was eight miles distant by carriage road, but only half that by a footpath across a mountain pass which was usually my route.

At first I took up arithmetic and English grammar in good earnest during the first fall and winter. And as poorly as I was qualified I taught a small school for a short time during the winter on Power's Hill. In the spring my said reverend teacher proposed, to my surprise, that I should take up the Latin grammar, which I did, though of English I knew so little; not the first rudiments of reading or spelling at all well, and nothing I might say of history or geography. I thought it strange that he should thus propose it, for I had not yet hardly dared to think it possible that I could think of anything more than a limited English education but his evident design was to lead me further.

Teaching

Come summer, as always after, until I graduated from college, I went home and worked on the old farm at haying and harvesting. The next fall I returned to my school pursuing my Latin and some other studies, also writing under a special teacher of that art. And come winter, knowing that I must do something for my own support, I started out to get a writing school. I took my bundle and went, of course on foot, through Plymouth and Rumney to Oxford. At the latter place I recollect I offered my services in that capacity, but my showing was not satisfactory or they did not need the instruction. So I went on to Thetford, Vermont, where I had a lady cousin, with whom I was acquainted. I do not now recollect her husband's name. With their aid I got, for a time, my writing school.

But the time not being long that I was patronized in that line, I went to Vershire in the same state to visit my uncle John Ball, for whom I was named. We were all named for father and uncles. There I engaged in teaching a small district school at some very moderate compensation, how much I do not recollect. There to extend my knowledge of men and manners it was my lot to board around, as was usual in those times, from house to house, according to the number of scholars or some other rule of ratio. It proved a new and interesting experience for everywhere I was a favored guest, for they lived on their best while the master boarded with them and I had the society of the young ladies and all the members of each family in their most approved form, but to me it was sometimes embarrassing, for up to this time my acquaintances had been very few.

This winter was a notable one in the history of our country. The war[2] had been conducted with few successes and some humiliating defeats, such as the taking of Washington, and now came the glorious news of the battle of New Orleans, and soon after the very welcome, and if I am right, unexpected news of peace. The overthrow of Napoleon and peace in Europe brought peace to us also. Oh! these wars and rumors of wars among people that in a boastful way call themselves Christians, claimed followers of the peaceful and loving Jesus Christ. Well might the Turk, of course a Mohammedan, say in satire when, a short time before this, he was witnessing from a neighboring eminence, the tremendous battle of Borodino near Moscow between the French and Russians, "See how these Christians love each other." Though I had then seen but little, very little for my age, even I had thought enough to give me then about my present views on that subject.

Salisbury Academy

Returning home in the spring, I made up my mind to continue the pursuit of an education if it was possible for me to do so. And thinking that the advantages would be greater elsewhere than at Mr. Rolph's I went to the Salisbury Academy, situated on the beautiful tableland in a small village a few miles west of Franklin, New Hampshire and about thirty miles from home. A Mr. Wells was the preceptor and there were some forty or fifty pupils, girls and boys, from about the country, forming agreeable society for us; there I pursued my Latin and some other studies, and after a time took up the Greek. Among the students I recollect William Haddock, a nephew of Daniel Webster, and a prodigy of a boy, who read Latin and Greek at the age of seven, or at eight quite fluently. When of sufficient age he went to college, but turned out poorly. My studies were this summer somewhat interrupted by a severe attack of measles.

The following winter I think I taught school in my native district on Tenney's Hill and in the following spring I returned to the academy, and went on with my studies, having made up my mind that I would try and fit for college. I studied hard, but from my prior limited opportunity and natural slowness my progress was not very rapid and I did not hope to be fit for admission to college before the next year; but to my surprise the tutor of the academy told me he thought if I studied well he could recommend me for an examination for admission at the close of the term about July. At that time, he said, President Brown of Dartmouth was coming there to examine some others for admission and he would propose me with the rest. Being so advanced in age it was very welcome news, and I, of course, exerted myself to be prepared for the trial. President Brown came and I was examined with the others and decided to be qualified. The college was the more desirous, at the time, to get students on account of the state's interference with its charter rights. My father had sent me word that he would be returning from a journey at the time of the closing of the term of the academy, and he would come that way and take me home. He did arrive the last of the week when the term had just closed, but the examination for the admission to college was not to take place till the next week, so I had to tell him what I was proposing to do and that I would wait and have the examination, and he might take my trunk, and, after President Brown had been there and examined us, I would walk home. And to show what my prospects were as to aid in my college course, I will state what he said. "What is that you say, John, if you are going to take that course you must not look to me for help." So he left me, taking my baggage, and I stayed, passed the examination successfully and walked home, and when there went as usual into the mow field.

[2] *The War of 1812.*

Dartmouth College, Hanover, New Hampshire, as it was in 1823, three years after John Ball graduated. [Reprinted from Autobiography of John Ball, *p. 16]*

DARTMOUTH COLLEGE
CHAPTER II

As the time approached for the fall term at the college I well recollect the anxiety and trouble I experienced in procuring the means to meet my expenses. But how I did get them I do not now recollect. During my whole course my father did loan me to the amount in all, at different times, two hundred dollars, but whether any at this time I do not remember. Still, by some means, I managed to join my class in due time and keep along, but with the most rigid economy in everything. When I hired my board it was at the cheapest place and I often boarded myself, preparing my frugal meals in my room, a room I took in the old college building at some low rent, and for the first year George Richardson of our class was my roommate.

On first meeting my fellow students for recitation, I well recollect my feeling of embarrassment for I really realized my lack of language, hesitating ways, and the better preparation of all of them than myself. In all I had been in school hardly four years while they, with probably a more ready capacity, had been preparing all their school years. Of the languages, Greek and Latin, they had read and re-read the required authors while I had not in either read what the college rules required, of Greek, but part of the Testament and in Latin, Virgil and part of Cicero. By great industry I managed to get a pretty good understanding of the lessons, still recited but poorly.

Class Work

In the recitation room we were arranged alphabetically, and as it happened, being no A's, it placed me at one end of the form so that in reciting it would often fall to my lot to be the first one called on to recite. Still on that account I seldom got the first part better than the whole of the lesson, feeling that it was of more account to know my full lesson than to recite a part well; but I often observed that my next fellow, Thornton Betton, who possessed fine capacity but fond of sport would often get his part of the lesson while others were reciting, and when they began with me he had to put forth his best exertion to get his paragraph. I thought the old professor of mathematics, Adams, and Tutor White, who were our main instructors through our whole course, ought some time to have called on him first. No, they seemed stupidly to commence with one end of the class or the other or about in the middle.

Dartmouth College is beautifully situated on a plain, high above the Connecticut River, which flows swiftly a half mile to the west, in which we bathed and such as could, swam, and I remember that I was usually the first in the spring to try its cold waters. The college building, for then there was but one, and a small chapel, was on one side of a broad green or common where the boys played football with great glee, and the best in the lot were the two or three Indian students, for by a condition of the charter and funds they still are required to have some of the people for whom the institution was founded in order to draw on certain funds in England and Scotland.

Sickness

Come winter vacation I went to my winter occupation, teaching school, and this time to be the one on what is called the Groton intervale, some four miles up the valley from our own village. I boarded at a Mr. Heath's. At one time I came near getting into serious trouble for having punished a refractory scholar, but by the kindly interposition of my old friend Mr. Rolph, the matter was adjusted.

One afternoon while in my schoolroom I suffered a severe headache, and, after closing school, with some difficulty reached my boarding place and feeling so badly I laid down on the floor before the fire and soon fell asleep or became unconscious. The next I knew, being towards morning, I found myself in a bed with a number of persons about me showing much concern. The fact was I had a severe attack of spotted fever, a disease till lately unknown in those parts.[3] Mr. Heath had lost two children the year before by the same disease. So seeing what my sickness was he did not wait for the arrival of the physician but immediately prescribed such remedies as were approved of in such cases.

The next morning my people and the doctor, they having been sent for, came and gave me all the care they could, thinking my condition very dangerous. I was fairly speckled with red spots on all parts of my body and suffering much pain. They gave me the best of care, among the rest a neighboring young lady, a Miss Shattuck, and I so far improved that in two weeks or so they took me home in a sleigh, but the shock was so great it was a long time before I regained my strength. In fact, I had strange and unusual feelings from its effects for months.

Classmates

There ended my school teaching for this winter, thus cutting short the means I was counting on. Still, in the spring I returned to my college studies, and by some means kept along, never knowing one quarter how I should meet the next. By this time the members of the class had become more acquainted and paired off more to each one's liking than at first. I exchanged my roommate Richardson for Jasper Newton, with whom I continued on the most cordial terms during all the remainder of our course. His father resided on a farm in the town of Hartford, Vermont, three miles only from Hanover. I often went home with him to pass the Sunday, when we could get the license so to do, and was received by his good people as one of the family. And such a family, ten boys, averaging six feet each! The father boasted that he had sixty feet of boys, and six daughters. Jasper, my chum, was the youngest, but one, so many of the other members were married and there were numerous grandchildren. Jasper was six feet and four, rather slim and finely formed.

I passed that year at college, was at home in haying time and until winter when I took a school at Thetford, Vermont, which is a small village on a hill two miles from the Connecticut River. At first I had a full school of many large and advanced boys and girls, some seventy in all, and I found it a laborious task to do them justice, as they were pursuing many, and some advanced, studies. But after a few weeks a new academy was opened in the place, which took off many of the older scholars so I got along better. There were here many refined families, all of whom treated me with much kindness. The pay for my services here helped me on, and I should mention another source. Powers, my brother-in-law at Lansingburgh, sometime in my course loaned me some money; and the faculty trusted me in part, on the required tuition.

By this time I had learned that a man could not, without danger to health, go from the active and hard life of the farm to the sedentary one of the student, and so, as soon as I perceived the bad debilitating effects I adopted the practice of daily exercise, principally walking, and thus kept up my strength. Every day I would take my long walks in all directions over that beautiful country about Hanover. I would start off alone if no companion was ready to accompany me, and though my dear roommate Newton and I were so much together in our room and in pursuing our studies, still he was my oftenest companion, and oftener than otherwise I walked to and from home, thirty miles away.

Dartmouth, a College or University

When I entered, and most of the time while in college, there were two institutions on the ground, the college and the university. The state had passed a law changing the name to university, and making many changes from the old English charter to the college, but most of the twelve trustees and the faculty deeming this act of the State unconstitutional resisted its provisions and continued the college in operation as though no such law had been passed. A Mr. Allen was appointed president of the new state institution, and also able professors. They took possession of the building, library and all the property, but having at most but a dozen students they rented the rooms in the main building to students that preferred, as ten-to-one did, the old faculty, and the old college people procured a hall for a chapel, and some private rooms so they continued their instruction at Hanover as in past times. The matter went before the Supreme Court of the United States and Webster, who was a trustee of the college, conducted the case in its behalf, and the

---

[3] A tick-borne disease for which rats are the carrier, characterized by fever accompanied by spotting of the skin.

court decided that the old charter was a vested right and no more to be infringed upon than the title to a farm acquired before our independence.

Though so limited in means and backward in my studies, I was ever treated with civility and kindness by my fellow students, and was aided by them in hard lessons. Members like G. P. Marsh, Thompson, Betton, Upham, Williams and Woodbury were provided with ample means, still they never assumed anything on that ground over their indigent fellows.

Studies

Now that we had reached those studies that were as new to others of the class as to myself, astronomy, natural philosophy, morality, I got along in playing my part much easier and more pleasantly, and for those I had more liking than for the languages and dry mathematics. Still our whole course there was much drier and less interesting, I presume, than in the same institution now. Nothing there at all in the natural sciences of botany, mineralogy and geology. Indeed such sciences were then untaught. How glad I am that we mortals are beginning to look at things near us and which more concern us than heretofore. The science of astronomy, however, I would not be understood to propose to neglect, for some knowledge of the vastness of the universe should tend to teach us humility.

In the winter of my junior year I taught school across the river in the town of Norwich, not in the village, but in a district next back, and a very good time I had of it for my school was tractable and the people intelligent, agreeable and very kind. Some of the families I have ever since recollected with much gratitude and pleasure.

Jaunt to the White Mountains

At the close of the spring term it was proposed by some of the students to take a jaunt to the White Hills, as then called, and though I could so little afford it, I could not forego the temptation to join them. My travels had been very limited indeed and I had from my childhood longed for a time that I could visit places beyond the hills and mountains that bounded the home. We had quite a broad view

Crawford's Notch House, 1838. Despite warnings from Mr. Crawford, John Ball and three of his classmates left from here to climb Mount Washington and were nearly stranded by a late spring storm. [New Hampshire Historical Society, #F960]

from the high hill of my nativity, and I had, from a rocky eminence back of the old farm, seen the mountains we now proposed to visit. Perhaps for this reason, I the more, wished to ascend them.

Four of us took our journey up the Connecticut from Hanover to Bath and then back to Franconia, visiting the iron mines and works and so through to Crawford's at the Notch, and we went much of the way of foot. Mr. Crawford had the only stopping place in those parts, he had then but a small house with three or four rooms, built to supply the place of a large one, lately burned down.

It was still in May, quite too early in the season for the undertaking of visiting those snowy regions successfully. A long rain storm came on, which detained us indoors on the second day of our arrival until noon; it cleared off then, and though advised by our landlord not to do so, we started out to climb the mountain. We were told that the ascent had never been attempted by strangers without a guide, but I told the boys that if we could not guide ourselves it was a great pity. So we started out going down the road some distance, towards the Notch, so as to reach a point where the ascent of the mountain would be more gradual. Then we turned into a forest, consisting mostly of firs; we went on for a time, but before we had gotten above the trees there came on a drenching thunder storm. It was curious to see the dwindling of the trees in their size as we ascended. Fir trees that were quite large at the bottom of the mountain further up were no higher than our heads, and the branches so spread and matted down by the winter snows, as to be almost impossible to get through them. The last trees were stunted white birch and then only ferns, wild grass, and moss.

When we had reached the naked granite ridge of the mountain that extends from the Notch to the foot of Mount Washington, the walking, over the often smooth rocks, soon became much better and so we hastened on. But long before we had reached the foot of Mount Washington we witnessed a most glorious sunset, for the storm had passed by; yes, saw the sun setting behind the Green Mountains of Vermont. We had expected to camp out one or more nights, but none of us had ever had that experience, and so we little realized what it was, or understood how to prepare for it. With later experience I have learned one can prepare to meet almost any weather or locality with comparative comfort. When night came on we concluded we could not camp on the bare and naked rock, but must get down the side of the mountain to where there were trees to shelter us and wood for fire. We did not, however, find much

shelter, and the wood was so green and wet we could not kindle fire.

After many trials, finding we could not get a fire, we laid down in our wet clothes with our blankets around us and huddled together to try to get some warmth. We suffered severely with the cold. My companions slept some, but I could not at all, and waited impatiently for day. When it came it was far from giving the expected comfort, for the whole mountain was enveloped in a cold dense fog. We felt it a bad and unpromising predicament for our grand purpose of reaching the summit of Mount Washington, and having the grand and wide view of the stretch of land from the mountains of Vermont to the ocean. We were then near the foot of Mount Washington, and as bad as the prospect was, after taking our cold breakfast, we commenced to climb the steep side of the mountain, composed mostly of huge rocks, making it decidedly laborious. We hoped that by the time we reached the summit the fog might clear away. Instead of the prospect brightening it soon came on to sleet and snow, and the wind to blow a gale. I was rather the leader of the squad, and when the others proposed to give it up and return back I would not consent, and said to them, "If we can do or see no more, we ought to see the summit of the mountain."

The Storm

But as the storm increased in fury I began to reflect that it might prove dangerous; we might get lost and possibly perish. So I gave up the ascent; but what was next to be done? We immediately concluded, on reflection, that we should perish in attempting to return in the storm, along the miles of the ridge of the mountain on which we had come, and for safety we must get onto lower ground as soon as possible. For that purpose we must descend right down the west side of the mountain, where it was the steepest and also in the direction of our hotel.

Dispute arose again, for I was going, as before, to be guided by my pocket compass, when my companions objected that the course the compass indicated was not west, and contended that it must be badly attracted by some iron ore. I grew alarmed and did not stop to argue, but leaped down the rocks, and they finally followed. It was almost at the risk of our necks, for the snow and hail had made the rocks slippery, so at every step we were in danger of plunging down some terrible precipice. Though freezing, notwithstanding our exertion, we dashed on and soon came to some bushes on to which we could hold to let ourselves down the steepest places.

After a time we got into larger timber and where the cold was not so severe, and on to the headwaters of the rushing Amonoosuck.

But there we got so entangled among fallen trees, occasioned by fires, that the only way we could get through was to go down in the icy water of the brook. Pressing on we got below the storm, and just at night arrived at Crawford's, glad to be safely out, as well we might be.

Winnipesaukee

The next day our party left to return, but by quite a different way from which we came. We went through the Notch, and down towards Maine to Fryeburg, near the boundary of the state, then, having got by the mountains, turned west to Centre Harbor and Plymouth to my home in Hebron. The divide between the streams that flow into the Connecticut River and through Maine must be before we reach the Notch, for through that flows the Saco; the pass there being between almost perpendicular mountains, rising thousands of feet on both sides, and so near for some distance that there is left between them only room for the road and the rushing river. The first house below was the Willey house, years after swept away by a mountain avalanche. Below this, the valley of the river broadens into quite a plain, still bounded by high mountains. The journey all the way was new and interesting. We passed Winnipesaukee Lake, the largest body of water in that state. And on the whole, we felt that our journey had been quite interesting and paid, notwithstanding the hardships and the failure from the storm to reach the summit of Mount Washington.

Passed the summer as usual at home at work, which probably had the good effect to keep up my strength and health. It made hands and sides sore for a few days, on the commencing to use the scythe and rake.

Professors at Dartmouth

In the fall returned to commence the studies of my senior year. As I have mentioned, Professor Adams and a tutor named White were for the most part my only teachers during the whole course — men who went mostly by the book. The question was always what does the book say? And if we ventured to doubt the book it was treated as an unreasonable presumption. It was their particular place to instruct in the mathematics, and books on other subjects, to them, had the same certitude.

But in one case the old professor was rather disposed to be governed by the majority. The class had for its lesson the calculation of an eclipse of the moon to take place some years ahead, and were to make a diagram showing the path of the moon in crossing the ecliptic, bringing it directly between the sun and the earth. The whole matter, the diagram and all, was laid down in a quarto volume — Ainsworth's Philosophy I think it was, including also Astronomy. And in the first instance my roommate, Newton, and myself, probably influenced by the book, made our diagram wrong; made the moon's path to cross the ecliptic obliquely, of course from south to north instead, as the fact was in our case, from north to south; drew it as though looking down on the moon instead of up to it in the heavens, which of course would reverse it. But fortunately Newton

Lake Winnipesaukee with the White Mountains in the background. John Ball and his companions passed by the lake on their return from Mount Washington. [New Hampshire Historical Society, #F3915]

discovered our mistake in time for us to correct our work.

But on going to the recitation room we found every member of the class had made the same blunder. But the moment G. P. Marsh saw our diagram, he said in an instant, that his own was wrong. Well, when we had got seated and the old professor had come in he called me up, as was usual the first to recite, and asked to see my diagram. He said "all right" till he found that Betton's and two or three of the next agreed with him; when he said that I was wrong. But feeling sure they were wrong I tried to persuade him they were, and explained why, but he would not listen to me till Marsh took the liberty to get up and say to him, that he thought my work was right, that he had made the same mistake. Marsh's scholarship was of so high a grade that he listened to him, and on inquiry found that no one was right but Newton and myself.

We were very unfortunate in having so little instruction in our course. No lectures except on Sundays from the pulpit from Shirtliff, the professor of theology and moral philosophy. And in that course he was our teacher. The books used were Paley's "Philosophy" and "Evidences of Christianity", Butler's "Analogy", and Edwards' "On the Will". Dry subjects except to the theological student, and Professor Shirtliff too, as implicitly relied on the author of the book as did Professor Adams.

As dry as the subjects were I read every lesson and thought of the subjects treated, for myself. And I well recollect that I could but think that they were sometimes rather partisan in their view. It seemed as if too often the authors felt themselves bound to sustain their prior conceived opinions and carry out, reasonable or unreasonable, certain theories. I well remember that Paley in his "Evidences of Christianity" seemed to treat the proofs of Bible miracles as most conclusive, while the claims of the other peoples, except the Jews and Christians, as improbable and hardly worthy of notice. He included the claims of the Catholics with the rest, as preposterous and unworthy of notice, but the Bible miracles and all, so easy of belief.

And in his preaching the professor was of the good old orthodox school, and as we were required to attend church, I always listened to all he said. But sometimes I thought I could detect the same contradiction as in other, "You must repent or suffer the fate of the wicked." Still before he got through he would tell us, "It was all of the Lord, we could do nothing."

In most things I observed strictly all the college rules and requirements, but the one that we must not leave our rooms on Sunday, except to go to church, I did not fully live up to, but would, as on other days, take a walk for the necessary exercise, but always in a most quiet and orderly manner.

Trip to Montreal

My means being so limited kept me very careful in all my expenditures, except seeing something of the world. The last part of the fall term of our senior year my classmate, McGaw, and myself concocted the strange plan of getting excused for the remainder of the term and taking a journey to see something of the world, and at the same time away off somewhere to get schools to teach for the winter, and strangely concluded to go to Montreal. So we started out, taking the stage to Burlington. The route led up the valley of the White River and so on — all the country to me new and interesting. Our attention was called to a little mountain rill that came down the mountain side to our road, where it divided, a part of it flowing into the White and the other into the Onion River. So its waters flowed into the Connecticut and St. Lawrence rivers. As we descended the Onion we had a good view of the north end of the Green Mountains. Burlington was then but a small village, still we noted the beautiful locality overlooking the lake, and the grand land scenery in the other direction.

To reach Montreal we must cross, or rather go down the Champlain Lake to St. Johns, the opportunity to do so was to take passage on a small schooner sailed by one man and a boy. A blow coming on we had to play the sailor and help them sail the ship. The storm was so severe it seemed all the four could do to keep her on her course. And we finally weathered it and reached the old village of St. Johns, situated on the west shore of the Sorrel river. Then we took the stage for Montreal, but this in fact took us only to the St. Lawrence at La Prairie, leaving five miles for the crossing of the river to the city. And what a strange old looking city it was, quite as I now know, a perfect likeness of the old French and German villages — entirely unlike anything I had seen, low stone houses with iron window shutters, on narrow streets. We gratified our curiosity by looking all about the town and noticing its strangeness, and ascended the neighboring hill, or mountain, that gives name to the place, from which there was a very extended view, the country round being so level that you looked right down on town and river.

Our funds getting short, we were put in mind of the necessity of soon getting employment, and school keeping being the only one we proposed, we made inquiry, and were referred to an American merchant by the name of Gage. But he gave no encouragement that we could get schools. After a few days we gave it up and made up our minds we must back out. The weather had become cold and there was some ice running in the river, but they could still cross to Longuel, which is about two miles distant, directly across the river. On reaching it we took stage for La Prairie and St. Johns in a hard storm.

And thus in getting back to St. Johns we used up the last of our money. I told the landlord of the hotel where we stopped our situation, and when we left that I would send him the pay for our bill, which I surely intended, but I am sorry to say I fear I have neglected to do so. I wish I could do it now. From there we induced the captain of a vessel to take us to Burlington, and I gave him a cheap watch I had to pay our passage, and he gave me a little to boot. With this money we started out on foot for Montpelier, and though we were tired and hungry I recollect we kept up pretty good spirits, laughing at the failure of our enterprise and our present predicament. I left McGaw at Montpelier and took the stage, promising to pay the fare on arriving at Hanover.

Nothing but my indomitable thirst for travel could have induced me, as I was then situated, to make the Montreal trip. I do not now by any means recollect all the inducements and reasons, but think that McGaw, who was rather of a wild character, instigated and planned it, and he carried it out better than myself, for he did not return, and I believe succeeded in getting a school in Vermont. Well, I borrowed money to pay my stage fare. It was so late in

the season the winter schools were all engaged. So after the close of the fall term I went with Newton to his father's, where I was always made welcome and spent part of the winter. In the spring we returned to the college and resumed our course.

Few, if any, of the students ever went at all into the very limited society at Hanover, so our only recourse was among ourselves — a life, that on the whole, but poorly fits one for after life, a life of abstruse learning and only coarse boys for company.

Senior Year

President Brown was then at the head of the college, and an able and worthy man. But very unfortunately for us he was all the while so out of health that he could not at any time fill his appointed place in our instruction. He finally, about the time of our graduation, died. I well recollect that after he had become very feeble he sent for our class to come to his room. And there he gave us some excellent advice as to our future lives. Part of it I well recollect, and if I have any claims to be in some degree learned, it has been by observing and following his suggestions. He said, "Young men, do not think you shall have completed your education, for it is but a beginning. You must still be pupils all your lives," or words to that effect. We lost much by not having his instruction.

There were two societies kept up by the students of the college. The Social Friends and Fraternity were the names, I think. They had libraries, and there arose a trouble at one time about them

Notre Dame Street in Montreal, painted by R.A. Sproule about 1829. The column honoring Admiral Horatio Nelson was erected in 1809 by joint French and English efforts. [Harlan Hatcher and Erich A. Walter, A Pictorial History of the Great Lakes, *New York, Crown Publishers, 1963]*

between the members of the societies, who belonged to the college and the university. They were in the old college building when the university had possession of it, and I think the university members of the societies claimed the libraries, and there was quite a battle on the subject; for the members of the societies belonging to the college were twenty to one, and claimed the ownership and moved the books away to another building. But before my course ended the United States Supreme Court decision was rendered, and buildings, libraries and all things were restored to their original status.

By the little I had earned and received from my father and friend Powers, I met my board and outside expenses, purchased second-hand books for my studies, and as for clothing I had little except what was supplied by mother, as I recollect. But my tuition had run on till there was something like a hundred dollars due. I called on the treasurer, Honorable Hills Olcott, to see what I must do about it, and he told me that if I could not pay I must get security. I told him there was no one whom I could get or at any rate was willing to ask and assured him that it should be paid if I lived long enough to earn the money, as I intended that that should be my first business. I explained that no one was in any way obligated to become my security, and I could not give it. I was answered, I could not then receive my diploma, parchment, as then called. As to that I thought it only a matter of form, and I could do without it.

Graduation

But I went to the pews appropriated for the class in the church, at the commencement ceremonies and listened to the parts acted by some of my fellows; for I, of course, was not an orator, or scholar enough to at all expect any appointment in any of the performances. The last performance of all was to be our march over the stage, in front of the pulpit, where all the trustees and the faculty were seated, and each receive his parchment. But when my fellow students, almost at the last moment, found that I was not to get mine they drew up a note for the amount due for my tuition, had me sign it, then nearly all of them did the same. Nothing in my life more touched me than this expression of their confidence and regard. As I now relate it the tears came to my eyes. But they did not pay the note, or any part of it. So then by that means I, with the rest of them, marched up and received my diploma, which is in the Atlantic Ocean; but of that hereafter.

CHOOSING A PROFESSION
CHAPTER III

That same day I left for Lansingburgh, where my brother-in-law, Powers, resided, to visit them on my way, as I intended going further south to seek employment. I started out on foot by the most direct route, without regard to a good or public road. But just the route or at what places I stopped I do not remember, further than that I crossed the mountains on the Rutland turnpike, and before I reached there turned southward and finally took a stage and passed through Salem and Pittstown to Lansingburgh, where my friends as always, welcomed me. They had then one son whom they named Albert Ebenezer, the middle name of our brother.

I had been there before, a mention of which I have omitted. I think it was in 1818, but well recollect many of the incidents of that journey going by stage down to Brattleboro and crossing the mountains to Bennington, and what I there and thereabouts saw. The great fire had just taken place in Troy and the burning grain in the warehouses was still smoking. We visited the Cohoes Falls, where there were no improvements, only some farms and two or three farmhouses in the vicinity. And I think it was at that time I first went to Saratoga, where then there were but few buildings, only one hotel of any account. There were the High Rock, Flat Rock, and Congress Springs; the last but lately found. Then, or later, I was at Ballston Spa, where I recollect of seeing Joseph Bonaparte. I think he was often in summer stopping there at the Sansouci.

Reading Law in Lansingburgh

On my informing Mr. Powers of my intention first of all to seek employment to earn money to pay up my indebtedness to the college, to himself and to my father, he urged me instead to select my profession and to begin the study of the same. I had not yet decided what should be my future pursuit, but had left that to be determined when my debts should have been paid. As I had but little gift as a speaker my classmates had set me down for the profession of medicine. For all college students were supposed to be destined for one of the three learned professions, as they were then called. The study of medicine I thought I should like well, but the practice seemed intolerable. Being heterodox I could not take divinity, so the law only was left.

So I yielded to my friends' importunities to stop with them and take up the study, and make the earning of money to pay my debts a secondary matter. I boarded with them and entered the law office of Walbridge and Lansing, (W. W. Walbridge, J. C. Lansing) who had their office on State Street, next to the book store and Lansingburgh Gazette office of Mr. Tracey. My friends then resided near the lower end of Congress Street, in a small old house. In fact, there were but few others then in that village, but small scattering wooden buildings — an old dilapidated village, good lots selling along those beautiful streets at $100 each. It was older than Troy, but the navigation of the river above being poor it was deserted by its business men for that better place. A handsomer place for a town can nowhere be found, a plain of dry gravelly soil requiring no grading, with the beautiful river on one side and the hills on the other.

Where the cemetery now is, on the hill, was all wild, and where the brook comes out, a Mr. Jones had a garden. For exercise I often climbed and roamed those wild hills. And there, on Van Schaick's Island, there was only the old brick Revolutionary house standing. Another one was on the bank of the river, called the Lansing House, now occupied by N. B. Powers. The old crazed Mr. Van Schaick, was then still living, and often saw in imagination the British Red Coats. He expected for sure Burgoyne's army would sweep over and destroy his farm. The back part of his island was then beautifully wooded, and a great pleasure resort for picnics, etc.

Teaching and Society

For my legal reading I of course was assigned Blackstone, which I pursued with due diligence, and also did some work in copying papers for the office.

A Mr. Simmons, was also a student in the office. He taught in the Academy, and after a time I got a department in the same to teach. My pupils were some twenty girls and young ladies, to govern whom to my mind I found it troublesome. The next year I taught a school of primaries, and gained some credit for my success. I soon made the little folks, some eighty in all, understand that I intended to make it pleasant for them – had lessons on large cards that could be hung up about the walls of the room. They were the same Mr. Powers had used before in teaching school on the Lancastrian plan. Six would stand around

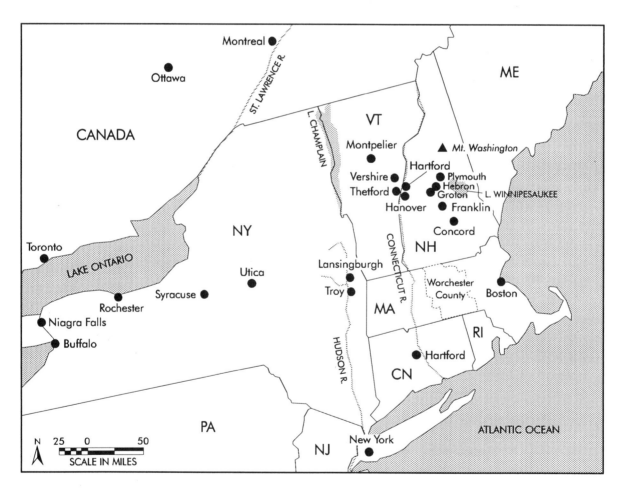

John Ball's Travels
Early Days In New York and New England

looking on the same lesson with directions to correct each other as they read in alphabets (little folks), who had sand smoothed down in which to make the letters with their fingers, with an older scholar to show them how. And I gave them liberal time outdoors, so it went merrily on. At the same time I kept up my reading in the office.

Though little in society for a time, I gradually got acquainted with the young people. There were a large number of young ladies accustomed to dance, but many of the young men were from the New England mountains, like myself, who knew nothing of the art, for there it was deemed very sinful. But having revolted from our education we employed a man, who was teaching some children, to give us a few lessons, intending to ask the young ladies to join us in the dance as soon as we were able to perform. But they mistaking our intentions, out of opposition some of them got up a sleigh ride with no men but the driver. At the first dance we had, we omitted to invite these, and the result was some unkind feelings, but before the winter closed it was all harmonious, and we got much reasonable enjoyment from our dancing.

New York City in 1821

The next spring after coming to Lansingburgh, the spring of 1821, I first went to the city of New York. I sailed down the Hudson in a sloop belonging to Mr. James Dougery of Lansingburgh. I had not before been below Albany, so it was all new and interesting to me — the varied shores, villages, the Catskill Mountains, West Point, highlands and palisades. Put up at a private boarding place on Pearl Street near the Battery, and the first evening I must see a theater, and went to some place up Broadway, for the Chatham had been burned. It seemed to satisfy my curiosity on that subject, for I never after felt much wish to go. The next morning, to see the city, I started up Pearl Street and some way crossed Broadway without observing it and came out into view of a broad water. And having started east I thought, of course, it was the East River, when in fact I had gone the circuit and come out on the Hudson. Then going up Broadway I came to vacant lots only two blocks above the Park. There was an open sewer in Canal Street and Greenwich was two miles out. Crossed over to Brooklyn and went onto quite a high hill, about I should think where the center of the city now stands, from which I got a very fair view of New York. There was little that you now see there except

the City Hall and Trinity Church. Returned by steamboat to Albany, taking about twenty-four hours.

I should have said when I had been in Lansingburgh a month or two my chum, Jasper Newton, called on me for a day or two, he being then on his way to Maryland, where he had a brother residing. We had a very pleasant visit, and he went on and joined his brother. We kept up a frequent correspondence, till at the end of about one year, I received instead of an expected letter from him, one from that brother telling me that he had from the unfavorable character of the country sickened and died. To me this was sad news indeed. No death, even of relatives, more deeply affected me. It seemed for a time as though my all was gone, and even now, after so many years, and the great number of changing scenes, through which I have passed, I still feel the loss of my youth's dear companion.

First Sea Voyage

When some two years or more had passed at hard work at Lansingburgh, I tired and longed for a change. So against all persuasion of friends I determined to put out somewhere, and perhaps the greater influence on my mind was to see something more of the world. So I went to New York with the view to ship to some place south, and on arriving there noticed on the North River a schooner advertised for Darien, Georgia. As that was about as far south as I could sail on the Atlantic side in the United States I engaged a passage aboard of her. She was to sail in a few days but was longer delayed than intended by a tremendous easterly November rain storm. It drove the water over the docks and into cellars. But at that time the lower part of the city about up to the Park had been deserted on account of the yellow fever.[4] The disease had subsided, and the residents were then about to return into this deserted section. It was indeed a strange sight to thus see a city without people — no shipping at the docks for a long distance each way from the Battery. A great share of the city business had for a long time been in temporary shanty buildings erected on the then vacant grounds up the Hudson, the shipping lying opposite in the river.

I was now to take my first sea voyage. We sailed as soon as the storm was over, in a high sea, for the wind had shifted to the southwest and blew hard. Before we had reached the Narrows I had the new experience of sea sickness. When we got out we

---

[4] *An often fatal disease carried by mosquitoes, characterized by fever and jaundice.*

could not so lay our proper course, but that we were by this southwest wind driven out into the Gulf Stream to stem its current. For a day or two it was pleasant, and from the novelty I enjoyed it and sang with Byron's Child Harold:

> *"With thee, my bark, I swiftly go athwart the foaming brine,*
> *Nor care what land thou bear'st me to so not again to mine."*

Then came on a northeaster, which against the Gulf Stream current raised a tremendous sea, making our little vessel roll and pitch awfully. At night I could hear the water splashing and whizzing by my ears, as I lay trembling in my berth, and by day the look out was in the thick rain storm and the foaming sea. Our table was on the cabin floor, and even then, as the craft rolled, we had to hold onto our plates and cups or they would have been in a pile on the one side of the cabin, and then on the

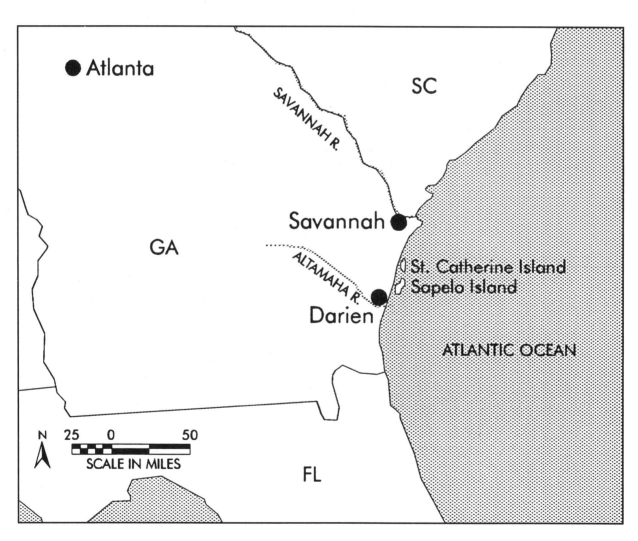

John Ball's Travels
Georgia, 1822-1823

other. When after three days it cleared off and we got an observation for the latitude, we had made but little headway against the current. In the pleasant weather we made better headway, so that on our twelfth day out we discovered land, which proved to be St. Catherine's Island, south of the Savannah River. Then, as fate would have it, there was brewing another northeastern November storm. The captain, a Swede who I fear did not know too much, said that to avoid the coming storm, instead of keeping out by Sapelo Island and entering the usual entrance to the Altamaha River at its south end; he would go in the entrance at the north end, between that and St. Catherine Island, which he well understood, and thus avoid the coming storm and keep down what is called the inland passage, and so up the Altamaha River to his port, Darien, which is some eighteen miles up the same.

Shipwrecked

But in the attempt he missed the channel and went onto the south bar about two miles from land, Black Beard, an uninhabited island near Sapelo. The sun was then an hour or two high, the wind not blowing very hard, and as they claimed, the tide rising, so they expected to get off. But, as it proved, it was high tide and the wind rose and the storm soon began, and all efforts to get the ship off were found fruitless. Some of the passengers and ship's men attempted to go to land in our only boat, to get help. They soon swamped, but got back to the vessel and got aboard, but lost the boat. Our troubles thickened fast, the waves so raised and lifted the vessel that it beat hard on the bar, making it necessary to lighten it as soon as possible. So they threw over the deck cargo and all the water with the rest.

Then the masts must be cut away, and they had only an old dull broad axe for the work. As it looked to me, there was no one who knew how to fell trees. So I took a turn at it, but had struck but a few blows when a wave came over the deck and knocked me down. Still I gathered myself up and chopped away, cutting the shrouds on one side, and pitching the masts over on the opposite side, where they were kept by the other shrouds. There was a break in the deck, so that the quarter deck was so much raised that the sea did not sweep over that part so much. As it was storming hard and there was nothing more that we could do, we went into the cabin for shelter. But before midnight the vessel from its beating broke, and the cabin filled rapidly. All scampered for the quarter deck, where we could just hold our own, about every third wave passing over us. The tide, after a time, went down so the vessel did not beat so

hard and we waited with some hope that if she held out till morning some chance of escape might be found, but the light only the plainer showed our perilous situation.

The danger had come upon us so gradually that it was met with more composure than one would expect, considering the diversity of persons on board. There were twenty-six in all – the captain, mate and common sailors, merchants who had been to New York to purchase goods, an Irishman, wife and boy of twelve, and three negro men, with others I cannot describe. There was little said during the night on deck, but probably much thought withal. My own recollection of the past was very vivid indeed. Things came to my mind that had not before, for a long time. I felt the chances for escape were very small, and that I should soon know whether a state of consciousness really existed after death – a matter of which I had doubts, and my then condition did not at all change my views, or produce any special alarm. Knowing that death was man's lot, I could see no reason why, if an hereafter existed, I was not as fitted to go into the other world then as I probably could, but made no promises of a better life, as imperfect as I felt that I had at all times thus far lived. But the grief that my parents and other relatives and friends would feel, if they learned that I was drowned or perhaps nothing of my fate, most deeply affected me. I much wished to be able to say to them I had safely completed my voyage.

The Rescue

The morning light showed a foaming sea all around us and the sight of low land in the distance, with the prospect of a continuance of the storm; so that no vessel out, would approach the shore, or the people on land, five miles off, would in any probability discover us. The tide being now at the ebb, our vessel lay almost high and dry, but she was so far broken that we could not hope she would stand through another high tide. There seemed a general consternation for a time, but it was said that as the tide rose it would set toward land, and that if rafts could be made out of the spars still floating by the vessel, we might still float to land. We immediately went to work to lash them together for that purpose, and even this desperate chance seemed to produce considerable sociability, even though our water had been thrown over and there was no food to be got at.

About the time that some were preparing to take the rafts we discovered a brig sailing down the inland passage, but as it was five miles off we had little hopes that they would discover our hulk through the storm, or if they did that they would come out to our relief. After watching them a short time we saw them change their course and put out, and we well knew it could be for no purpose but for our aid. Then for the first there was marked feeling shown aboard the wreck. It was as the news of pardon, and tears were shed. But still there were many difficulties to meet. They well knew the channel and kept it, sailing forward and back, but on account of the bars and shallow water they could not come near us, even with their well manned boat. So to reach them we had to wade some distance through the rolling waves.

The first effort was to get off the woman, but in the same boat went the sailors, the officers having lost all control over them; then others, as many as it was thought the boat could safely take. It was said they could take but three at a time, and then that they could take more when they found that they should not get us all off. I had stood by, feeling my claims were no better than others, and some were out some distance waiting on a bar for the boat, when it was said that they could take one more. I asked if any one would go, but the tide had risen and it looked so bad, they declined, so I jumped in and rushed for the boat. Before I had reached it the waves broke over me several times. I braced against them till passed, and then rushed forward in the trough, I was much exhausted when I reached the boat, and was told often by my shipmates that the men would have rowed off and left me if they had not urged them to

hold on. I was the last that was taken off, for none after could leave the wreck for the boat. Still on board were the captain, mate, three Irishmen and three negroes. These took the rafts and all drifted ashore except one of the negroes who was swept off the raft and drowned. Our vessel sailed back into the channel and landed us on Sapelo Island. At a Mr. Hopkins' plantation we were kindly fed and warmed. All was satisfactory except the thought that our ship fellows left on board must in all probability perish, for we did not know of their escape till their arrival the next morning.

The storm had passed, and the next morning on going out we found the sun shining brightly on a landscape all new to me, the foliage, fields and fruits being tropical. There were fields of cotton and orange orchards. The thought struck me, have I indeed changed worlds? Never in life did I experience a more thankful, soothing feeling.

The poor woman, when she found her husband and son were left on the wreck, was frantic, saying if they had left her with them she would not complain. But their arrival relieved her distress.

The wreck did go to pieces the night after we left, and the next morning we were informed there were wreckers all along the shore ready to seize every bale of goods and every trunk the moment they reached the shore, and secure them for their own personal benefit. In some cases the clothing of our people were afterwards seen on others' backs.

The busy docks at New York City in 1828, just a few years after Ball took passage for Georgia. [Collections of the Library of Congress, #LC US262-24285]

A WINTER AT DARIEN, GEORGIA
CHAPTER IV

The vessel that saved us was bound for Darien, so the next day after the taking us up, they continued their voyage on to that place, where they arrived before night. On the way up we made from our scant means a purse, for the brave men who had risked their lives to save ours, and we soon by donation or other wise, got what would make out one full suit. I escaped with shirt, coat, vest and pants and my small means which were in bank bills in my pocket. My hat, boots and baggage, in which was my college diploma, went to the waves.

I found Darien a small village with a few stores built in the Spanish fashion, they being the first people here. A mortar made of lime, sand and oyster shells filled into a mould formed the wall of the building, and when dried, the mould was raised up and filled in again. The door and window frames and timbers for floors were then put in.

This is the county seat of Mackintosh County, and the harbor on the Altamaha River, as Savannah is on the Savannah River — sea vessels coming up to this place, and keel boats, then going above to Macon and Milledgeville, propelled by negro power, for there were then no steamboats in that state. But a little above the town, on the river, there was a powerful steam saw and rice mill — that is for the rice mortars to pound off the hulls, and gangs of saws to cut from the pine, ship-stuff sixty feet long.

Teaching Again

Well, at Darien I boarded at a Mr. Hunter's, and succeeded in raising a small private school, and there passed the winter of 1822 and 1823, and the spring till May. Being latitude about 32 degrees, ten further south than I had before resided, I found a great change in the climate, December the tempera-ture of the North in October, and January cooler, and one severe turn in February — so cold that it froze quite hard, injuring their orange trees. During the cold spell the pigeons and robins came calling along in great numbers, getting such food from the berries in the swamps and otherwise as they could. And when a few days after it turned warm, they all came back and passed North in one day, and so thick that they darkened the air.

Life of the Slaves

I was here in the midst of Negrodum, only a fifth of the people of the country being of the white race, and very few free negroes. The Butler plantation, on an island, in the river against the town, had its 400 slaves with only one overseer — the owner, Mr. Butler, living in Philadelphia. On Sunday they would come into town by thousands, usually bringing a chicken, tarapin [large turtle], fish or some little thing of their procuring, for trade, the stores being kept open till ten o'clock. All the negro families have their little patch of ground by their cabins to culti-vate and raise their chickens, etc. They would meet acquaintances in town on these Sundays and talk and laugh — a more happy, jolly set of creatures I never saw. There was one church in the place, and such of them as chose, but there were very few, could go into a small gallery.

Guard Duty

At all times, at the ringing of the eight o'clock town bell, on all days, they had to go home, and any found in the streets after were taken to the guard house. And every white resident was enrolled to take his turn about once a week or two, to patrol the streets and guard the place on account of the slaves, fearing an insurrection or some mischief from them, and I had to take my part. I saw no severe punishment, the usual punishment for bad behavior being imprisonment in the public goal [jail] or short feed till they promised, as they soon did, good behavior.

I witnessed a sheriff's sale of the whole people of a plantation, some 60 or 80 men and women and of all sizes. And there was great grief among them, that they would be bid off separately and thus parted. But the matter was compromised, and when they were told that they were all going home again together, you never saw a happier set. I noticed that when anything happened to them, like the loss of a child, their grief seemed deep and the manifestations boisterous. But in a few days, all was apparently forgotten and the afflicted mother as gay as ever.

Saw much that satisfied me that the African and Caucasian are constitutionally unlike, and cannot by any education be made, even to fully understand each other, any more than the ox and the horse. Each may have good qualities, but each in his own way. The negro docile or he could not be enslaved, cheerful under all circumstances, never committing suicide.

My landlord however, had a very capable slave, Sam. He was chief butler to the whole establishment, did the marketing and oversaw the cooking and dealt the rum to visitors — no, not rum, but good brandy or gin, and these we always had on the table to temper the poor water. In following this prescription I feared I might make it a needful habit, but it did not prove so, I left the habit when I left the country and without remorse.

Because one meets occasionally a smart negro like Sam, some seem to think all of them can be made the same. I account for most of the smart ones in this way: tho' all the slaves imported may have been bought by Christians on the Guinea Coast, they were by no means all raised there. But by their wars and trade inland and even across to Madagascar and Abyssinia, the captives in war and others may have been sold as slaves on the western coast, and thus have brought to the States people, tho' dark, with more of the Caucasian than Guinean in their veins. There were a set in Carolina and Georgia called the round heads markedly different than the usual stock.

Savannah

As the days lengthened, tho' slower there and the change not so sudden as at the North, I felt it was hazardous to health to stay longer, so took my very limited earnings, bid goodbye and started out on foot for Savannah, stopped at a plantation over night, and the next day, taking the stage that came along reached there.

This gave me the opportunity of seeing something more of the country. But everywhere far back from the coast it is quite the same — the plains with long leaved, straight bodied, tall pine, or the river and creek bottom swamp, rice lands, when with much labor cleared. For in these grow the magnolia and many forest trees and thickets of vines and on their margin, the live oak. It looked odd to see large leaved evergreen trees and the mighty flower of the magnolia and the trailing moss, hanging from high trees almost to the ground.

But I omitted to mention that I continued my legal studies at Darien, and should have been admitted an attorney had I been there the required six months. I read their statute laws much of which I found related to the institution of slavery. Some of the provisions seemed strangely inhuman, such as the making it penal to teach them to read, and others quite humane, making it lawful for any one to take an old and decrepit slave who was neglected by his owner, and care for him and enforce the owner to meet the charge. And oh! while residing there, though I saw nothing of the barbarous physical treatment of the slave that has been so much talked of at the North, nor do I believe it ever existed only as an exception to the general rule, with brutal men, whose natural cruelty is shown elsewhere towards domestic animals, still I saw and felt its terrible blighting effect on the country and its inhabitants and ever after viewed it as a national curse.

After spending a few days in the beautifully laid out city of Savannah, I took passage by sea for New York. It was very warm and there were many passengers, who being uncomfortable below, ladies and all sought the shade of the sails, on the bales of cotton. But before we arrived in New York it became uncomfortably cold. I felt not only seasick but sick otherwise, during the whole passage, and so continued my voyage up the Hudson to Lansingburgh, which I had left some seven months before and with little gained except additional knowledge of the world, and with the loss of having contracted the ague, that kept me confined for two months, cared for by my kind sister, Mrs. Powers.

BEGINS THE PRACTICE OF LAW
CHAPTER V

As soon as I was any way so far recovered as to be able to do so, I took stage for New Hampshire to visit my old home and friends, and recruit [recuperate]. And I did recruit on breathing my native mountain air so fast that I enjoyed it right well, roaming about the fields, hills and mountains. I think no case of the ague was ever known to originate in that mountain region, probably from the good reason that the granite soil has not enough fertility to produce enough vegetation, that when decayed vitiates the air. After my shipwreck, residence South and sickness, my friends in New Hampshire were indeed rejoiced to see me convalescent.

After thus spending nearly a year away from my legal studies in the state of New York, I returned to Lansingburgh and resumed them for another year. For by their rules no legal student could apply to be examined for admission to the bar as an attorney till he could produce a certificate from a practicing one, that he had studied in his office for three years. This certificate I obtained the next summer of 1824 and went to Utica, where the Supreme Court was in session, and was examined and admitted as an attorney of that court, but still no counsellor. I went from Schenectady by boat on the then new canal. It was not yet completed through to Buffalo. We arrived at Little Falls in the night, and there came on a thunder storm with most vivid lightning, so that during the flashes, the rocks and scenery thereabouts could be seen as plainly as in full daylight, giving a more striking and lasting impression than seeing the same by day. The scenery all along the Mohawk is interesting and the spreading out of its valley about Utica with its fertility in that part truly so.

Meets Aaron Burr

Spencer was then Chief Justice, and Platt and Woodworth Judges. But there was one attending at the court at the time who attracted more notice than the court itself. This was Aaron Burr, who was attending to argue some important causes before the court as counsel. He was said then to be nearly eighty years old, small in statue, his head white, but erect and mentally in full vigor. When he came into the courtroom, there was shown a sensation by all, even the Judges on the bench. I met him once afterwards. It was on a steamboat ascending the Hudson at night. During the evening he led the conversation, relating many matters of history, and of course he was listened to with deep interest by all.

Law Partnerships

When thus licensed to practice law, I went into partnership with an old practitioner at Lansingburgh by the name of Walter Raleigh.

* * *

About a year later it was proposed that I should go in with another of the practicing lawyers, Jacob C. Lansing, one of the men with whom I had read, he and Walbridge having dissolved. He was much out and rather negligent of business, and his friends seemed to want someone they could find in the office. I recollect his own brother, Abram C. Lansing, used to apparently with design, give his business to me. I was too diffident to ever appear in court to make motion or try a case. But office business I strictly attended to, and pretty well understood. But

*Jacob C. Lansing, John Ball's law
partner in Lansingburgh, New York.
[Lansingburgh, New York, Historical
Society]*

as it again happened the partnership of Lansing &
Ball continued but about another year.

Justice of Peace

Justices of the Peace, in the State of New York had
always been appointed by the governor of the state,
for all the cities and towns, till the year 1827; when,
by a change of the constitution, they were to be
elected by the people, four in each township, for a
term of four years. But for the purpose of electing
one each year, at the first election, choose the four;
and the four elected draw lots to determine who
should hold, the one, two, three or four years. When
the election was to come off there were many aspir-
ants for the office. Mr. Lansing wanted it, but our
friend said he was much out and I always in the
office, it better be given to me. And I was nominated.
Still Lansing ran, being much dissatisfied, as he
wanted it, that I should consent to be a candidate.
Mr. Walbridge was also a candidate. And come to the
election, neither of them were elected, but I was
among those who were. And as fortune would have

it, come to the drawing for the time of service, I drew
the four years. And Mr. Lansing was so much dissatisfied at my election, that he informed me that we
must dissolve partnership. And as the whole thing
had been done without my solicitation, I did not feel
myself to blame, so I readily assented to his wish in
the matter. The election was the first of November,
and I was not to commence acting in my office of
Justice till the first of January. So I embraced the
opportunity to visit my friends in New Hampshire,
going by the way of Boston. November was very cold
that year, so I had a bleak time on my native hills. I
returned through Vermont and to Whitehall and on
my journey from there it came on to thaw.

Now I opened an office alone and prepared to
commence to officiate as a magistrate. And soon
there were suits commenced before me, mostly for
the purpose of making collections. A justice's juris-
diction extending, I think to the sum of $200. The
civil suits were not often litigated, the plaintiff
making proof of the indebtedness. On the first contested trial where counsel was employed on both
sides, the old fellows, who opposed my election,
came in to see me break down. But seeing their
object, it did not happen, so they came in no more
from curiosity. I had most of the justice business of
the village and some of the best business men gave
me their law business, so my prospects for a livelihood were looking quite promising.

Mock Marriages

In one instance soon after my term commenced,
there was quite a gathering of young people at a Mr.
Gaston's. Among the rest a Mr. Ford, a sadler, and a
daughter of a Mr. A. C. Lansing, who took a fancy to
play marriage, and called on me as a justice to officiate. So, and perhaps improperly, I in a very informal manner married them. But it did not end
with them, they soon paired off and most of the
party were married in like manner. It was treated by
all as a part of the sport of the evening. But next day
some mischief makers got hold of it, and claimed
that it was all binding, and all but persuaded parties
concerned, that such was the case, producing quite
a village sensation, and the strange news was spread
through the country, even published in New York
papers. The first I knew of the commotion one of the
parties, a Mr. Ives, came into my office under much
excitement, and exclaimed, "Ball, what have you
been doing, they say all those marriages last night
are binding and I had rather give a hundred dollars."
There was amusement as well as alarm out of it. But
it was concluded that intention was needed to make
it valid.

I have omitted to speak of my admission as counsellor-at-law, which by their rules is allowed in three years after admission as attorney. I went to New York City at the sitting there of the Supreme Court in the summer of 1827.

Philadelphia

The time appointed for examination being some few days ahead, I thought I would go and see Philadelphia, having never been there. So I took boat for Elizabethtown and before reaching there the passengers were assigned to coaches of a certain number, so that there might be no delay, and on arriving there in a twinkling we found ourselves on our journey in some twenty carriages at full speed. And when we had reached the place for changing horses, they were already in the harness and hitched on as soon as the others could be loosed, so in two minutes, I should think, we were again under way. And on arriving at Bordenton away we scampered on to a steamboat that took us down the Delaware to Philadelphia before night.

On going out the next day to see the city, I was struck with its contrast with New York, streets all regular and much less bustle in the same, people very civil, answering all inquiries in the most civil manner. I visited the old state house and saw the bell that declared the glad tidings at the Declaration of Independence. And while looking about the ground near the same, a gentleman asked me if I was a stranger in the place, who, on being informed that I was, spent some hours in showing some of the objects of greatest interest about the city, among the rest, West's picture of Christ healing the sick. The city then extended about half of the way from the Delaware to Schuylkill, out to which I went to see the waterworks. Returned to New York, was examined in the old City Hall, passed and was admitted counsellor, which then entitled me to be examined for practice in the court of Chancery. So on my return stopped at Albany for that purpose, and the chancellor gave me a solicitor's license.

Voting for Jackson

In that same year came on the political campaign when General Jackson was first elected president. And I was out and out a Jackson man, and I also was at the previous contest in 1823, when he, Clay, Adams and Crawford were candidates, resulting in no choice, and Clay and Adams joining, the states chose Adams. At the election Jackson was my choice out of the four, but he received but two other votes in the village.

Lansingburgh, New York, 1840, with Hudson River in foreground. Powers oilcloth factory is in center. [Sketch by John Barber, original in Lansingburgh, New York, Historical Society]

FAMILY TRAGEDY
CHAPTER VI

First Oilcloth Factory

My friend Powers was then an Adams man. And he had now shifted his business from school teaching to the manufacture of floor oilcloth. There was then little if any made in this country, that used here being imported from England. He knew nothing of the business, but being of a mechanical and inventive turn, could make it. So after experimenting for a time in a small way he succeeded in making an article that was well received in the New York market. He then proceeded to make preparation to extend the business, by erecting a brick factory of five stories and 150 feet in length. And commenced his business in the same in the spring of 1829. Up to which time my own business had prospered fairly and I deemed myself a permanently settled citizen of Lansingburgh, well known to all and generally commended, taking a part in its concerns generally, its amusements, especially the dancing of winter evenings — never, however, neglecting my business, my Justice business requiring me to be in my office punctually for the convenience of the numerous callers in that line. One evening my friend Powers called there and said he wished to speak to me about his own business and situation, or to that effect; he wished me, should he pop off, those were his words, to look to and aid his family. I told him I was as like to pop off as himself, but should anything happen, after what he had done for me, he might well suppose I would do it without the asking.

Being a prudent, thoughtful man, it was natural that he should feel a concern for his family, should he be taken away. I say he was prudent, perhaps his ambition to extend his business had carried him beyond what was strictly so, for in erecting his building he had gone, for a man of his means, deeply in debt.

From what so soon followed, one might well ponder, whether his conversation with me that evening was not a presentiment of what was so soon to happen. For in a week from that time, news was brought me, that he was badly burned. I hastened to the factory, for the family residence was in a part of the same building, to witness a scene indeed of horror. He was burned to a crisp, almost from head to foot and my sister and one or two of the men badly burned in their effort to save him.

Advertisement for William Powers oilcloths, 1817. [Lansingburgh, New York, Historical Society]

Detail from lithograph of Lansingburgh, New York. Powers oilcloth factory is No. 58. Buildings across the avenue are also part of company. [Burleigh Lithograph, 1891, copy in Lansingburgh, New York, Historical Society]

Death of Brother-in-Law

It was this way. He was making a copal varnish, a composition much used in his work, in a high sheet-iron kettle over coal on a movable, or hand furnace, standing at a fireplace in the opposite end of the factory from the dwelling part. The varnish caught on fire, and in his effort to extinguish it, his clothes caught, which being a cotton shirt and linen pants, he was soon enveloped in flames. His wife happened to be near on the sidewalk and some of the men, when they reached him, made the effort to get his clothes off of him, so they too were burned. He was so deeply burned that it seemed to have destroyed his nervous sensation, so he did not complain of his suffering more than they. He seemed fully conscious of his situation and thought with all around him, that there was no hopes for his recovery from the terrible injury. The next day he became unconscious and in a few hours died, and in less than 24 hours from the time of the accident.

While conscious his friends came to him to converse, among others a Dr. Spafford, a Swedenborgian.[5] He answered him, "Doctor, we have talked of all this before now." Seemed quite composed in his mind, considering his hopeless condition, said

his books would show the state of his business matters. And as to the future our condition after this life, he showed no fears, thought of those matters as he had often before expressed to me, that it was a subject of conjecture of which we could know but little, in fact nothing. The young Presbyterian minister of the place came, wishing to talk to him, but feeling that it would only annoy him without any possible good, I objected to it. And when he seemed disposed to protract the conversation, I told him he must excuse me now, as I must attend to my dying friend. But when there was a proper opportunity if he wished to say anything to me on the subject of religion, I hoped he would not defer it till I was on my death-bed.

Thus died William Powers the third, for I had known his father and his grandfather, who bore the same name. Not only his family but the whole community seemed paralyzed at the shocking manner of his death. All the business men of the place had full confidence in his punctuality and ability to accomplish what he had undertaken, and as far as asked by him, aided him in his enterprise. When we had laid him in his grave and looked about to see what was to be done to fill the large place he had filled, it looked hopeless. His very art seemed to have been lost with him. Some of the compositions for his cloth, he prepared with his own hands and the workmen did not understand them. My sister was suffering for some time from her burned hands, and the men had no heart to go to work. So for a time everything lay as he left it.

Carrying on Mr. Powers' Work

His two boys were young, Albert E. twelve, and Nathaniel B. but six. And it seemed so hopeless to even carry on the business so as to pay the debts, being some $8,000 and all the property besides the factory not amounting to near that sum, my sister offered the creditors the factory and all, if they would take it and say they were paid. This, most of them being neighbors, they promptly declined, saying they would give time for their pay and the business must go on, for the benefit of the estate, and said, and did all they could to that end. So hopeless as it seemed, the men were induced to go to work and make the effort to carry on the business though it was even feared a merchantable article could not be made. Mr. Calvin Barker, the heaviest creditor, was very kind and a Mr. John Neil showed the men how to mix paints and shade the colors.

---

[5] *A follower of Emanuel Swedenborg, the religious and scientific writer.*

As for myself, I at once proposed to assist in settling the affairs of the estate and do some of the outdoor's affairs in carrying on the business, little expecting at first that the death of my friend would result in the entire change of the business of my life and residence. I went to New York to purchase paints and all the credit I could get was to the amount of $300. The business was carried on in the name of my sister as administratrix and she soon put some cloth on the market, which was well received. And when we could give the creditors orders on good carpet merchant houses in the city, to pay for the stock of paints and other materials wanted, our credit became good and the business went along.

Closes Law Office

But I soon found that I was devoting so much time to the factory business, my own office business would leave me. So after consideration, feeling that I must abandon one or the other, I concluded to shut up my law office and give my whole time to the business left by my friend. So I went and boarded with my sister and gave my whole soul to the work of extricating her affairs. Acted as foreman in the factory, directing the whole business of the same. And from the aid of the kind neighbor painter, soon learned to compound paints and in fact to do any and all parts of the work. But I was engaged mainly in planning the work for the men so as to make the most of their labor. The greatest economy was practiced by my sister in all things to increase the means, being so limited, to carry on the business. She hired a woman to keep her house and went into the factory and in the ornamenting took the place of a man saving so much in wages. Even Albert was turned to account in running errands and doing chores, which he attended to faithfully, if he did not meet with a book, which if he got hold of, everything else was apt to be forgotten. He could read at three years old, and is still reading. I have never known a person who could read understandingly so fast.

Business Trips

And as for myself I never worked harder, for I saw daily more to do than could be accomplished. For I shirked no part of the work that I could lay my hands to. And when I went to New York on business I left by stage for Albany just in time to reach the night boat, so to be in the city in the morning for the day's business and probably returned by the next night's boat, neither using the means nor the time for theater going or other outside matters. In the spring after the death of Mr. Powers, I took some

samples of the cloth and patterns stamped on paper, so as to make but a light roll to carry, and went to New York, Philadelphia and Baltimore to get orders. I was gone but a week or so, though I had to travel across New Jersey by stage and to Baltimore by the Delaware and Chesapeake canal, and in that one trip procured advantageous orders for a whole year's work. So that we now felt assurance that we should work out successfully, pay up the debts and go along if no disaster overtook us.

For the first year I claimed no compensation for my services but the next year proposed to my sister as her business was proving successful, that I should have one-third of the net profits, which gave me some $1,600. At first she seemed much to rely on me in all matters of business, but after a time she showed a readiness in taking a part in all the concerns of the establishment. We well agreed in all things except the working hours of the men, she thought ten hours not enough.

In the spring following, 1831, a Mr. J. E. Whipple came to the factory and engaged to work on the same terms as the other men, at one dollar per day. He was a brother of a Rev. Mr. Whipple, the Episcopal clergyman of the place, and who had been very friendly to my sister in her troubles, though she was not of his church, or indeed of any other. And it was through him his brother was introduced to us. I thought it a little strange that he should take the place, as he had been for some time a clerk in Boston and had some means. But it was not my business to inquire why, as he took hold of the work assigned him faithfully and in earnest. And the business continued to prosper. I made a proposition to my sister to rent the establishment, but she did not wish to, saying she wanted the boys to learn the business. I told her I did too and that need not be in the way.

New Partner

When Mr. Whipple had been in the factory say six months he said to me one day, "Your sister has proposed to me to go into partnership with her, in this oilcloth business." And said, he thought considering my relation to it he ought first to speak to me on the subject. I told him at once, I hoped he would do so, if she wished it. And if he would, I would give him all the information I could about the business and introduce him to our customers. So the partnership was agreed on and the terms arranged, and to commence on the first of the coming January. Up to that time I was to continue to conduct the business.

My sister expected me to remain in the place and return to my law business, and proposed to give me a salary of $500 to aid them in sales and business outside. But I made up my mind that I would have no connection with the business unless a controlling one, and that I would not go back to hunt up my old law business, that had all gone into other hands. But having worked hard all my life so far, I would take a little recreation, and for that purpose having learned that a Mr. Wyeth of Boston, North Cambridge, was making arrangements to cross the plains and mountains to Oregon the next season, I wrote to him to inquire if I could join his party. He answered that I could and informed me of his plans and time of leaving. So without consulting any one and before I had even hinted to my sister or any one else of my intentions on the subject, I had engaged to meet him at Baltimore in the coming spring and accompany him to Oregon.

Leaves Lansingburgh

I then gave general notice, that all business of my own and of the Powers floor cloth manufacturing must be settled and closed up before the first day of January 1832, and it was accomplished fully to my satisfaction. And on that day I bade goodbye to my Lansingburgh friends, went to Albany and the next day started for the city of New York, going all the way by sleighing. There I collected dues to the factory and remitted the same. But I should have said that before I left, all the old debts were fully paid and there was left on hand a heavy stock and ample means for my sister to carry on the business without any of Mr. Whipple's. As I have said I conducted the business in Mrs. Powers' name as administratrix. And the new firm was D. Powers & Co., and so she has continued at the head of the firm.

John Ball had his portrait painted in 1831, the year before he joined the Wyeth party bound for Oregon. [Oregon Historical Society, #69869]

After deciding to close out his affairs in New York and head west, John Ball bought basic supplies in Lansingburgh for the trip ahead. This receipt from J.M. Caswell & Son lists powder, a shot pouch, a "percussion rifle with extra shot barrel," and a screw driver and hammer. [John Ball Collection, Grand Rapids Public Library, Box 25, Folder 498]

34

BOOK THE SECOND
Across the Plains to Oregon and the Return Home by Cape Horn 1832 - 1835

❧

The city of Washington, D.C., in 1834. John Ball visited two years earlier, before leaving for Oregon. [I.N. Phelps Stokes Collection, Miriam & Ira D. Wallach Division of Art, Prints, & Photographs, New York Public Library Astor, Lenox and Tilden Foundations, #1833-E-47]

1832

Bot of Berry Pike & son

Doll

Feb'y 20th

1 Pocket Sextant — 25 —
1 " Compass — 1 — 75
1 " Thermometer — 2 — 25
1 27ft tape measure — 1 — 75
                                     30 — 75
1 Mountain thermometer, rather altitude   2 —

Rec'd Payment — Berry Pike & son

While in Washington, D.C., John Ball purchased a sextant, compass, thermometer, tape measure and "mountain thermometer" to make scientific observations during his trip west with N.C. Wyeth. [John Ball Collection, Grand Rapids Public Library, Box 25, Folder 498]

~

NEW PLANS
CHAPTER I

While in New York I sought out and found some of John Jacob Astor's[6] Oregon men for the purpose of gaining information from them about that country. There were the Messrs. Seaton's who sailed around Cape Horn and to the Columbia River and assisted in establishing the trading post Astoria, and Ramsey Crooks, who conducted the land party for him across the continent, reaching Astoria the second year. They told me much of their experiences there. I then went to Philadelphia and Baltimore and made collections in each place for the oilcloth contracts, for my sister, and sent her back after my leaving, in all, some three thousand dollars.

Notables in Washington

Having the time, before the arrival from Boston of my Oregon traveling companions, I went for the first time to Washington. Put up at Brown's Hotel, standing there almost alone, on the Avenue, Washington then being comparatively but a village. General Ashley, who had long been in the fur trade from Missouri to the Mountains, was stopping at Brown's. So I took the liberty to call at his room and inform him of my intended journey and asking from him advice and information. He kindly answered many inquiries. But finally said, "Young man, it would be as difficult to tell all about it, all that may occur or be needed on such a journey, as for a carpenter to tell every blow he had got to strike on commencing to erect a house." He had sold out his fur business to William Sublette of St. Louis and others, and had been elected a member of Congress.

While thus spending a few days at Washington I took the opportunity with other things to attend the sitting of the United States Supreme Court. And then I listened to Chief Justice Marshall's celebrated decision of the Georgia and Cherokee case, with regard to the Cherokee lands. And, of course, attended the sitting of the houses of Congress, Calhoun, then Vice-President, presiding over the Senate, in which Benton, Clay, Webster and other celebrities were then members. As a presiding officer I have never seen Mr. Calhoun's equal, or a finer man to look on. And, as then constituted, it was indeed an august body and in the House were then Adams and Choate. The latter I knew well at College and there were others in both houses with whom I might without impropriety have claimed acquaintance. But no, I poked about as a stranger. And as such presumed to call on General Jackson at the White House without any introduction. He however received me kindly.

President Jackson

Then, as always through life, I neglected to make use of men in place and of notoriety, as I perhaps might have done to my great advantage. Had I then told the President and others of my proposed journey they might have taken such interest, as to have given some aid, or more notoriety to my journey and personal advantage after its performance. But so it has always been, I have never felt much deference for men barely on account of holding office or claiming consequence. Had I studied to make use of such and shown them more regard and aid, who knows but some more notorious place might not have been

---

[6] *B. 1763, d. 1848. Businessman and fur trader, founder of the American Fur Company.*

Nathaniel C. Wyeth, leader of the expedition that took John Ball to Oregon. [Oregon Historical Society, #OrHi 3632]

mine. But there is this consolation, I have no less self respect, and may have escaped more severe troubles than have now been my lot.

Captain N. Wyeth

After spending a few days at Washington I returned to Baltimore and awaited the coming from Boston by sea of Mr. Wyeth and his party. And they in a few days arrived, numbering about twenty. Mr. Wyeth I found a man of some intelligence and great energy in his undertakings. He had been a shipper of ice from a pond, Clear pond, in Cambridge. But his men were such loafers and laborers mostly, as he had picked up in and about Boston by high representations of the pleasures of the journey and the fortune-making result of the enterprise, none of them, as time showed, at all understanding what

they were going into. A Mr. Sinclair, myself and one other, I think joined them here. While at Baltimore I stopped at Belsover's, where was one of the best tables I ever sat at. And I made the best of it, knowing when I left it, I should go into camp life. I had always liked Baltimore, so beautifully located and its fine fountains of water.

Leaves Baltimore

Having arranged matters for our journey, about the middle of March we left Baltimore on the Baltimore and Ohio Railroad for Frederick, sixty miles, by horse power. That sixty miles was then more than all the other railroads in the Union. It had been built at enormous labor, graded down, and part of the way through the mountains to a dead level and the stringers, on which was riveted strap iron, were of cut granite rock. But they had been so moved out of place by the frost of the previous winter, that the cars moved roughly over them. From Frederick we took our journey on foot, having a wagon for our baggage. In fact commenced our camp life, sleeping at night under tents and cooking our grub at a fire by the roadside. And so for some days we trudged on. At Cumberland visited the coal mines, which to me were quite new and interesting as were many other things on our way, for I had never been before in these parts. And so we continued along on the National Cumberland road to Brownsville on the river Monongahela. There we took a steamboat for Pittsburgh, where on arriving we looked about to see its wonders; for from its history, its commanding location, at the junction of those two mountain streams to form the Ohio, and its coal and iron made it one of the most marked places in the country. In passing thus slowly the Alleghenies, I noticed with much interest the geology of the country.

Bound for St. Louis

From Pittsburgh we took passage in a steamboat bound for St. Louis. And as we descended the river I noticed its high bluffs, where at first the openings to the coal mines were high up the same, but as we sailed on, they gradually opened lower and lower, till the coal veins passed below the river. We stopped for a time at Cincinnati; which was then but a village, with few buildings but of wood and these of no great pretentions. That spring the river had been so high as to flood much of the town, doing a good deal of damage. Among the passengers on the boat, bound to Cincinnati was the Reverend Lyman Beecher,[7] and

[7] B. 1775, d. 1863. Religious leader and social reformer associated with the anti-slavery movement.

one pleasant day, as we were smoothly gliding down the stream, he and also Wyeth and myself were promenading the deck which had no bulwarks. We noticed that **he** turned many steps before he reached the stern of the boat, while we went so near that our next step would have been overboard. My companion remarked, "How is it that Mr. Beecher is so much more cautious than we sinners?" Implying that Mr. Beecher doubtless claimed that all would be right with him should he be drowned, while with us we made no pretentions in that direction.

We had a pleasant sail down the river, running the rapids at Louisville, and stopping there and at a few other places, but not at Cairo, for there, all was swamp about the mouth of the Ohio. And when we entered the Mississippi we found it a muddy instead of a clear stream like the Ohio, and that we made much slower progress in stemming its current. The first sight of this mighty river strikes one as a thing almost sublime, thinking of the thousand streams so far away that make up its rushing volume. Arriving at St. Louis, I found it then but a village, mostly consisting of old French buildings along the levee and a street near the river, but few good buildings in the place. Draw a line then from there to, say Detroit, and the entire white population beyond I do not think was ten, if five thousand. I saw a steamboat sail, while there to go up the Illinois River, with the United States soldiers to fight Black Hawk,[8] who was overrunning the country about where Chicago now is.

---

[8] B. 1767, d. 1838. Sauk Indian leader associated with the Black Hawk War in which he led his tribe back into Illinois lands previously ceded to the United States, causing an armed response by the U.S. government.

Like all members of the Wyeth party, John Ball signed a pledge agreeing to terms established by the American Society for Encouraging the Settlement of the Oregon Territory, and received Certificate No. 106 from the society. [John Ball Collection, Grand Rapids Public Library, Box 26, Folder 534]

St. Louis was a rapidly growing Mississippi River city when the Wyeth party arrived on the way west. [Collections of the Library of Congress, #LC USZ62-49333]

~

ACROSS THE PLAINS
CHAPTER II

Sail up the Mississippi

Here we expected to settle about the manner of performing our further journey. We did not propose to undertake it, without guides or inducing some experienced mountaineers to join our party. And we learned that a Mr. William Sublette of St. Louis, successor with Smith & Jackson, of Gen. Ashley in the mountain fur trade business, was now fitting out in the upper part of the state for their annual trip. So thinking that we might probably join his party in the journey, we determined to go right on up the country. So took a steamboat for Lexington which is in the west part of the state and near where was then his party. So we sailed up the Mississippi in company with the boat with the United States soldiers to fight Black Hawk, and parted with it at the entrance of the turbid waters of the Missouri into that river. It is a very interesting thing to observe long before you reach the junction, the clear waters of the Mississippi of the east side of the river and the turbid waters of the Missouri commingling with them, giving the riled look to the whole river.

The Missouri

The waters of the Missouri I have compared in color to that of your creamed coffee or kind of ash color. For the purpose of cookery and drinking if one chooses, the waters of the river are put into a cask and left to settle. But I noticed that the boatmen preferred it fresh from the river, drinking it down with apparent relish – and this, though when left to settle in the bucket there would be an inch of sediment at the bottom. On drinking it raw I could perceive the grit between my teeth. It comes sweeping along for thousands of miles from the summit of the Rocky Mountains. The country to the foot of those

mountains seems to the sight not to rise, still there is sufficient ascent to give a constant and rapid current to its waters, so rapid that we found our boat checked in its velocity the moment we entered the same. And we steamed on, day and night, varying our course to avoid snags and sand bars.

The country along the lower part of the river seemed well improved and occasionally a small village. And when we got a short distance above Jefferson we came to a bar that extended entirely across the river, with no place over three feet of water, and our boat drew six. And the way in such cases is to run the boat's bow hard into the sand and when the water has washed it away about the same, push it in farther and in that way, in time, work through it. But some of us tiring of this slow navigation, quit the boat and journeyed on foot. And thus got to Lexington first. This gave us the opportunity to see more of the country and the ways of its inhabitants. The country seemed rich and then but thinly settled, woodland and prairie interspersed. There were but few taverns along the road, but when we called at the cabin, the most were constructed of logs, we were hospitably received and lodged and fed in their best manner and at a very reasonable rate. As to their mode of cookery I noticed one thing to me peculiar, they cooked thin bread as well as meat and vegetables at each meal. It was a corn hoe or Johnny Cake of wheat flour biscuit, and the Johnny Cake made only with salt and water. Some think such is not good but I do.

Joins Fur Traders

When all had arrived at Lexington, we went on to Independence, near which Mr. Sublette and his party were in camp. And on meeting him he readily consented that we might join them on this condition: that we should travel fully under his discipline; take our due part with his people in guarding camp and defense in case of attack by the Indians, which he rather expected, from a personal dislike they had to him. They charged him with leaving the year before a horse in the country packed with infected clothing, to give them the smallpox. I hardly think he could have been guilty of it. We then traversed the country and purchased horses and mules for our journey over the plains and mountains. Rigged them with saddles for riding and packing, made up those packs by sorting out the goods; for Wyeth's party had brought on much more than they could pack. But for myself I had brought but little so had nothing to throw away. But Wyeth would start with so much, that he had to drop some things by the way. Among them a small anvil and blacksmith's tools.

Order of March

A Mr. Campbell of St. Louis also with some men joined Mr. Sublette's party, making in all some eighty men and three hundred horses. For with the traders, each man had the care in camp and charge in marching three horses, one to ride and two with packs. And besides they took an extra number to supply the place of any that might fail in strength or be stolen. And thus rigged and ready we started on our march from Independence, on what was then in much use, the Santa Fe road or trail, leading off in a southwest direction, crossing the west line of the state some twelve miles south of the Missouri. Our order of march was always double file, the horses led, the first attached to the rider's and the third to him. So when under way our band was more than a hundred horses long — Mr. Sublette always giving all orders and leading the band, and Mr. Campbell as lieutenant bringing up the rear and seeing that all kept their places and the loose animals did not stray away.

Leaves Last Settlement

Our last encampment, before crossing the west line of the state, was at a Morman settlement. They had come and settled here the previous fall, on this extreme border of the settled world. We procured from them some milk and they otherwise treated us very kindly. They thought then that they had found a permanent home. But no, like all new religionists, they were doomed to much persecution. I remember when the Methodists were slighted. It was the 12th of May that we left this last settlement and continued our march on said Santa Fe road over a beautiful

John Ball made careful scientific observations, including these mileage calculations, throughout his trip west. Note that after leaving Independence, Missouri, on May 12, the party made 27 miles on the Santa Fe Trail two days later. [John Ball Collection, Grand Rapids Public Library, Box 26, Folder 536] prairie country, some two or three days, then left it and turned to the northwest and in a few days more came to the Kansas river, at a point I think near where is now Topeka. Here we found means to cross the river and swam our horses. For here was one white man, acting I think as a gunsmith for the Indians. He was the last white man we saw except of our own party.

Kansas River

We continued our march up the Kansas river along the edge of the prairie back of the timber bordering the river. For on most the larger western rivers and often on the smaller, as far as the land is moist, there is timber, but beyond grass. And in the spring or fall, the fire sweeping through this grass kills the timber on its border. But then it will, if the seasons are wet spring up again. So there was a constant warfare between the fires and the trees till these prairie fires were stopped by the settlers.

At this time I think the Indians were away, but we passed one of their villages where I noticed their mode of building. They dug holes in the dry ground some five or six feet deep and then built a roof of split plank, so made quite a warm winter house. When we had reached near the mouth of the Big Blue river, we left Kansas and traveled for days over the rolling prairies, encamping at night on that stream. One day on this prairie march with our band of packed horses, we overtook General or Captain Bonneville, who had also started out on a trading excursion, but with wagon, and with which he went all the way to the mountains, but with much difficulty. We halted for a few minutes to salute them and passed on, traveling with double the speed. The last time we encamped on the Blue, it was but a stagnant pool. And the next day's usual march, about 20 or 25 miles, brought us to the Platte about where is now Fort Kearney.

On this first part of our journey we did not depend at all on game for subsistence, but on supplies packed along on our horses. Mr. Sublette's party had also driven along cattle to slaughter on the way; as the horses never went faster than a walk, they could keep up. Then were some deer seen, but as yet no buffalo, so there was no reliance on game, or intended to be, till we should reach the buffalo. And now we continued our march over the smooth bottom of the turbid Platte river on the south side, the river riley, broad and rapid, no falls, but a sufficient descent in the country to give a rapid current — from a half to a whole mile wide and very shallow. It gives its full share of the mud of the Missouri — some timber on its islands and on its shores, bottoms broad and rich, bounded by broken bluffs and all the country beyond rolling.

Hunting for Provisions

Our provisions were becoming nearly exhausted and we were daily expecting to see our future resource, the buffalo, but none were met with, till the day we reached the forks of the Platte, when nearly our last meal on hand had been consumed. And the same day too, we had the last shower of rain of any account. Up to this time, about the first of June, we had occasional rains, and the prairies had become green affording good feed for our animals and the wild ones too on their native range. Not far above the junction of the North and South Forks of the Platte our band forded the south branch without any serious difficulty, the depth of water not being so great as to come over the saddles or wet many of the packs. But there being some fears of a quicksand bottom, its safe accomplishment gave great satisfaction. A short ride over the bluffs brought us to the north and main branch, in all its characteristics like the main river below the junction.

Mode of Encampment

Now came a march of day after day up this North Platte of great sameness. The main band keeping straight on the way, when the buffalo were not met with crossing our tracks. A few of the best hunters, each with two horses, one to ride and another on which to pack the meats, would leave the band and range the country back, kill and dress the animal and bring the meat to our night's encampment.

And I should have before described our mode of encamping. Mr. Sublette leading the band, always selected the ground, having reference in doing so to water, always encamping on the river or other stream, to feed for horses and the safety of the place for defense in case of an attack, which he seemed to rather expect. And if such place was reached by that time, he usually ordered "halt" by the middle of the afternoon, so as to give the horses time to feed and make full preparation for night. The horses were unpacked and men or messes arranged in a manner to leave a large hollow square, the stream forming one side. And then the horses were immediately hoppled, four feet tied together, and turned out of camp and a guard placed beyond them, to keep them from straying too far or drive them if attacked. Then about sundown he would cry out "ketch up, ketch up" always repeating his order. Then each man would bring in the horses he had charge of, keep them still hoppled and tie them to short stakes carried with us, driven close into the ground, giving each one as much room as could be without in-terfering with others, so that they could feed also during the night. Then a guard, changed every three hours, sat for the night. As soon as light in the morn-ing the order would be "turn out, turn out." And all would rise from their earthly beds, turn the horses out to bite, get a hearty breakfast, then the horses were saddled and packed and formed in line and the order given to "march." And as a reward for their expedition, the first ready took their place nearest to the commandant. In the middle of the day a stop was made, the horses unpacked to rest them, but not turned out, and a lunch taken by the men, if wished, of meat already cooked, and in half an hour pack up and march on.

Buffalo

We had now reached the region where there was no growing timber even along the river. And our fuel for cooking was the dry buffalo droppings. We usually in this part of our journey cooked our meat by boiling it in our camp kettles. And it was rather hard fare, for the buffalo were still lean in flesh, they getting quite reduced in flesh during the winter from their poor chance. The men felt the change from common food to this lean meat only and with-out even salt very severely, and rapidly grew weak and lean. The men would almost quarrel for any part of the animal that had any tallow, even the caul. But as soon as the buffalo improved in flesh and we got where there was wood to roast whole sides by, the men rapidly improved. I was a little surprised that I stood this change of life and living about as well as the mountaineers, and better than most of the new ones at it, and as to a camp life I rather enjoyed its ways. I had for bed purposes, the half of a buffalo robe, an old camlet cloak with a large cape, and a blanket. I spread the robe on the ground, wrapped the blanket about my feet and the cloak around me, throwing the cape loosely over my head to break off the moonshine, and a saddle for my pillow. And oh!

I always slept most profoundly. We had tents, but it never raining and but little dew, we did not use them. I felt less discomfort from the change of life than I expected, and much enjoyed every day's march. For at every mile I met with much that to me was interesting, while Wyeth's men dwelt on the hardships and privations and cursed the day they were induced into the undertaking.

North Platte

At times we would not see a buffalo for a day or two, and then in countless numbers. One day we noticed them grazing on the opposite side of the river on the wide bottoms and the side bluffs beyond like a herd of cattle in a pasture, up and down the country on that side as far as we could see, and con-tinued the same during our twenty-five miles' march and no end to them ahead, probably, 10,000 seen in that one day. The greatest unevenness of the endless plain, the bottoms of the river over which we were marching, were the buffalo paths made by following one path, direct from some break in the bluff, back to the river. For they range far back for their feed, but must come to the river for their drink. We saw not a spring or crossed a stream in traveling hundreds of miles up the North Platte. But we crossed many what are called dry rivers — beds of gravel and sand — where torrents must have run at the melting of the snow in the spring. And after many days on the close-fed plain and bluffs of earth back we came to an interesting change. We saw a whole day's march ahead on the plain, what looked a big castle, or small mountain. But on nearing it, we saw that it was a big tower of sand-stone far detached like an island, from the bluffs back, which had now all become of that kind of rock, high and perpendicular, and strangely worn into many fantastic shapes. The de-tached mass first seen is called the Chimney Rock, a striking landmark in this prairie sea. The upper, perhaps 100 feet of naked rock and the lower 50 a spreading pedestal, well grassed over.

~

THE MOUNTAINS
CHAPTER III

Crossing the Laramie

Finally we came to a big, rapid, turbulent tributary, the Laramie from the mountains of the same name, and to a dead halt at the point where since has been Fort Laramie. For here we had to make what proved a serious undertaking, a crossing of said river. And fortunately here was plenty of timber, out of which we made rafts on which to take ourselves and our goods across, and made the horses swim the river. It was so broad, say half a mile, turbid and turbulent, they were unwilling to go in, but were drove in and then headed back until they were compelled to seek the other side, but were so swept down by the current they landed far below. And I do not know that we should have got them to head across at

all had not two or three courageous men mounted some and made them swim ahead to give a lead to the rest. There was still snow in sight on the Laramie mountains, the melting of which made the high water of the river. With some difficulty we all got safely over, but some of the traders' goods were lost.

Now for two or three days' march there was a great change in the country, hilly, brooks of water, partially wooded, and better feed for horses. And we traveled back from the river. What we were crossing is a spur of the Black Hills, that extended to and far beyond the Platte toward the great bend of the main Missouri. It was a pleasant change from the monotonous plain. But we came again onto the river with its bottoms, but hills and mountains all the time in

Well over a century after the last Oregon Trail traveler passed by, Independence Rock in central Wyoming still bears the names of western immigrants etched in its granite surface. [Wyoming State Museum]

At the South Pass in Wyoming, the Wyeth party crossed the Great Divide on their journey west. [Wyoming State Museum]

sight to the south. And after some more days' march we came to where it comes from the southwest, and our route required its crossing. And here we crossed it, but with less difficulty, in the same manner we had the Laramie. And the next day we reached the Sweet Water, a branch coming in from the northwest, and encamped at the Independence Rock, a granite bowlder the size of two or three meeting houses, having got its name from some prior party having stopped here and celebrated the 4th of July on it. From it you behold a grand mountain and valley scene. And we now continued on our march up the valley of the Sweet Water, a beautiful, clear, cool stream, a great luxury as one may judge after quenching our thirst so long from the warmer, turbid waters of the Platte. It comes down a plain some few miles wide between high ridges of naked rocky mountains. And up this valley we wound our way till the stream was but a rivulet that you could step across — and so high we overlooked all the mountains we had passed, and snowdrifts around, though the middle of the summer.

South Pass

Here we were at the celebrated South Pass of the Rocky Mountains, said by his political friends, when a candidate for President, though he was not there till ten years after, to have been discovered by General Fremont. And it was by no means then new to our fur traders. It has its name from Lewis and Clark and other early travelers always keeping on the main Missouri which led them to a crossing far north and more difficult. In two of three hours from our leav-

ing this headwater of the Sweet Water that flows eastward to the Mississippi and to the Gulf of Mexico, we struck a small stream, a branch of the Colorado that falls into the Gulf of California. And here we were traveling over as level a prairie as I have ever seen, except bottom lands — stretching far away south and west with hundreds of buffalo feeding on the same. But stretching off to the northwest we looked out on the towering snowclad Wind River Mountains; the very crest of the Rocky Mountain range. For on the north of this, rise all the higher main branches of the Missouri; and on the west, branches of the Columbia river; and on the south, these waters of the Green and Colorado rivers.

And we continued our journey off northwest as near the foot of these mountains as the traveling was good, crossing the cool snow-formed streams of the Green river for perhaps one hundred or more miles. But our trappers now moderated their march, expecting before this to have heard from their mountain partners, who had passed the winter there or rather farther west, trapping and trading. For they knew the time they might expect Sublette out and the route he would come. And they were to send an express to meet him and inform him where they had rendezvoused to receive him. One of these days while we were laying over, a few of the party went out to hunt, and our horses were quietly feeding in the brook valley where we were, only a short distance from our camp. And these hunters, for mischief, as they came on the bluff gave an Indian whoop and fired, and the horses all came to camp for protection like scared children.

Indian Attack

One night in this part of our journey when we were encamped in the usual way, in messes all around, leaving quite a space within for our horses to feed, and the usual guard. But unperceived by the guard, Indians approached near camp and raised their whoop and fired guns and arrows, and so frightened the horses that they all broke loose from their fastenings and rushed by us out of camp. And all were instantly on their feet ready for fight. For myself the first consciousness I had, I found myself on my feet with my rifle in my hand. For always all were required to sleep with their rifles by their side, well loaded for action. But the Indians were not to be found. And we soon collected our horses and tied them and laid down to sleep. At least I did so, showing how a man will become, in a measure, indifferent to danger. I felt some fears before getting where there were Indians, but felt but little after. But this time we found in the morning, they so far did what they aimed at, had stolen some dozen or more of our best horses, those probably which ran farthest out.

Fremont's Trip

The only means I had to ascertain our altitude was the temperature of boiling water by my thermometer, and which I made in that way to be between 8,000 and 9,000 feet. But Mr. [John C.] Fremont,[9] who was sent out by government, supplied with barometer and all needful instruments, made it something less. His account of that exploration is very interesting. He was an intelligent and industrious traveler, but sometimes too rash and venturesome. As in this case in crossing the Nevadas in the deep snow, and still worse when he was sent on a railroad exploration, and was caught in midwinter in the mountains and escaped into New Mexico.

No rain of any account in all this part of our journey. Sometimes a small cloud would form attended with thunder, and rain be seen falling part way to the ground, and all evaporate. Perhaps a few drops of rain or hail would reach it. Nights clear and cold, often below freezing and days, hot sun and up sometimes to 80 degrees. But on the 4th of July as we approached and arrived at the first waters of the Columbia, we had an hour or two of snow.

Hunger

Now we came into a rough and mountainous country, more difficult than any we had experi-

Fremont's Peak in the Rocky Mountains was viewed by John Ball and the Wyeth party ten years before the famous explorer claimed discovery and gave it his name. [Henry Howe, Historical Collections of the Great West, Vol. 1, Cincinnati, Henry Howe & E. Morgan & Co., 1854, p. 326]

enced. And to add to our troubles our animals had become, from their long journey, much worn out, and the men though in like feeble condition had to walk. And food too became short, for we met but few buffalo, but some game of other kinds. And nothing came amiss. And we ate of everything that fell in our way, but the snakes, I think. Sublette had before this met with some of his mountain trappers who guided us on our way to their rendezvous. And in four days of hard working our way through ragged ravines and over steep ridges brought us out on to a fine grassy plain among the mountains, called Pierre's Hole and to the grand encampment, where they had for some time been awaiting our arrival.

Grand Rendezvous

Here we found not only Sublette's traders and trappers, but a party of the American Fur Company, and bands of Nez Pierce and Flat Head Indians, who had by appointment met the traders here with their furs and five or six hundred horses. Many of them

---

[9] *B. 1813, d. 1890. Soldier, explorer and political leader associated with extensive exploration of the American western regions.*

they sold us to take the place of our lean ones. They would allow something for the lean ones for with them, in their slow way of journeying they would recruit. But the full price of a pony was but a blanket and a cheap knife. So we supplied ourselves with all we needed. These mountain horses are of the Arabian stock, brought to Mexico by the early Spanish settlers – light of limb and fleet. It was a grand sight to look on their immense herd out on the prairie of all colors from white to black and many spotted ones. For during the day they would send them out on to the open prairie to feed with the mounted guard with them, to run them into camp, if the Blackfeet, in whose country we were, should make dash down the mountain side to steal them. At night they would bring them into camp where they would quietly remain among their owners' tents till morning.

Pierre's Hole

Here in Pierre's Hole was for us a grand time of rest and recruit. The Indians had an abundance of good, dried buffalo meat which we bought of them and on which we feasted, took a bite of the fat part with the lean, eating it like bread and cheese, uncooked or slightly roasted on the coals as we chose. And I never witnessed such recuperation of men as during the two weeks we lay at our ease in this camp, feeding on the dried buffalo meat, and our drink the pure cool mountain creek, a branch of the Lewis river, on which we were encamped. And among us, a varied congregation of some two hundred white men and perhaps nearly as many Indians, there was quite a social time, and a great exchange of talk and interesting indeed, from the wide and varied experiences of the narrators. There were cultured men from city and country down to white men lower than the Indian himself. Men of high-toned morals, down to such as had left their country for its good, or perhaps rather personal safety.

Some made the season's trip from the miasmic air of the Mississippi and its city follies to recuperate their bodily and mental derangement. And it proved a grand specific. This mountain-pure air and ever-shining sun is a grand, helpful thing for both the soul and body, especially when feeding on only meat and water.

And here we had the test of the honesty of the Indian. When we had purchased a horse and it had got back into the immense herd, we could never have reclaimed it, or perhaps known it if seen, but they would bring them back to us, and again and again, if needed. And if any of our property, tools or camp things seemed lost, they would bring them to

us, were in all things orderly, peaceful, and kind. And the Flat Head chief used of an evening to mount his horse from which he would give his people a moral lecture. A white man who had been some years in their country and well understood their language, told us what he said. And it was of a high, moral tone, telling them to be punctual in their dealings with us and orderly among themselves.

Here we were more than a thousand miles from the white settlements and had met no natives till now. And not having then ever seen much of them, I observed with much interest their ways. Their usual dress was a frock and leggings and moccasins made from dressed deer skins, and a well dressed buffalo skin with the hair on for a blanket, to ride on and sleep in. The frock of the women was longer than that of the men. Both had their dresses somewhat ornamented by a projecting edge of the leather, cut into a fringe, shells, feathers and beads, when to be had, worked into their dresses, or in their hair. The women, these mountain women were extremely diffident, would blush if looked at. And though they and their friends deemed it quite an honor to be married by a white man – one of these traders or trappers, who had passed years in their country – they, that is the father or nearest male relative, would never consent to any intercourse with these women, but for life. But I fear that the more virtuous and honorable Indian was sometimes betrayed into an alliance that the white man betrayed and annulled when he quit the country.

Sublette Returns

Mr. Sublette had here reached the end of his journey, and in a few days, but not till we left him, would commence his march back to St. Louis with his seventy horses packed with beaver, worth as he estimated, some $50,000 in the New York market. No other fur was deemed worth packing so far, not even the otter. And the pressing question arose with us Yankees as to the manner and safe means of our future and further journey. Many of Mr. Wyeth's men had long before they got here become disheartened and disgusted, but they could not stop or return alone. But now they decided to return with Mr. Sublette's party. And all decided to go no farther, except twelve. For myself I never turned my face back for a moment and resolved to go on, if it was in the company of the Nez Pierces whose country was down near the mouth of the Lewis river. But a Mr. Frapp and Milton Sublette with a trapping party of Sublette's men were to go off trapping somewhere westward, so we resolved to go on, joined their party of some forty whites, half-breeds and Indians, and so keep on, thinking some way to bring out rightly.

JOURNEY CONTINUES WITH TRAPPERS
CHAPTER IV

Mr. Sublette had come out with arms, ammunition, traps, etc., for his business and new men to take the places of those whose term of service had expired, so there was much fixing up to sort out the parties for the different purposes. And our party of trappers under Mr. Frapp one afternoon left the main camp and went out some seven or eight miles and encamped on a prairie near some timber on a little creek, as usually there is timber on the streams and mountainsides.

We had a quiet night but in the morning, as we were about to commence our day's march, Indians were seen in line of march on horseback off across the prairie, say some two miles. And the trappers at once decided they must see who they were. So Frapp told Antoine, the half-breed, to take a good horse and have an Indian of the party go with him and go out and see who they were. As Antoine approached them he saw they were Blackfeet, and their chief left his party and came out in a friendly way to meet him. But his father having been killed by the Blackfeet, he was going to have his revenge. So he said to his companion, "I will appear to be friendly when we meet, but you watch your chance and shoot

Under attack and carefully watched by Blackfeet Indians, the members of the Wyeth party, like this mountain man, had to move carefully through the Rocky Mountains. [California Historical Society]

49

him." His plan was carried out. He was shot down. Antoine caught his robe, a square of blue and scarlet cloth, and turned and the Blackfeet fired after him, when they saw his treachery. He escaped and came into our camp, said they were Blackfeet, and that he had killed their chief and there was his robe in evidence.

"All right" they said, "they would play friendly now but at night attack our camp." But we twelve could not appreciate the reasoning. But here we were in the company that thus decided. But as we watched to see what they would next do, they seemed at first to break up and scatter, but soon we saw that a large band, the warriors, seemed coming directly towards us to make fight. So we immediately tied our horses to bushes near and put up our saddles as a kind of breastwork. But before they reached us, they turned off into some timber on a stream, built a kind of fort of logs, bushes, their saddles and blankets, as a shade, if we attacked them, and took their horses into the fort with them.

Fight with the Blackfeet

The moment that Antoine gave the information that they were Blackfeet, an express flew off back to the old camp to tell we had met the enemy, and in the time, it seemed to me, that race horses could have hardly gone over the ground, some of Sublette's men and the friendly Indians came rushing into our camp inquiring where were the Blackfeet. And on soon finding where they had fortified themselves, each white or Indian, as he felt that his gun was right, and all things ready for his part, would start off. And so they went helter skelter, each on his own hook to fight the common enemy. For the friendly Indians had their own wrongs to avenge. As they thus almost singly approached their brush and saddle fort, they could only see the defences whereas, they, the Blackfeet, could see everyone who approached them. They soon shot down some of the trappers and Flatheads, for the timber was not large enough to shelter a man. And soon wounded men were brought back to our camp.

We twelve Yankees felt that we had no men to spare to be killed or wounded, that we were not called upon to go out of the way to find danger, but had they attacked our camp, we should have taken our full part, to save ourselves and horses. But we readily assisted in taking care of the wounded and in other ways aid, as far as we felt belonged to us. They kept up a firing at them, at a safer distance, but did not rout them. Six trappers and as many friendly Indians were killed or mortally wounded. And as night approached it was determined to retreat. And

the whites took a wounded man on a horse, others riding each side to hold him up. The Indians fixed long fills to a horse letting the ends draw on the smooth ground and fixed onto them a kind of hurdle, onto which they laid the wounded and drew them off easily over the smooth prairie. A better way than ours.

When night came on we encamped in the best manner of defence we could, and the next day expecting surely an attack from them, built a high fence and strong pen for our horses in such case, and a guard on the open prairie to run them in if attacked, and then awaited the result. Their fort was finally visited and a number of dead horses found. But of course they had secreted any men they lost from scalping. We did not go back so far as the old camp.

Buried the Dead

The man who died in our camp we buried in the horse pen where the ground was so trodden that the enemy could not find the body to scalp it. Another badly wounded was sent to Sublette's camp on a bier suspended between two horses, one ahead of the other. And when we found that the enemy was not near, after a few days, we took up our line of march as originally intended. And after two or three days reached the main Lewis river. To cross its water, and such others as they could not ford, the trappers had packed along, what they call a bull boat, green buffalo hides with the hair off, which they soak in water till limber, then stretch this hide over a temporary frame made from such saplings as could be bent into shape, and then turn their rude boat up to the sun to dry, and thus keep in shape long enough to cross two or three times, before so soaked as to be unmanageable. The men with the goods, traps, etc., were crossed in these and horses swam.

And so we traveled on slowly in a pleasantly rising country back from the river, the trappers stopping to set their traps for beaver on the branches, that showed signs of their residences in and on the same. Not far from this part was afterwards built what was known as Fort Hall. And we were at one time in sight of the American Falls, also of the Lewis river, and a man of our party, who had been there said at one time we were within twenty-five miles of the Salt Lake. And so we kept on southwesterly with a low ridge of mountains between us and the river. And finally came to a stream running to the south or southerly, the country apparently descending in that direction. The trappers had poor luck and said they would now quit and turn back. Sixteen free trappers, as they were called, men on their own hook, said they would go down that stream, I now know it to be the Humboldt, and go to California and get mules. None of our party had been so far in that country before and knew nothing of the country beyond in any direction. And for aught I know the free trappers are still going, Frapp and his party turned back, and we twelve turned northward to again get onto the Lewis river.

Other things I should have before said – one, the great clearness of the air of the Rocky Mountain region, from the dryness of the same, no mist or haze to prevent a distinct view of very distant objects. Objects, on our march, that seemed as though we should reach in a few hours, would perhaps take as many days, being accustomed to judge of distances through a humid atmosphere. We were soon now to pass the range of the buffalo. So while in the country where they ranged, say north of the Salt Lake, we halted a day or two to dry, in the sun and on hurdles over a slow fire, some of their meat to pack along for our future use, a wise forethought for game was scarce.

Birth of an Indian Baby

Mr. Frapp had an Indian wife who traveled along with him, and the Indians of the party, some of them, had their wives, these women as good horsemen as the men, always riding astride. One day we delayed our march, we knew not why, till after a time we heard an outcry for a few minutes from Frapp's wife, out to one side in some bushes. And we soon learned, the cause of our laying over, was to give her the opportunity to lay in, give birth to a child in camp and not on our day's march. But the very next day, she sat her newborn baby, feet down, into a deep basket that she hung to the pummel of her saddle, mounted her horse and rode on in the band as usual. And she had another child of two or three, who had his own horse. He was sat on the saddle and blankets brought around him so as to keep him erect, and his gentle pony went loose with the other pack horses, which kept along with those riding and never strayed from the common band. I mention these things to show something of the Indian ways in their own country, and that whites in their country readily from necessity and convenience, fall into like habits, and soon find but little inconvenience from the same. The Canadian Frenchman seems to adopt their life as readily as though raised in that way, and others the same after a little time.

Trapping for Beaver

I have been writing from recollection mostly. But on turning to the scant minutes I made at the time I

Trapping beaver in the Rockies required steel traps and a willingness to endure long, isolated winters and bone-chilling mountain streams.
[New York Public Library Picture Collection]

find that there were Trois Tetons and other snow mountains all the time in sight. The country we passed through zig-zag, as Milton Sublette, a brother of William, and Frapp were after the beaver, and went up and down the mountain streams hunting them, set their traps at night; and the second of more, if the game was found plenty, on the same ground. Three boys left our party soon after crossing the Lewis river to make a season's trapping by themselves on the mountains to the left in the midst of the Blackfoot country, showing the strange, wild, fearless habits formed by these mountain trappers. The sixteen free trappers left us on the Humboldt, but Sublette and Frapp kept on westward and we parted with them on the creek that ran north and which we followed.

We were with these trappers more than a month, parting from them the 28th of August. I had during the time made many interesting observations of things around, the weather clear, and days hot and usually frost at night, ranging from say 30 to 80 degrees often. Soon after crossing the Lewis river I observed for the first strata of the igneous or volcanic rock in conglomerate. And ever after met with it and saw beautiful white and variegated marble bowlders, and lime and granite rock partially melted down, but still showing the original rock. The vegetation was much diversified, timber of various kinds and extended prairies. Though but little or no rain, grass was often good and occasionally we met with fruit, which, you may well think, was very acceptable to us — a berry growing on a shrub they called a service berry, resembling what is called in New England the robin pear, and red and orange colored currants, all of an excellent quality. I brought the seeds home, but they did not grow.

TWELVE OF WYETH'S PARTY
GO ON ALONE
CHAPTER V

The first day after leaving the trappers, we traveled over a rough country of all sorts of rock, burnt and unburnt, and encamped in what is now called a canyon, between high basaltic rocks. We twelve thus for the first time alone it seemed a little lonely. And though not fearful, there was something like a deep curiosity as to the future, what might happen to us in that unknown land. Our aim was to get back on the Lewis river and follow that to its junction with the Columbia. And I now presume we were on the headwaters of the Owyhee, the east boundary of Oregon. And the next day and for days we kept on the same or near. We pursued it till so shut in that we had to leave it by a side cut and get onto an extended plain above, a plain with little soil on the basaltic rock, and streams in the clefts or canyons. One day we traveled 30 miles and found water but once, and in the dry atmosphere our thirst became extreme. On approaching the canyon we could see the stream meandering along the narrow gorge 1,000 feet down, and on and on we traveled not knowing that we should survive even to reach it to quench our thirst. Finally before night we observed horse tracks and that they seemed to thicken at a certain point and lead down the precipitous bluff where it was partially broken down. So by a most difficult descent we reached the creek, dismounted and down its banks to quench our thirst. And our horses did not wait for an invitation, but followed in quick time. The bluffs were of the burnt rock, some places looking like an oven burned brick kiln, and others porous. And laying over the next day and going a short distance down the creek, we found Indians who had our future food, dried

salmon. And getting out on the other side we traveled on and when we came again to the river we found it, though now quite a stream, decidedly warm, made so by hot springs gushing in from porous bluffs. Quite a stream came in of the temperature of 100 degrees.

Shoshone Indians
The creek finally comes out of the ravine into a better looking country, and here we met other Indians. They call themselves Shoshones and seemed very friendly and sold us their salmon for such of our goods as they seemed most to need — awls of iron to prick their deer skins for sewing into garments, and knives, for they hardly possessed an article of our manufacture. They used a sharp bone for an awl, one flattened for a chisel, stone knives and hatchets. Ourselves and all we had seemed to them great curiosities. For their country being poor in furs it had not been visited by traders.

In some ten or twelve days after leaving the trappers, we reached the mouth of the creek where it joins the Lewis river. And here we found a large encampment of Indians, being a favorable site for fishing. The first thing on arriving the chief, in their usual hospitable manner, sent us a fine salmon for our dinner, and would have deemed it an insult to be offered pay for it. We were strangers and his guests.

Indian Fishing
Their manner of fishing was ingenious. The stream was shallow and they built a fence across it near its mouth and then some distance above, leaving weirs at one side, so that the fish coming down

or going up would come in, but would not find their way out. They had spears with a bone point with a socket that fitted onto a shaft, and a hole through the point, by which a string tied it to the handle. At sunrise at a signal from the chief they rushed in from both sides, struck the salmon through with the spear, the point came off, and held by the string to the shaft, they towed them to shore and so soon had hundreds on land.

Near, up the Lewis river, were bluffs of basaltic rock thirty feet high and resting on the sandy shore, the pentagonal columns tumbling down into the river as the earth was washed away, showing that there had been melted overflow of rock, which then cooled and crystallized into rock and in this form in blocks, one above another.

Beavers

As we occasionally saw the fresh marks of beaver on the streams, we set our traps and occasionally caught some, preserved and packed along their skins, knowing that they would be acceptable to the Hudson Bay people in exchange for such things as we should need from them. And at times we had nothing else to eat but their meat, which having nothing else, we relished right well. About the beaver building houses, they only do it when the land along the streams, where they are, is low. For when there are high banks they burrow up and make their nests in the earth, but always have the mouths of their

holes under the water, so even when the streams are frozen over they can come to the water under the ice. They subsist on the bark of small trees, but for winter's use cut, with their chisel teeth, small trees into blocks and store them in the mud at the mouths of their burrows or in the same, as the squirrel does with his acorns. And the muskrat too makes his nest of grass or rushes in the swamp, raising it above the water. The beaver is an intelligent and interesting animal and so are all others, birds and all, each in his way.

Reckless of Danger

In this part of our journey we twelve were often very reckless of danger. For the purpose of this trapping we would separate, for a night or for more. When in full camp our horses were always picketed near us and some two or more always awake as a guard. But when two or three were away for a night's trapping, we slept with our horses' long halters tied to a bush near us or sometimes in our hand. One night when thus encamped I had my old camlet cloak stolen from my saddle and our horses' halters cut, but they, the horses, did not leave us, and we did not see by whom done. At another time we found the Indians about at night, for though generally friendly, they could not forego the attempt to steal away in a quiet manner, our horses, of which we had two to a man.

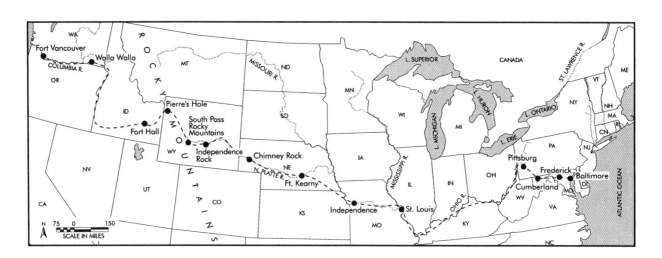

John Ball's Travels
Oregon, 1832-1833

We traveled some days along or in the vicinity of the Lewis river after meeting Indians, and subsisting mostly on fresh or dried salmon bought or given us from them, and making short or long day's journeys and laying over to catch the beaver. They are a night animal.

At one night's encampment, we made the Indians understand that we were going to Walla Walla, the name of that place being the only word we had in common. All else was by signs, talk with the fingers. Inquiring the way, one of the Indians said that he had been to Walla Walla and made in the sand a map of the country. He said that such a mark meant the river and another the trail, that the road kept down the river three sleeps, always reckoning distances by day's journeys, or in two if we whipped up; that then the river went into the mountains, it does pass through a canyon and for a hundred or two miles, and the road left the river and up a creek, and then we should go so many days and come to a mountain, go over that and encamp, then over another and encamp, then a plain and in two days Walla Walla.

I felt confident that I understood him, though this all by signs, and it proved just as he had said, and of great help to us. But as we traveled on we met with no more Indians from whom to buy our fish, and we met with no game that we could kill. And not taking the precaution to pack along much, we soon got short of food. And we hurried on making thirty miles one day, crossing a most beautiful fertile plain surrounded by mountains, the same I think is called the Big Pound. And came to the mountains, the Indian described, the Blue Mountains. And here we were in a bad plight, our horses, some of them at least, exhausted by hard travel, and ourselves the same, having been some days on short allowance and now nothing left. So for food we killed an old horse. But hungry as we were, this did not relish well. But I will show that horse, in good condition is good food, for I afterwards tested it.

Wyeth Presses Ahead

Here, the next day, Wyeth took four of the men and the best horses and started off express for Walla Walla, requesting me the next day after to follow on and he would get food and send back for us. So the next day following I told the men they better pack along some of the horse meat they had dried, and some of them did so. And we ascended the mountain on the Indian trail and found a quite level road

along its ridge, and scattering pine and cedar timber on its sides. After many hours' travel the road led down the mountain to the west into a valley where we found water and encamped. Here the men who would not pack along any of the horse, stole from those who did. As for myself, as each one looked out for himself, I had saved to this time some dried salmon, having eaten but one meal per day for many days.

Mount Hood

The next day we ascended another ridge and kept along the same, hour after hour. And it was a clear bright day except some cumulous, or thunder clouds as some call them, and I noticed one, on the western horizon, that seemed stationary. And after watching it an hour, I made up my mind that it was no cloud but white, snowy Mount Hood and called the attention of the men to it, and hailed it as the discovery of land — an object on which men had looked and of which they knew something of its locality. Just at night we came down to a creek and out of the mountains, and encamped, ourselves weary and our horses more so. An old pack mule turned round to me the moment I dismounted to be unpacked. Here for food we found a few blackthorn berries and rose berries.

The next day we started out onto the plain, but found so many trails we did not know which to take. But we traveled on the deepest worn, but not as proved the most direct one. Encamped at night and found some stagnant water and next day hard traveling brought us to a fine creek running west which proved to be the Walla Walla creek.

And now I proposed to the men, as we had been so long without food, to kill another horse and the best conditioned one in the lot, but they thought they could stand it another day, so we did not kill the horse. The next day we started early down the creek, for I thought that would bring us out right, and in a few hours we came to an Indian encampment, where we got some food. They had dried-bear and other meat and elderberries, and we bought and ate, for they had learned of the whites. For myself I did not eat so ravenous, but the men ate till I urged them to desist, for I feared the result. We soon after encamped, and the next day arrived at the fort, where we found Wyeth who had been there two or three days.

Inside Fort Walla Walla and other primitive Hudson Bay Company outposts, company representatives negotiated with Native Americans, exchanging guns, traps, knives and other trade goods for furs. [Western Americana Collection, Yale University Library]

Fort Walla Walla was an outpost of the Hudson Bay Company and a welcome sight for the remaining members of the Wyeth party. [Alexander Ross, The Fur Hunters of the Far West, *Vol. 1, London, Smith Elder & Co., 1855, frontispiece]*

OREGON
CHAPTER VI

Fort Walla Walla

The said fort was a small stockade of upright timbers set in the ground some fifteen or eighteen feet high with stations or bastions at the corners for look-outs. And the company kept here for the purpose of trade a clerk and some half-dozen men. We were kindly received and here for the first time since leaving the forks of the Platte the first of June ate bread, being now the 18th of October. The fort is at the mouth of the creek on the Columbia nine miles below the mouth of the Lewis river. It was an interesting sight to look on the Columbia, after the long, long journey to see the same and to get to it.

The country about looked barren, for the fall rains, if they have them, had not commenced — little or no timber or shrubs, except the Artemisia, wild sage, which grows from one to five or six feet high, and is found everywhere on the mountain plains. It has an ash-colored leaf as bitter as the garden sage; still when nothing else can be found it is eaten by the buffalo and deer. I am informed that there is now cultivation in these parts and crops raised; but I presume it must be only by means of irrigation. Here we decided to leave our faithful horses and descend the river by boat. Oh! the horse is appreciated, when one for months has passed with him, his days and nights.

Down the Columbia

We procured at the fort a boat and two Canadians to take us down the river and started the day after our arrival. And in descending soon came into the high perpendicular basaltic bluffs with only river and a narrow shore on one or the other side, of grass and sand, the current of the clear water with a slight blue ocean shade sweeping swiftly on. And when we encamped at night, if we could find a place that we could ascend the bluff we found no timber, but a dry, grassy plain stretching far away to distant mountains, in the west the Cascade range and snowclad Mount Hood. At one night's encampment the Indians, being acquainted with our boatmen, gave them a young horse to kill for our supper. And though we had received a plenty of food for our voyage at the fort, I tried the horse and found it as good meat as I had ever eaten, it·being in better condition than the one killed by us at the Blur Mountains. And we voyaged on past the big falls and came to the Dalles and then stopped to see the Indians and found there had been great mortality among them. We walked by the wonderous chute of flume through which all the water rushes at its low stage, but passed the boat through it.

Saw the basaltic columns at places along the bluffs standing out prominently, or even singly, all pentagonal, blocks or sections piled one on the other, the upper side of the block dishing and the next fitted to it, and all as compact as iron. Lewis and Clark called them "high black rocks" as well they might. Finally we came to the cascade where the mighty river rushes for some miles through the break in the Cascade range of mountains, a continuation of the Nevada range of California. The mountain on the north side somewhat subsides giving a land pass way, but abrupt and thousands of feet high on the south side, down which leap from the immense height beautiful cascades. These passed we came to the tide waters of the Columbia. On the mountain is evergreen forest to the snow line, east of the mountains no timber on the plains but west, timber and prairie interspersed.

The Hudson Bay Company's Fort Vancouver, established by Dr. John McLoughlin in March 1825. From a drawing by Lieutenant Henry J. Warre, an officer of the English Navy, in 1845. [Reprinted from Autobiography of John Ball, *p. 90]*

Dr. John McLoughlin's factor's house at Fort Vancouver. [Fort Vancouver National Historic Site, Washington]

Fort Vancouver, 1832

Stopped over night at a sawmill of the company on a creek, and saw there, two strange looking men, saw at once they could be neither Caucasian, Indian or African. And so it proved, they were Kanakas, Sandwich Islanders,[10] in the employ of the traders. And the mill was under the superintendence of one of Astor's men who had remained in the country. And the next day the 29th of October we arrived at Fort Vancouver, which is on the north side of the river, and not in Washington territory. It was quite an extensive stockade enclosure, on a prairie, some little back from the river, with the store houses, the houses for the Governor and gentlemen, as partners and clerks were called, and quite a garden, and for the servants, the Canadian Frenchmen, little houses outside the fort. This was the main station of the Hudson Bay Company[11] west of the mountains. And to this place came up their shipping, what they called 100 miles up the river.

Indian Burial

Though a hard looking set and unexpected, we were received very kindly and treated ever in the most hospitable way.

Some of us did not feel that we had reached the end of our journey till we had seen the Pacific. So a few days after, five of us took an Indian canoe and paddled down the river, passed the mouth of the Willamette river, found the country for miles level, prairie and timber, met a company's sloop, and often Indians singing as they paddled their canoes swiftly along.

Encamped one night near one of their burial places. Their way of burial here was to wrap their bodies in their clothing and mats, and place them in canoes, which they place on some conspicuous place on shore or on an island, one is called Coffin Island, then cover the boat with boards, split slabs, and load them down with stone so that the wolves or other animals could not get at the body and put the deceased's property in and about the canoe. To steal from a grave they view a great crime.

Fort George

After a time in descending the river the country becomes very broken and heavily timbered and after some days reach and encamp on Tongue Point, where we could look out to sea, and next day go to Fort Astoria, or as they called it, Fort George. We were there kindly received by the clerk and fur people. A fallen tree near the fort, one writer calls 45 feet in circumference and another seven fathoms, and I thought it no exaggeration.

And on going into the standing forest out towards Youngs Bay, the bay in which Lewis and Clark wintered, I saw many trees of enormous size, in girth and height. The whole forest was nearly 200 feet high, for the small trees had to grow so high to get the sun, and so dense that I should think more weight of timber on one acre than on four anywhere east that I have ever seen. And the brakes and other vegetation of annual growth were equally gigantic of their kind. Still on their little clearings about the fort, the potatoes and other things were small and the soil looked poor.

Hudson Bay Company chief factor Dr. John McLoughlin hosted Wyeth and John Ball shortly after their party arrived at Fort Vancouver. [Fort Vancouver National Historic Site, Washington, #2587]

---

[10] *The Sandwich Islands, as they were called then, are known today as the Hawaiian Islands.*
[11] *British fur trading company.*

We got a yawl and one of their men to sail it and crossed over to Chenook Point and returned across the broad boisterous bay to Clatsop Point on the inside and encamped. And I urged the men, or some of them at least, to accompany me around the point to the seashore, but they declined. So the tide being down, I alone footed some three miles, fairly around on the beach to where I could look out on the broad Pacific, with not an islet between me and Japan, look far down the coast and Cape Disappointment across the mouth to the northwest. Here I stood alone, as entranced, felt that now, I had gone as far as feet could carry me west, and really to the end of my proposed journey.

The Pacific

There to stand on the brink of the great Pacific, with the rolling waves washing its sands and sea-weeds to my feet! And there I stood on the shore of the Pacific enjoying the happiest hour of all my journey, till the sun sank beneath its waters, and then by a beautiful moonlight returned on the beach to camp, feeling that I had crossed the continent. Cape Disappointment is in Lat. 46.19 N. and 123.59 W. Mount Saint Helens being due east, majestic and symmetrical in its form. This was the 9th of November and we had left Baltimore the 26th of March, seven and one-half months before. We returned slowly up the river, seeing something of the Indians, always peaceable in their ways, for these traders had the good sense and tact to keep a good understanding with them, though they had to deal with them quite in their own way, the Indian always knowing just how much he was to get for his furs in the articles he wanted. I should mention the fact that the Columbia in parts, as we passed, seemed alive and white with geese and ducks.

Death of One of the Twelve

When we got back to Fort Vancouver, we found that one of our fellows, and one who had stood all the hardships well, was dead and buried. He had eaten heartily of peas for his supper which gave him the colic and before morning he was dead. It was new food for him for we had lived on animal food. Mr. Wyeth as captain of the party and myself from some cause, were invited by Dr. McLoughlin, the oldest partner and nominal governor, to his own table and given rooms in the fort, and the others of our men to quarters with his, out of the fort. And I soon gave him and Mr. Wyeth to understand I was there on my own hook, and that I had no further connection with the others, than that for the making of the journey. We were received at the fort as guests without talk of pay or the like, and it was acceptable, or else we should have had to hunt for subsistance.

First Teacher in Oregon, 1832-1833

But not liking thus to live gratis, I asked the doctor, as he was always called, being a physician, for some employment. He at first told me I was a guest and did not expect to set me to work. But after further urging, he said if I was willing he would like to have me teach his son and other boys about the fort. I, of course, gladly accepted the offer. So he sent the boys to my room to be instructed, all half-breed boys of course, for there was not then a white woman in Oregon. The doctor's wife was a Chippewa woman from Lake Superior, and the lightest woman, a Mrs. Douglas, a half-breed woman from Hudson Bay. Well, I found the boys docile and attentive and making good progress, for they are precocious and generally better boys than men. And the old doctor used to come in to see the school and seemed much pleased and well satisfied. And one time he said, "Ball, anyway you will have the reputation of teaching the first Academy in Oregon." And so I passed the winter. The gentlemen in the Fort were pleasant and intelligent, a circle of a dozen or more usually at the well provided table, where there was much formality. They consisted of partners, clerks, captains of vessels, and the like — men to wait on the table and probably cook, for we saw nothing or little of their women, except perhaps sometimes on Sundays out on a horse-back ride, at which they excelled.

The National boundary had not then been settled beyond the mountains, and these traders claimed that the river would be the boundary, and called the south side the American.

Hudson Bay Company

The fur trade was their business, and if an American vessel came into the river or onto the coast for trade they would at once bid up on furs to a ruinous price — ten to one above their usual tariff. And as the voyage around Cape Horn from England was so long to bring supplies, they got a bull and seven or six cows from California and in seven years had about 400 cattle. They had turned the prairies into wheat fields and had much beyond their wants, ground by ox power and made good flour. Salmon was so abundant that the men would throw it away to get some old imported salt beef, for they had not yet killed any of their own raising.

To show the climate, the wheat green all winter, for there was no snow, still spring and summer so cool that harvest did not come till last of July or

August. Rained from middle of November till New Year's incessantly with the temperature day and night about 40 to 45 degrees, then rain and shine till May, frost, clear nights and vegetation nearly stationary, grass for cattle, but cold for them out, the summer cool and dry, still the wheat first rate, the berry large and good, corn did not mature. Potatoes and vegetables seemed to do well, and were dug in winter as used.

Wyeth Returns East

In the spring Wyeth and two of his men returned home across the mountains, some way successfully. Others went into the company employ. I wrote to my friends in New Hampshire and New York and by the Hudson express that leaves Fort Vancouver on the 20th of March, goes up the North, the main branch of the Columbia, to about the latitude of 52 degrees and by men on snow shoes over the mountains in about two weeks to where they take bark canoes on the La Bashe, that flows into the Arctic Ocean. Descend that distance then make a short portage at Fort Edmanton to the Saskatchawan and down that to Lake Winnipeg, and by its outlet, the Nelson, to Hudson Bay and also up the said Lake to Lake Superior, etc., to Montreal, from which place my friends got my letters by September.

Thinking I might long stay in the country, believing after so much had been said on the subject, that others would come soon to settle, though urged by Dr. McLoughlin to continue the school and stay at the fort, I determined to go to farming. And when I learned that some of the Company's men had turned farmers and gone up and settled on the Willamette river, I went there to see the country and found it very inviting. And when the doctor found that I was bent on going to farming, he kindly told me, he would lend me farming utensils, seeds for sowing and as many horses, as I chose to break in, for a team. So I took seed and implements by boat, getting help up the Willamette to the falls where the city of Oregon now is, passing the site where Portland stands, carried by the fall, boat and all. First stopped with one of the settlers, a half-breed, with two wives, his name J. B. Desportes. Yes, two wives, seven children, and cats and dogs numberless.

Farming

Caught from the prairie a span of horses only used to the saddle, made for them a harness and put them to work. Stuffed some deer skin sewed in due form for collars, fitted to them for harness crooked oak limbs, tied top and bottom with elk skin strings, then to these, straps of hide for tugs, which tied to the end of a stick for a whiffletree, and the center of this I drew out logs for a cabin, which when I had laid up and put up rafters to make the roof, I covered with bark peeled from cedar trees. And this bark covering was secured by poles across and tied with wood strings, withes, at the ends to the timbers below. And out of some split plank for no sawed boards, I made bedstead and table. And so I dwelt in a house of fir and cedar.

And with the aid of my neighbors and their teams I broke up quite a large field of rich prairie lands. Drew out fencing stuff with my own, to enclose the same, and sowed and planted my farm, a farm that butted half a mile on the river and extended back to California. My family consisted part of the time of a Mr. Sinclair, one of my mountain companions, a young wild native to catch my horses, and some of the time entirely alone. Got meal from the fort to make my bread, my meat some venison and some salmon from the falls, for being 60 feet high they could not jump them.

A rather primitive lonely life I found it and not seeing when it was likely to be less so, and having seen something of the country and experienced its climate, and the Hudson Bay people having entire control of the country, and no emigrants arriving, I began to think I might as well leave could I have the opportunity. Yes, this primitive life of the plains, mountains, and keeping house with only Indian neighbors, had lost its novelty and I wanted a change. To be sure the Willamette valley is a fine country, being a valley watered by a stream of that name, fifty miles wide and say one hundred fifty long with a coast range on the west and towering Cascade range on the east, crowned by Mount Hood, in the bright summer days ever in sight. And I was near the river, handy for a summer bath, and out of its bank a short distance from my house was the fine cool spring from which I got my water.

Indian Customs

Near by was the graveyard of the Indians, and on one occasion I attended with them the burial ceremony of one of their young men. They dug a grave as we would, put down some slabs at the sides and bottom, wrapped the body in his clothing and over these some mats, lowered it down to its place, put a board over and filled up with the earth. Then they built a fire on the grave and sat on the ground around and for an hour chanted a mournful dirge, all very orderly and impressive. And for a long time after his mother would come almost daily to place food in the earth at the head of the grave for his use on his journey to the other world. At the head of a man's grave they stuck a paddle and at the woman's a camas stick, a crooked pointed stick used by them to dig the camas root, with them a great article of food, the digging of which is woman's business, while paddling the canoe is that of the man.

The camas grown on the prairies is the size of an onion, a stem, say a foot high, having a blue blossom. It is as palatable and nutritious as the potato. The wapeto, another root they eat, is not so good but grows larger. It is the root of a kind of plant like the waterlily, which grows in the shallow waters of lakes and streams, and which they gather by wading in the water, often up to their arms, and break off with their toes, when it will rise to the surface. A common way of cooking these, as also sometimes meat, is to wrap in leaves and place in a hole in the ground, heated by a fire in it, then buried in same and a fire above, a very good way to cook.

Chenook Language

There was in use a mongrel language between the Indians and traders, called the Chenook; but unlike theirs, which was said by a man well acquainted with that and other Indian languages, to be the most copious of any. But this comprised hardly three hundred words, and probably not half of these theirs, but composed in part of words of other tribes, English and French. Things new to the Indians were called by their accustomed names. The hog had its French name, the ox the Indian name of the buffalo where the buffalo ranges in the mountains. The Indians on the Williamette, as most of the Indians, talked much by signs and sounds. One word was used for bird, for instance, then by imitating its cry, would express that it was the swan, goose or duck. One word meant growing vegetables; then by an adjective, or some motions, show whether grapes or trees were meant.

In enclosing my lands I fenced in a portion of their road or trail, and they went around, never crossing my fields. And in all things they were kind and just, as far as I observed, so I am disposed to ascribe our troubles with the Oregon Indians to injustice, or indiscretion, on the part of the whites. And this was the cause of the trouble, in most cases, from the first settlement of the country.

Ague and Discouragement

I suffered much while residing on my farm from the ague, a disease said to be unknown to the Indians or traders, till within some four or five years. It first broke out among the Indians near the fort, and spread far into the country, except near the ocean. And with the natives it proved very fatal, sweeping off whole bands, partly probably owing to their plunging into the water when the fever came on, and other improper ways. Still they seemed wonderfully aided by the use of such medicines as they procured from the whites. As an instance, to show the fatal effect, a trader returning to the fort came to their lodges on the river, just below the mouth of the Willamette, and he found numbers dead and unburied. The only one alive was an infant child at its dead mother's breast. He carried it to the fort, and it was living when I was there. When the disease broke out, they seemed to think they must have it, and die from its effects, so gave up and died.

For myself, I had no superstitious fear about it, but I suffered severely, and the more so on account of my unfavorable condition to meet sickness, my living poor, and no nurse but my friend, Sinclair. And at one time I had to send him off to the fort for medicine, to be gone some three or four days, leaving me alone, and so poorly that I hardly knew whether it was day or night. But still I mustered strength, when I became very thirsty and out of water, to get out and down the bank of the river to my spring for more. And when the medicine came it helped me, and then I would be taken down again, and so kept in rather a feeble state of health.

LEAVES OREGON
CHAPTER VII

No immigrants arrived from the States, as I expected, and the Hudson Bay Company having control of the country, so I could do nothing but subsist in the way I was pursuing. And tiring of the life I was leading, I saw no object of staying longer in the country, than for an opportunity to get away by sea. For once crossing the mountains and plains, I thought enough. I had passed nearly a year there, and experienced its climate and seen its lands and waters, and become acquainted with the natives and traders. And the company being about to send a vessel to the bay of San Francisco and the Sandwich Islands, I exchanged my crop, now mostly harvested, for a passage in the same.

So about the 20th of September, 1833, I quite my home on the Willamette with something of regret after all, but on the whole gladly went down the river by boat, and when I got to the falls an Indian boy of perhaps eighteen assisted us in carrying our boat by. On inquiring of him how his people were, he said, they were sick and dying, and when we came back, as he expected we would, he should be dead. Asking the chief to the band below the falls for two of his men to row us to the fort, for I was feeble and had with me only my friend, Sinclair, he answered that his men were all sick or dead, so he could not supply us. So we had wearily to paddle our own canoe.

Boards a Hudson Bay Company's Ship

After some days delay at Fort Vancouver, the ship *Dryad* made sail down the Columbia, with a Mr. Douglas, a botanist, a Mr. Finelson, a member of the Hudson Bay Company, myself, Sinclair, and two others of the Wyeth men. We stopped at Astoria, Fort George as they called it, and a long time in Baker's Bay, under the shelter of Cape Disappointment, which is a high promontory, the north cape at the mouth of the river, from which there is a splendid look out over the river and bays, the land and the ocean. There again I suffered severely with another attack of the ague, the chills lasting all day long.

On October 18, 1833, we sailed from Astoria, the wind having subsided, but we still found the swell in crossing the bar tremendous, and much of wind and storm as we sailed down the coast. So with the combined seasickness and ague I was not able to leave my berth for some days. But after a time both left me and I was able to look out on the sea, and occasionally the land. Still we kept at so respectful a distance that we saw little of it, and no harbor was then known between Columbia river and the bay of San Francisco.

Golden Gate

After a half month's voyage we neared the coast and on the 4th of November entered at the Golden Gate, but some fifteen years or more before it received that name.

The only buildings then seen about the bay were just at the turn, on the right, as you enter the same, called "The Presidio," which we passed and came to anchor some mile or so south, near the shore of little valleys and sandhills, all in their natural forest of bushes and trees. And here, and hereabout, they say is now the city of San Francisco. Some mile or two beyond and back from the bay was a mission called Dolores, consisting of a few, small adobe buildings; and back on the opposite side of the bay were some farmers. For I recollect from them our vessel got some pumpkins and other vegetables. I met there but one resident not Spanish or Indian. This was a Mr. Forbes, a Scotchman, but who said he had

The Mission Dolores, founded in 1776 by the Franciscans and now situated in the heart of San Francisco, was seen by John Ball in 1833, long before there was a city of San Francisco. [Reprinted from Autobiography of John Ball, *p. 100]*

resided in the United States. He seemed rather a shrewd man for as no one, unless a Catholic could hold real estate, I noticed, when with them, he was a good one too. How often do we see that one's religion aids his business, a great thing with many for this world. Rather a digression.

Lassoing a Wild Bullock

And here our ship lay for many days. On one, I saw a Spaniard noose with his lasso a wild bullock on the shore, or rather two of them. And thus mounted on their horses, used to the business, one threw and caught him by his horns, and then wound his lasso around the high pummel of his strong, well girthed saddle, and the horse stood and held him. But they wishing to throw him down, so as to butcher him, the other man threw his so accurately that by his first move the ox stepped into the noose, which caught him by his foot. Then each turned their horses in opposite directions and starting up they laid him flat on the ground in a twinkling. And then the horses keeping their stand, one dismounted and cut his throat. And quicker done than said. The only vehicle I saw was a drag made from the crotch part of a tree. On this a man placed a barrel containing whiskey, perhaps, and to this drag he tied his lasso, mounted his horse and tied the other end to the pummel of his saddle, and so drew alone the barrel home on the drag, the lasso passing by the horse's side.

Dolores Mission

One day I went to the Mission, on another through the woods and over the hills to the seashore, and up to the Gate where I found in the grass, dismounted some three or four cannon, which were once probably used to guard the entrance to the bay. But the fatigue of this day's trip again brought on the ague, so I did not go much more, staying aboard the vessel.

Upper California was then, and till acquired by our war with our neighboring Republic, a Mexican territory. One day its governor came aboard the ship to dine. He had come, I suppose, all the way from Monterey, his capital, for that purpose. His name was Figueroa. There is much said of John Augustus Sutter,[12] as an early settler in this country, but this was long before his time. The only trade to these

---

[12] B. 1803, d. 1880. Founded settlement near the junction of the Sacramento and American rivers, where gold was discovered on January 24, 1848, initiating the great California gold rush.

parts seemed to be by vessels from the States with calico and the like to exchange for hides, their only product, the country being full of cattle, and vessels came in for that purpose while we were there. And not having heard from that country for nearly two years, I inquired with much interest for the news, but was much disappointed in not getting more. He knew that Jackson was still President, and that the nullification business[13] was all settled, but there came the puzzle, what nullification was. I had never heard the term, and he could not define it any further than it was something about South Carolina.

And a whaler came in to get supplies from the Japanese Banks, as the fishing grounds were called, where they had been on a cruise. They told the time they had taken, which was very short for a well-constructed sailer, whereas their ship was an old Gerard Philadelphia Square, built over forty years before, showing the constant prevalence of a westerly wind in that latitude on the Pacific and in fact the world around. And here all our Americans except myself quit our vessel and went aboard this whaler, it being of their own country, so to them attractive. I said all were Spanish except Mr. Forbes. No; I also met here

Russians, who resided at some point up the coast, and raised wheat to supply their trading posts at Sitka and other places in Alaska.

When here I had somehow a presentiment that we should some day, by purchase or otherwise, become possessed of this splendid bay of San Francisco, and the surrounding country. Oregon I felt sure we should not relinquish to the English, and if we held that we also needed this. I thought those Hudson Bay men seemed to be very civil to their neighbors here, and that it was reciprocated by the call of the Governor, etc. All the trade that came to my notice was the purchase of some tallow from them. It was put up in hides sewed up into a kind of bag, and the melted tallow poured in, making a snug bale of goods. And if it be asked for what these traders wanted the tallow, it was mainly as a portion of the rations to their French and Indian employes, which with corn and other grain made their soup.

While we lay in the bay the weather was very pleasant, uniform, and of an agreeable temperature, being from 52 to 60 degrees. And we were a long time there, from the 4th to the 29th of November, with them probably a pleasant part of the year.

---

[13] *The principle, championed by some Southern states, that state power superseded federal power, and that a state could thus refuse to obey a federal law if it violated a state's "rights."*

A whaling expedition at Kealalealua Bay, Hawaii, 1841. [New Bedford Whaling Museum, #5787-088]

SANDWICH ISLANDS IN 1833
CHAPTER VIII

And now we repass the Gate and bear away for the Sandwich Islands, not direct, but bearing southerly, so the sooner to fall into the trade winds. We had a diversity of weather, but none very bad, and with the aid of the sea air I soon got clear, and for good, of my ague. And so we sailed on prosperously and in three weeks, the 22nd of December, 1833, entered the port of Honolulu, having as we approached a splendid view of those high volcanic mountains that constitute all of the higher parts of all these Pacific Islands. I was told before, as I found when there, that all the rock were either coral or volcanic. The island is 14 miles long, and some half that in its widest part, and the mountains 3,000 feet high, a portion of the valley and side mountain, susceptible of cultivation, well watered by streams from the mountains. An old crater called the "Punch Bowl" immediately in rear of the town, say some two or three hundred feet high, was used as a fort, being a basin some half mile across with a grass plot and rocky border.

An Old Friend

Before I went on shore myself, the officers of the ship who had been, informed me that they met a man on shore who knew me, and that his name was Brinsmade. As I knew no person of the name except Dr. Brinsmade of Troy, who was my most intimate friend and correspondent, and his two brothers who were clergymen, I took it for granted that one of them was there as a missionary, but when they told me that he was a merchant it seemed a great puzzle. But on meeting him I found that one of the clergymen, from loss of voice or some cause, had changed his business and joined a brother-in-law, a Mr. Ladd, who had come there before, and my friend was indeed a merchant. I will mention here that they had two Chinamen, as clerks in their store, who dressed in their native costume and had the cue of hair. My friend told me that one of them was a great accountant, quick and accurate. Their trade was mostly cash, receiving in a day some hundreds of dollars in Spanish gold ounce pieces, and dollars and shillings in silver. To test his accuracy and honesty he had abstracted from his drawer a sixpence, and after fussing a long time over it would tell him he could not make his accounts balance.

Japanese

There were strangely here too, four Japanese, and in this way. A strange looking craft was seen off the harbor, and it was found to be a Japanese junk or vessel with but four men alive on board. They were brought in and were kept by a Mr. French, an American merchant, and when they had so far learned English that they could talk with them, they said they got lost, had been out so many moons, that being their way of reckoning time; that the rest had perished for want of food. They had been there about a year when I saw them. When the merchant proposed to take them home, for they thought they could use them to open a trade with that exclusive people, they declined to go, and for why? They answered that they would be executed for having been in a foreign land, and so would not consent to go. A strange contrast with the present, now that they are sending many of their own boys to all the countries of Europe, and to this, to be educated and to learn our ways.

The meeting of an acquaintance here proved a great pleasure and advantage to me. My Hudson Bay friends could learn something of me, not from myself. There was but a poor understanding between the missionaries and merchants, and he being a kind of middle man, I was introduced to both, and though I boarded ashore with a Mr. Reynolds, I was often at his house. This Mr. Reynolds had passed most of his life in the Islands, and about the Pacific, and possessed much knowledge of all pertaining thereto. Had a half-breed native wife, whose father was Spanish. Their children were nearly white. I think a cross with them lighter than with the Indians, and as to those Islanders, they are a fine formed and featured people – honest, generous, but as lascivious as the monkey, their intercourse being quite promiscuous. The introduction of the venereal disease by the whites has proved their ruin. A Dr. Judd, a man who has since acted an important part in those Islands, told me that though the disease did not prove immediately fatal, it undermined their constitutions and shortened their lives.

Traders and Missionaries

The American consul's name was Jones, a Boston man. Mr. Reynolds was from Charlestown, Massachusetts. When the first missionaries, Mr. Bingham and others first arrived there in 1818, he received them kindly and did much for their comfort. But when he found they had written home, and their letters were published to be read by his family and friends, representing the resident whites as being a dissolute and wicked set of men, he felt that they had acted an ungrateful part, and in fact, there soon grew up a great dislike between the merchants and missionaries, their business and views clashing severely. So when there I found there was no friendly intercourse between them, the residents having their own minister, a Mr. Deal. I am of the opinion, that as to the change in the ways and opinions of the natives, the missionaries claimed more than their share of being the instruments. Kamehameha First,[14] a short time before their arrival, had abruptly at a feast gone over to the women's table and eaten. And then, in the surprise and commotion arising from a violation of all their fixed customs and usages, he came out in an able speech showing the folly of this and many of their customs and opinions, which so satisfied his people of the truth of his views that on the ground they assailed and broke down their images.

The Catholics of Mexico also sent missionaries to the Islands. But when it was found by the Protestants, that they were rapidly gaining ground, they induced the native government to send them away and punish their adherents by putting them to hard labor on the public roads. This looks a little like persecution.

King Kamehameha

An American merchant by the name of Hinkley occupied their mission building, one of the best there. To this, for a Christmas dinner, he invited all the resident white gentlemen and ladies, except the missionaries, and the King Kamehameha Third and a few men of his cabinet, but none of the native women. And I was informed that they found them so easy in their manner that the whites, even the missionaries, could not tolerate them in general society. Being an invited guest, it was the means of much extending my acquaintance. The king and other natives present spoke English fluently, and seemed entirely at their ease and gentlemanly in their ways.

Here, as is usually my practice, I acted no exclusive part, but sought also to become acquainted with the missionaries. So I called on Mr. Bingham, in his house, carried with him when he first went there, not whole surely, but put up after brought to the ground. And there I had much interesting conversation with him and information from him. He told me of his visit to the neighboring islands, and to the great volcanic crater on the greatest of the group, Owhyhee (Hawaii). I attended their meeting in a large booth kind of a building, where were a great audience of natives, and their native school. Mr. Bingham made an alphabet for their language, of sixteen letters I think, so they had their own books. There was a paper printed, one side in English, the other in native, and it is a very sonorous and beautiful language, many vowel sounds.

Natives

I went some about the island, climbed up the steep side onto the Punch Bowl, from which one looks right down onto the town, the harbor, the sea, and some of the other islands of the group. Went also out some three or four miles to the Pava, a break in the mountains where one can look out on the ocean on the other side and on the perpendicular side of a once volcano some two or three thousand feet high, rising abruptly from the ocean which I suppose had swallowed up the other side of said volcano. On this trip I saw many of their taro patches on the border of the sea, low lands watered by the mountain brooks and their orchards of bread and fruit trees, the orange, lemon, banana and other

---

[14] *Hawaiian king.*

tropical fruit. The bread fruit and taro are their main articles of food. And these usually cook by roasting in heated holes in the ground, an excellent way of cooking. The bread fruit when cooked, more resembles bread than any other vegetable. Taken warm with butter it is as palatable as biscuit, and the taro root, which is the size of an English turnip and quite as palatable, is as nutritious as the potato.

The natives are indolent and apparently happy in their ways. You would hear them chatting late of the moonshine nights. Still they are strong and enduring. They are often employed aboard whale vessels, and a whaler told me that they were so docile and obedient that if you put a gang in a boat they would row all day long unless told to stop. Still these people, like our Indians, are fast passing away. Mr. Bingham told me they had been dwindling, but he thought at that time, under their influence, they were keeping their own. And that then he estimated the population of the island at 200,000 but he was greatly mistaken. They have constantly dwindled in number, swept off by, to them, new diseases. The measles proved to them as fatal as the plague, in times past, to whites. The same disease very differently affects it seems different races of men. And so it seems there must be an eternal round of races to inhabit this, our earth, island and continent. All races have and probably will have their turn.

I found, on arriving at Honolulu, a trunk so far on its way to the Columbia river from Boston, for me, it being my directions, when I left Lansingburgh that they should thus send to me, if opportunity offered. It contained some clothes and other things, but what just then proved most interesting to me was a file of newspapers. For though all of them a year old or more, I never read news with greater interest. And among the other documents I found General Jackson's nullification message, by reading of which I learned fully what nullification meant. And that very able state paper added to my great faith in my always favorite statesman. Had we had a Jackson at the helm, when the Rebellion was brewing, I have always thought that things would have taken a different turn.

Climate

In these tropical islands, far away from any extended continent, there is a wonderful uniformity in the temperature. I met here a Hollander who had observed the weather here closely for the four prior years, and he informed me that the lowest he had seen the thermometer was 70 degrees and the highest 85 degrees so only 15 degrees difference, night and day, year in and out. And this coincided with my own observations. The temperature of the ocean on both sides, within the tropics, was 80 and 81 degrees, so of course, it must be nearly the same on the neighboring lands, if not vastly extended or high.

Honolulu was the principal harbor visited on those islands, whose central position about on the northern tropical line is usually a stopping place for vessels bound to China, or the northwest coast of America, and also was much resorted to by the sperm whale fishermen for repairs and supplies. There was a large number of vessels in at the time, giving an active business to the merchants, and indirectly to the natives, of whom there were some 7,000 in the village, all living in their own built houses scantily furnished, as of past times. Only they had generally exchanged their native tapa cloth for our American cotton white or dyed, not often figured.

The women preferred the dyed, say blue, to the white, as it would not so soon show the dirt. Of this they made a loose, long chemise or frock, which with most of them was the only garment. And as for the men, if they wore anything, it was a piece of the same around the waist or body coming down to the knees. But their ladies of rank, princesses of the royal family, tried to dress like white ladies. But as pointed out to me by a resident, they never got their dresses on right, like the improper garment hanging the lowest and the like. The men and women too were very fond of the water, would swim like frogs.

When a ship came in off would go their scant dress and away to the ship as readily as they would walk the land. And the whites, even the missionaries, could little control their movements. When at Mr. Bingham's, a chief lady came in to ask some advice about government affairs. She was nearly dressed like the whites, as she knew how, but while talking with him carelessly threw her enormous form on a sofa. She was the largest person I ever saw, weighing some four hundred. These islanders have a tradition, it is said, that in times past there came to them by the north and around from the east a few persons of great size and superior wisdom who became the rulers — but probably enough of this.

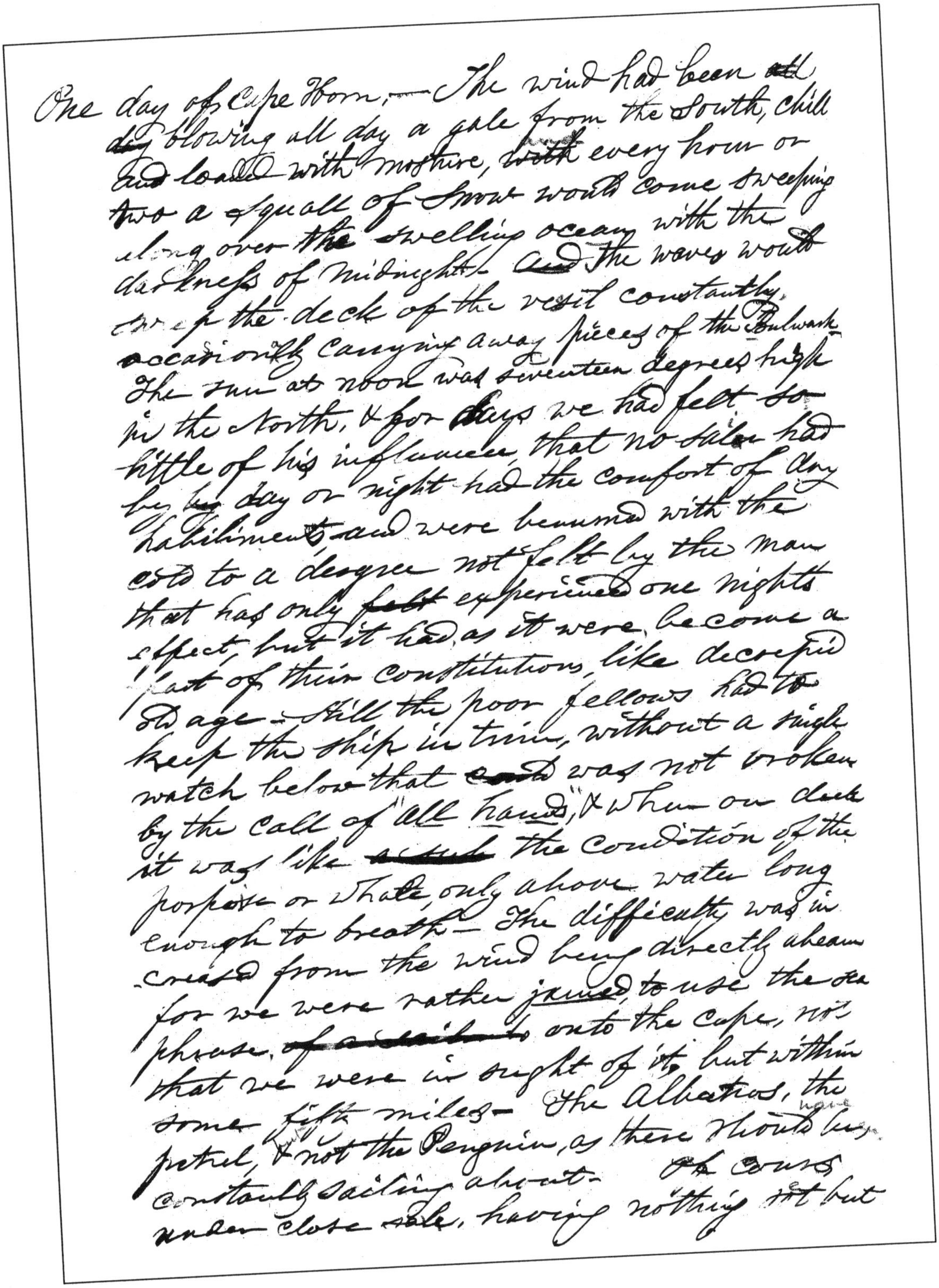

One day off Cape Horn,— The wind had been ~~all~~
~~day~~ blowing all day a gale from the South, chill
~~and~~ loaded with moisture, ~~with~~ every hour or
two a squall of snow would come sweeping
along over the swelling ocean with the
darkness of midnight. ~~And~~ The waves would
sweep the deck of the vessel constantly,
occasionally carrying away pieces of the bulwark.
The sun at noon was seventeen degrees high
in the North, & for days we had felt so
little of his influence that no sailor had
by ~~by~~ day or night had the comfort of dry
habiliments, and were benumbed with the
cold to a degree not felt by the man
that has only ~~felt~~ experienced one nights
effect, but it had, as it were, become a
part of their constitutions, like decrepid
old age. Still the poor fellows had to
keep the ship in trim, without a single
watch below that ~~was~~ was not broken
by the call of "All hands", & when on deck
it was like ~~actual~~ the condition of the
porpoise or whale, only above water long
enough to breathe. The difficulty was increased from the wind being directly abeam
for we were rather jammed to use the sea
phrase, ~~of a sailor~~ onto the cape, not
that we were in sight of it, but within
some fifty miles. The albatross, the
petrel, & not the Penguin, as there should be,
constantly sailing about. Of course
under close sail, having nothing ~~set~~ but

John Ball kept a diary throughout his trip. This page recounts, "One day off Cape Horn – The wind had been blowing all day a gale from the South, chili [sic] and loaded with moisture, about every hour or two a squall of snow would come sweeping along over the swelling ocean with the darkness of midnight." The diaries were used extensively by his daughters to create The Autobiography of John Ball. *[John Ball Collection, Grand Rapids Public Library, Box 26, Folder 541]*

ON BOARD A WHALER
CHAPTER IX

I did not come here with the expectation of staying long, but to find the means of further return toward home, which I expected would probably be by an American whale ship. I was pleased with the country, and would perhaps have stayed had I found anything to do, and as it was, thought that I would probably return with goods for merchandising. In no place of my long journey was I so much interested, or enjoyed myself so well, but I must go, so I sought a vessel in which to take a passage. And I found the whale ship *Nautillus*, whose captain was named Weeks, and the first mate, Harding. It was nearly full of oil and bound home to New Bedford, would only stop to catch any whale they might meet with on their way. So with the scant money I had, I engaged a passage on her around Cape Horn.

After spending two weeks on this island Oahu, including Christmas and the New Year of 1834, on the sixth I bade farewell to my *Columbia* and Honolulu friends, by all of whom I had been treated most kindly, and went aboard ship and sailed. It was a great change indeed, from the society of intelligent men and the agreeable family of my friend Brinsmade, to that of Captain Weeks' only, a man who never in his life had been three miles from the sea — born on Martha's Vineyard and raised almost from childhood on shipboard. He knew well how to sail a ship and to catch a whale, but little more. Well we made sail, and here however he did not show the knowledge of the winds and lands that he should have possessed, for we soon fell into a calm from approaching so near Owhyhee (the island of mountains, as high nearly as any except the Himalayas), so high, in fact, as to entirely break off the northeast trade winds. There we floundered for nearly a week before we could get away, and when we did we bore off towards the line, soon losing sight of these islands, and after a time came near the Meldron Islands, which are low coral islands inhabited but little, rising above water.

Seasickness
Soon after going aboard, to add to my rather disconsolate situation, I became seasick, induced or at least increased from the cabin assigned me being poorly ventilated, and the offensive smell of the ship. The sickness did not, as is usual with that kind of sickness leave me, but continued for weeks, and I lost all appetite for my food, and so became quite weak and emaciated. I stayed on the deck during the day, but at night turned into my close stateroom. I wished to stay on deck at night, but the captain would not give his consent, I know not why, till I told him I could not live in that way any longer, when he finally consented. So I stayed on deck at night too, stowed away in some corner, with a sail above to break off the dew, after which in a few days I was right well.

Whaling
And as it was my privilege to see something of whaling, I will give some account of how it is carried on. The ship is manned with a captain, first and second mates, boat steerers, carpenter, cooper, etc., in all some thirty men. A less number of men will sail the vessel, but when on whaling ground they need that number for properly pursuing the business. So instead of shipping the whole number at home, they sometimes filled up their crew with the islanders, who they found made good seamen. Our ship not being full after crossing the line, we cruised about for a whale, and they caught some six or eight while

I was aboard. An interesting sight to see them take the huge monsters of the deep. When on fishing ground three men all the day are aloft on the top masts galent trees looking out for whale, and they can see them blow, as they call their breathing, a long way off. For understand, the whale, porpoise and some of the other creatures of the sea are not cold blooded like most of the creatures deep, but warm blooded breathing the air like land animals, and bringing forth living young, and suckling the same.

And there are different kinds of whales, the right whale, that mostly inhabits high latitudes and feeds on insects and small fish, that they gather into the mouth by thin whalebone apparatus. Those I have not seen, but these sperm whales of the tropics have teeth in their lower jaw, and feed on a strange gelatinous creature that lives deep in the sea. The whale for the purpose of feeding will dive down and stay under water a whole hour. Then he must come up to breathe and swims along with a waving motion and about once a minute throws his head up and breathes, blows. He has but one nostril, and that right at the top and forepart of his huge, square kind of head, and this has a kind of lid that closes under water. So when he breathes out he throws his misty, vaporous breath high in the air, and thus swims along and breathes, if not disturbed, a whole hour, and then sounds, as they call it, or goes down again.

"There She Blows"

The cry always given when the whale is sure to breathe at a distance is "there she blows" and if so far that the officer on deck can not see, he asks, "Where Away," and the answer is "Astern," off to the starboard," or the "larboard" as the case may be. And if near enough to be reached before going down again, the next order is to lower away the boats. These are suspended over the sides of the ship, and each has its crew of six, one of whom is a mate or a boat steerer, to take the helm and give commands. Then comes the contest, which boat shall first reach the whale. As they approach the whale, the forward oarsman is ordered to "stand," which he does, lays in his oar and takes the harpoon, a lance-like instrument with a heavy handle to give the harder blow, and to this harpoon is tied a rope 80 fathoms long.

Harpooning

And they row up behind the whale, and when near enough, the order is "strike," when the harpoon man throws it with all his might into the back of the animal. It generally goes deep, and from the wound the whale starts off swiftly and takes the rope attached

to the harpoon from the tub in which it is coiled, through a groove in the bow of the boat, but in a short time they snub the rope by a turn around a projection at the bow. And then he takes the boat, sweeping over the water like an arrow, and so they let him run till he is tired, then they haul up by the rope till they come along by his side and kill him by thrusting a lance into his vital parts. For the harpoon only holds him, but if instead of running on, or near the surface, he sounds, goes down, till he takes the whole rope, they loose him and the rope too. But in such cases if they can attach the rope of another boat, and any way hold onto him, he is so out of breath and worried, that he will soon come up again to breathe. When killed they either take him in tow to the ship with their boat, or if the wind favors, make sail to where he lays with the ship.

The first that I saw of the business was under the most favorable circumstances to witness a great diversity of its attendant features. All of a sudden, a whole school, a half dozen or more, came up near the ship, and all the four boats were immediately lowered and made chase. To see the performance the better I went aloft where I could look right down on the whole scene.

The Chase

Soon the men of one of the boats struck a whale, but as quick as thought the same or another whale, they could not say which, by an upward stroke with his fluke stove the boat into a hundred pieces and sent the men sprawling in every direction. Still none were seriously injured, and another boat near picked them all up, and the game was not yet all over, for still one of the boats caught a whale of the same school and brought him alongside of the ship. And to keep him there they noosed a cable around the smaller part of the tail, if we may so call it, between the fluke and body. Then they first cut off the head with heavy chisel-like axes on long handles, so as to stand on stagings and strike down; hoist in the whole head, out of which comes most of the sperm. Then cut through the blubber spirally and hitch onto it and strip it off of the lean flesh below and take it aboard in pieces. And then let the body go, unless sometimes they take off a piece for a fresh steak, tolerably good when no other fresh meat is to be had, still, rather coarse. Then comes, the trying out the oil in three large caldrons set in arches back of the forward mast, and after the first fire of wood to start, the scraps furnished abundant fuel to try out the rest. And the oil was filled into barrels brought from home for that purpose. The largest that I saw taken made some forty barrels, but they told me that during their cruise they had taken one that made a hundred.

And when they had taken more whale and filled the last barrel they made sail for Tahiti, of the Society Islands, to repack and get some supplies before doubling Cape Horn. I watched the whaling while it lasted and the albatross, and other birds and whiled away the same time as best I could. Usually at noon with a little sextant, I had bought in New York, took the sun's altitude and worked out the latitude. And it now being the latter part of February we passed the sun in latitude about 10 degrees south. And on the cruising grounds in the neighborhood of Meldron Islands we were in from 155 to 156 degrees west; Oahu is some 158 degrees. There was great uniformity in the temperature, differing not more than three or four degrees in the twenty-four hours, sunshine mostly, but often cloudy and occasional showers and sometimes squalls, one, on the first day of March that carried away some of our spars.

Society Islands

The next day, to our joy, we came in sight of land. Bolobolo one of the Society group, looming up in the far distance, with one of its sides apparently perpendicular. And as we sailed on came in sight of others and finally Tahiti with its castelled mountains. And finally, on the 7th of March, two months after leaving Oahu we entered its coral bound harbor, found in the harbor some ten whale ships and three brigs, one of which was freighted with shells, the mother-of-pearl, the oyster shells being very large and the inner shell very beautiful. From these are made your pearl buttons, and all those things of use and ornament. Strangely, the tide here is high at twelve o'clock day and night year round. This island being within the tropics has also the eternal summer, even summer temperature of Oahu, and still more beautiful, if possible, in its diversified lands and luxuriant productions, thickets of guava, with the fruit rotting on the ground, the banana, citron, lemon, orange, and all the tropical fruits in the greatest abundance. The price of the same is but nominal. I boarded on shore while there and went considerably about the island, and much enjoyed the change.

When we were entering the harbor the captain asked me what day of the week it was. I answered Saturday, but when we got to shore, he said it to be Sunday. And so we found it and went to church. Our ship had sailed by Cape Horn, I had crossed the continent and the whites at the Sandwich Islands had in reaching there gone towards the setting sun also, and we all reckoned time alike. But the English

missionaries at Tahiti had reached there from the opposite direction around the Cape of Good Hope, so it made one day's difference, setting them one day ahead. English missionaries had been here thirty years, still, as far as I could judge, they had made but little impression on the ways of the natives. They still even made and wore their native tapa cloth, when they wore any dress, and I saw them make it. They take the inner bark of the bread fruit, or other tree, lay it on a square block of wood, then with a mallet pound it out thin; then lay onto the edge of this another strip of bark, which by pounding is made to adhere to the first; and so add on and on till they have made a piece, say a yard or more square. And this they sometimes dye into divers figures. This cloth is pliable and has so much strength as to be quite lasting. And a piece of this brought around the body and fastened at the waist, by just a turn under of the corner, constitutes a full dress for the woman."

Mutineers of the Ship "Bounty"

One day I made a long trip to a part of the island where the ship *Bounty* lay [Tahiti] to take in the bread fruit tree to be planted in the West Indies, the crew of which soon mutinied to get back among the fascinating natives and went and stayed at Pitcairn Island. On my way back the natives became very civil. One climbed a cocoanut tree to break off some of the nuts that I might have some of the milk to drink, and dealt out some of their poc, made of the roasted tarro root and ripe banana pounded and mixed – a very good porridge. But as with them, the finger is the only spoon, it bothered me by its sticking to my fingers. They laughed at me and handed me a calabash of water into which first to dip my fingers so it would not stick. They accompanied me back to port, civilly packing me across the creeks. All of which was explained when I got to port. They had taken me for a runaway seaman, for the return of whom they got pay from the vessel.

These natives of the Society Islands are quite the same race of people as those of the Sandwich Islands – the same in looks and character, and speak a dialect of the same language. Whereas the inhabitants of other islands, nearer to either of these groups than they are to each other, differ much every way speaking entirely different languages. For a wide sea rolls between these groups, say 40 degrees of latitude, 2,500 miles. In both they make boats in which they navigate far from land, passing from one island to another of the same cluster, if not further. Their construction is quite ingenious, and they are furnished with what is called an outrigger, a timber so attached by cross pieces from the fore and after part of the boat so as it just rests on the water off some six or eight feet from the boat, and prevents the boat from rolling and upsetting.

The ruler at the time was a woman, and quite a Morman in her ways, having two or three husbands, and for use too, for she said one was not enough.

The outer coral reef breaking the ever rolling of the sea beyond made a still harbor within, on which there was a beautiful row, in boats, over the coral forest below and a delightful walk along the shell strewn beach. And much more might be said of these Elysian Islands of the seamen, but their great fascination for them, was none for me, and I was impatient to be away.

The cargo of oil having all been re-coopered and re-packed, and a supply of fruits and vegetables taken aboard, oranges, bananas, yams and sweet potatoes — and they say the Irish potato will become swart [sweet] after two or three years' planting here — we bore away with the easterly trade wind on our lee beam to propel us, and in three or four days passed in sight of the last of the group, Toabouai, the last of land we saw that side, being about 23 degrees south and 149 degrees west. And on and on we sailed, the albatross and other sea birds always about.

Seafaring

And now as before, all the way from the whaling ground, I, every night, unless it rained, slept in one of the boats hanging on the davits over the ship's side. Had my overcoat around me and a sail spread loosely over the boat to break off the moonshine. And the swinging of the boat rocked me to sleep, and never was it more profound, and far more conducive to health in that warm climate than it would have been in my stateroom, which when we got into a high latitude and the weather became cold I had with reluctance to take.

The days sometimes passed rather dully by, still every day, even on the broad ocean, to one who observes, brings some changes. The changing clouds and winds, the calm or crested sea, the petrel ever following the ship to pick up the crumbs for a living, and at times, a fish would show its back and down would swoop the albatross or man of war bird to take him. For thus alone can these birds subsist, as far from known land as is Europe from our own shore. But still, to lay their eggs and hatch their young they must find some shore or islet, and such they have sought for ages, as is shown by the vast deposits of guano.

Aboard the ship there was no library, and mine consisted of only the Bible, Byron and Bowditch Navigator. I would make observations with my sextant, and from the tables of the Navigator calculate the ship's place for myself, so they should not deceive me. And then read the sublime of the Bible, Job or the Psalms, and Byron's inimitable description of sea scenes and sea doings in his Child Harold or other parts — "Roll, roll, thou dark blue ocean, roll."

Meager Living

The ship's provisions, except the supply at the island, was salt beef and pork, sea biscuit and flour laid in when they left for the cruise three years ago. The beef as hard as a brick, the flour musty, mouldy, and biscuit full of worms which we knocked out on the table as we ate. And after the fruit and vegetables were gone the living seemed rather hard, not half equal to good buffalo alone. And our vegetables grew scarce, the yam holding out the longest, being a kind of potato-like tuber of great size, sometimes weighing twenty pounds, and much used on long voyages. But to close the fresh vegetable business, a sea one night swept our decks and away they went. And there we were brought to our old three-year-old provisions, and nothing else.

Our captain more fearful probably than he need to have been of getting near the land, with unfavorable winds to keep off, bore up and up to the southward instead of off more direct to Cape Horn, reached its latitude hundreds of miles to the west of it, and still sailed away further up, with a constant westerly wind. And, oh, what a sea this strong constant wind from one direction raised. The ship would climb up and up to the crest and slide down seemingly half a mile. I have never elsewhere seen anything to compare with these off Cape Horn sea waves. And about the time we had probably reached the longitude of the cape the wind shifted to the northeast and drove us into a still higher latitude, probably as high as sixty. I say probably for we did not see the sun for two weeks, so of course we could not know our place.

Boy Overboard

And could we have seen the sun, its altitude at that season would have been but about 17 degrees high in the north at midday. So the days were almost all night, and as dark as death, squalls of snow, tearing winds and now from different points. The sea constantly sweeping across the deck from side to side, and sometimes over the stern top rail. The seamen were all drenched the moment they came on deck, and often to adjust the yards and sails all hands were called. And the ship was so damp below too, that not a stocking could be dried, so when they turned in for sleep it was in their wet clothes. And no fires except at the caboose to cook by. So they became tired and benumbed and with difficulty did their duty.

One day, as it was closing, they were ordered aloft to clue up the sails, and one of them, a youngster, out on the lee yard, fell clear of the ship into the foaming billows, and it was the last he was seen. To show his pluck to the end, the man next on the yard seeing how exhausted the benumbed he was, said to him, "You better go down." "No," he said, "I can stand it as long as you," and, next minute from the violent rolling of the ship, fell.

The same night a big sea struck the starboard side, and at the time also the windward side of the ship, and swept over it with that violence and in so large a body that it carried off everything on the deck, and swept away also the lee bulwark. So that come morning it was as clean as a new mopped floor. My stateroom was on the wind side of the ship, and when the sea struck her it seemed as solid and hard a knock as though another vessel had come against it. It seemed sinking and I supposed it was all over with us, but she tremblingly came up and floated on again. The same sea carried away the boats on the lee side, and we had now but one left.

Rounding the Horn

The wind and ocean current favoring us, some days we made in our old barnacles, lumbering ship not less than 200 miles, which in this high latitude thus sailing toward the rising sun, would shorten our days some 20 or more minutes. and after we had sailed on and on eastward till Captain Weeks felt doubly sure that we had far passed the Cape, he on the 5th of May, at noon, gave orders to change our course and bear off northeast. Never did I listen to so pleasing a sound. I felt as though we were indeed bound towards home, and almost that we were near there. Supposed to be in about 57 degrees south and longitude 64 degrees. New York, say 41 degrees north and 74 degrees west, equals 98 degrees of latitude difference, making nearly 7,000 miles, not far. and we sailed on, and soon got into better weather, and could see the sun to get our latitude. But as to the longitude, the captain had no chronometer, so had to get that by night observation of the moon and stars as best he could.

When we got down into about 45 degrees off Buenos Aires, a long way too, in the morning watch a squall struck the ship and so knocked her down, that in righting, the main yard and top sail yard and many of the sails were carried away.

I was in my berth and the captain in his near by and the ship went down so far and we being on the lee side it rolled us over onto the side of the ship, and while righting the captain sprang and climbed up to get out and when he saw that she had come up said, "Something is gone or she never would have righted." And on going on deck the ship's rigging, spars and sails, seemed mostly gone. The main yard snapped in the middle, and these spars and most of the sails overboard.

Loss of Rigging

But the squall had already passed, and they went immediately to work, got things rebound, for all still hung by the ropes to its side. The whole was the result of carelessness. The second mate, shipped at the Sandwich Islands and a favorite with the captain, was the officer of the watch. It was already morning, the ship was under full sail, and when they saw the squall coming he sat the men at the halyards to cast off when ordered but did not give the order till a tremendous gust struck her down, as you would upset a chair. The seamen said it was all to be seen that such would be the result, but they must wait for orders. Oh! how the captain did swear at his favorite, and the first mate, Harding, said "Had it been in my watch, Weeks would have thrown me overboard."

They had no spar to replace the one broken, and they soon found the sailing apparatus of the ship was so badly damaged they could hardly sail at all, except with an aft wind, which they could not expect to have anything like constantly. So they must change and give up their original plan of keeping out and on direct to New Bedford without stopping at all, unless they got short of water. Now they saw they could not do it, but must put into some port for repairs. And though Rio de Janeiro was far away, as it would take them less out of the course, they made the best sail they could for that port, and being much of the time favored with an aft wind, in some 20 days we made land. The weather was pleasant, and we now occasionally saw the nautilus, flying fish, and Mother Cary's chickens.[15]

---

[15] *"Mother Cary's chickens" are petrels, long-winged seabirds that fly far from land and feed on surface creatures and the refuse from ships. Their name comes from the slang "Matra Cara" for Virgin Mary, the protector of sailors.*

Land in Sight

On the 30th of May unexpectedly saw high land off north by west, and on asking the captain what land it was, he answered, "Cape Frio, the cape east of Rio." "But what was our latitude yesterday?" I asked. "Well so and so, 200 miles to the south of Cape Frio, and we were about in its longitude," he answered. "But at our slow sailing have we made 200 miles?" Well, he was puzzled, and finally concluded it must be some other land and it proved the coast southwestward of Rio, at a distance of more than 100 miles. Now, this showed that the day before he had mistaken his longitude a whole degree, and was trying to persuade himself that we had sailed 200 miles instead of 50. Two days after at night, we descried the city's lighthouse light, but he was so afraid of land, by standing off south it took us two days more before we got into the splendid bay of Rio de Janeiro, and to anchor.

It had been nine weeks that we had not seen land, and ten from sailing to landing. And oh! never shall I forget those ten dreary weeks of monotony, even in sunshine and at the best, too much of storm and perils on three-year-old feed. And worst of all the low character and conduct of Captain Weeks. He was jealous if I made any conversation with the other officers or men, though he knew little himself, but as you see to sail his ship, and as you further see, hardly that. One time, when off the Cape, he found so much fault with me about something, that I told him if he was not satisfied he must throw me overboard, if he chose. I had no passport, and was entering a foreign port, and he tried to get me to put my name on the ship's papers and pass as one of his men to save difficulty, and repeatedly urged me to do so. But I felt myself already as far in his power at I could consent to be, and would not.

ON BOARD THE UNITED STATES SCHOONER "BOXER"
CHAPTER X

The approach to the coast showed a variegated landscape, and the entrance to the bay a very striking scene. A little detached mountain on the left, of say a 100 feet in height, rose abruptly from the sea and the narrow entrance, and from the land on the other sides, in the form of and called the Sugar Loaf. So steep on all sides that it had never been ascended till some ingenious Yankee hit on the plan, by the aid of a kite to fly a small rope or cord, so as to fall over its top, and tie to this a larger rope and draw it over and fasten both ends, and then ascend the mountain by this rope. The bay is some 60 or 70 miles in circuit, and of a circular form, and the varied land seen rising from it on every side. The most beautiful bay in the world.

Wishes to Leave Whaler

The city and its harbor lies along a mile or two on the left of the bay from said Sugar Loaf, with no docks, but the best of anchorage, and the city built mostly of granite, on narrow streets, and quite in appearance like an old European city, which then having never seen, looked to me strange. But I had not yet got ashore. When we had come to anchor a harbor officer came aboard to see who we were, and on examining the ship's papers and counting noses I was found supernumerary. So, as in duty bound, he proposed to take me ashore and to the calaboose, prison, but when he found that I was quite willing to go, he concluded to leave me till the next morning. And he did not do it then. I did not feel much concerned as to what next might happen, if I could leave the old whale ship prison. For I had safely had such a diversity of experiences that I feared nothing worse

for the future. Nothing in any way insurmountable I was sure could happen.

Rio de Janeiro

I saw that there were two or three United States Men-of-War lying in the harbor, and soon one of their boats came to ours. On learning my case they offered at once, as they had the right to do, to take me on shore, which gave me the grand privilege of once more feeling terra firma, and looking about the city and country. And I enjoyed it much. The only impediment, I could not talk the Portuguese

It was aboard Lt. Farragut's Boxer, *a United States 10-gun Schooner of War similar to this artist's rendering, that John Ball completed his remarkable journey. [Reprinted from Nathan Miller,* The U.S. Navy: An Illustrated History, *American Heritage Publishing Co., New York, 1977]*

language, and they would not, like the Indians, understand signs. Still I got about and went some distance into the country to see its ways and productions. Of the latter I saw nothing new, except their ground product, coffee. This I found on the trees in its full growth, the berry the size of a small cherry or plum. Our coffee being only the pit of the plum, and this grows on a tree the size of the common plum tree, set out in extensive orchards. I called on our consul, a Mr. Baker, though I had no special need of his aid, which, however, it was my intention to seek should need be.

I had made up my mind long before reaching Rio to quit Captain Weeks and his ship, though my passage aboard of her was paid to New Bedford, and when I now told him of my intention he urged me strenuously to continue the voyage with him to its end. Said it would not take long to get the ship so repaired that he could sail. I had made up my mind I could stand that life no longer, let what might next come. I would stop here and run my chance as to the means of getting on further.

Calls on Lieutenant Farragut

There was in the harbor Men-of-War vessels, the *Natches, Boxer,* and I think one other; this being one of the United States stations for armed vessels. And I soon learned that one of them, the schooner *Boxer,* of 10 guns, was soon for some purpose to sail home to Norfolk. And though I knew the vessels of the navy did not take passengers, in my desperate necessity, considering my limited means and all, I wished to get along. I called on the commandant, Lieutenant [David G.] Farragut,[16] and informed him of my case, and asked him if there was not some way I could go with him.

I gave him a concise statement of my journeyings, and by what means I had reached there, and my wish and necessity of getting on, to all which he listened with much apparent interest and kindness. And then told me, as he had no clerk and was entitled to one, if I would like to ship in that capacity he would like to have me do so. Of course, I did not hesitate long in the acceptance of the place, and blessed my good fortune for the chance. And when on board was duly assigned my proper place to quarter and mess with the midshipmen. Still from their curiosity or courtesy, or both, most of my waking time was passed with the commandant and his officers.

Lieutenant David G. Farragut hired John Ball as his clerk in Rio de Janeiro, providing the traveler with an opportunity to return to New York. [Reprinted for A. T. Mahan, Admiral Farragut, D. Appleton & Co., 1892]

This Lieutenant Farragut was the same who afterwards became Commodore, and he well deserved and merited the promotion. Never was I acquainted with a man that showed the talent to control and command others. For he too could govern himself. He told me that often suffering at times from the failure of water at sea, and knowing the liability of such failure in spite of all precaution, he made up his mind to school himself by the daily use of very little, to so accustom himself to it as to escape the suffering in case of failure. And he had fully succeeded. A gill a day, I think it was, that sufficed him.

But there is more that I should say of Rio. There are beautiful islands in the bay and Fort St. Croix on the right at the entrance, from it we were hailed as we entered. And there was music and firing of cannon in the evening, and much that I had not for a long, long time been accustomed to see and hear. In one

---

[16] *B. 1801, d. 1870. Later to achieve fame in the Civil War as the Union naval commander who declared "Damn the torpedoes!" during the capture of New Orleans.*

day two American, four English and one Brazilian vessel came in, showing that it was a place of business, as indeed it was, and then I think next to New York in size in America. I was surprised to see so many vessels. The coffee was brought from the country on mules and from the warehouses to ship borne on the heads of the negroes. And I noticed that many of them were deeply tattooed, showing that they were of late importation.

Southern Skies and Magellan Clouds

And it is strange that I have so long omitted to mention the celestial aspect from this southern portion of our earth. Before reaching the Sandwich Islands, one observes the decline of the North Star and Ursus Major. And on sailing from there south when you reach the equator you have sat the same, except during the night when the Big Bear happens to be the highest, and in the same degree the stars of the south rise above the southern horizon. When leaving the Society Islands the seamen said we should soon come in sight of the Magellan clouds, and being asked about them they said that they were clouds, two white ones and one black one, but always seen in clear weather, and in the same position. And I was puzzled about it, till by the time we had got into 40 degrees south there indeed were the white clouds and to the left some degrees the black one. And I at once saw their purport. The light ones were bright, distinct nebula, and the black one a hole, as you may say in a bright part of the milky way – angular and very distinct, entirely without the luminous appearance of its other parts, the brightness of which around gives it the dark look. And the Southern Hemisphere having many more stars of the first magnitude and bright clusters gives the heavens of the night a most glorious aspect.

On the 8th of June, with some difficulty from the harbor regulations I was transferred from the *Nautilus* to the *Boxer* with my trunk, a trunk now right here made by Ira Ford of Lansingburgh, sent by my directions to Boston to be forwarded from there, which I found at Oahu.

Leaves in U.S. Ship

On the beautiful evening of that day we made sail, passing out by the Fort and Sugar Loaf, and leaving behind the old whale ship so long my home without regret. The only drawback to my full satisfaction at the change was a fear that my company might be irksome to my new ship companions. And as we sailed from the harbor and bay the look all around was most beautiful. And the moon and stars shone forth in all their beauty and brilliancy too. The

Southern Cross and other bright constellations had much lowered, the latitude of this being about 23 degrees, and now being at its height we could see in the north our old friends the stars of the Dipper.

And we sailed merrily on eastward in the sight of the coast and the next day at evening passed Cape Frio and tacked northward. And as we sailed on we were seen by a British Man-of-War, watching off the coast for slavers and taking our schooner *Boxer* to be one, made chase. But she could outsail them, and though Captain Farragut well understood their mistake he chose to have some fun out of it. So he would slacken, let them approach and show United States colors, and leave them again. Till on the third day of the chase he let them come up and speak us. And we entered the harbor of Bahia June 14th together, and there we stopped but three days. And I went ashore and found the lay of the land, deep ravines and abrupt shore, but few vessels in the harbor except the steamer *Fulton*. On the 17th sailed and on the 21st arrived off Pernambuco and came to anchor some distance from shore. I did not land.

In sight of the shore all the way from Rio for some distance abrupt, but from Bahia low, still distant mountains in sight. But in two days after lost sight of both low shores and the distant mountains. The weather clear and cloudy, showers, squalls and sun shining as is usual at sea within the tropics. And I found the temperature of the water and air the same as the other side, 81 degrees. And the upper clouds sometimes moved eastward against the lower wind. And we were sailing in the right direction to be favored by these almost constant trade winds. So with our fast sailing clipper-shaped vessel we made fine progress and on the 25th we crossed the line. Our latitude at noon 21 minutes and our longitude say 37½ degrees equals 40 degrees east and 40 degrees south of New York. And we being bound for Norfolk made our course just about northwest.

Duties as Ship's Clerk

I could not but feel that I was indeed nearing home, and at night and day too the heavens began to look more natural. The sun in 23½ only in the north at midday. No, I should have said nothing about the sun, for instead of his being at the equinox he was in the summer solstice. But the planets were about and above and the stars of the north fast rising, and the north star soon was seen above the horizon. For the purpose of education the midshipmen made the observations and kept the ship's reckoning, and all the duty I had to perform as captain's clerk was to transcribe their record to the captain's journal, some ten to fifteen minutes' labor. And at the time with me passed pleasantly along. The living a great improvement on that of the **Nautilus,** and the company ever pleasant and often instructive. And most of the time with the captain and officers, who always treated me, waif as I was, with the greatest kindness.

So we sailed on and on for some days with a fine trade breeze and good enough sea and little, to at all, vary the scene, few fish or fowl to be seen, and had not, as is usual, a calm in what is called the horse latitudes. But when we got into the Gulf Stream we met with some weeds, birds, and the flying fish, and as we neared the coast some vessels. And on the 16th

of July we descried land and entered the bay, passing Cape Henry and came to anchor in the Hampton Roads, making 37½ days from Rio. And here our captain was at home, (of course a commandant is always captain to those aboard his vessel, no matter his grade.) At home for here Lieutenant (Commodore) Farragut found his wife. I went ashore at Norfolk, and the next day with the midship boys to the Navy Yard at Portsmouth. And the day following bade farewell to my kind ship fellows and went aboard a steamer bound for Baltimore.

John Ball's Travels
Sandwich Islands (Hawaii), and
Cape of Good Hope to U.S.

HOME AGAIN
CHAPTER XI

We stopped at Point Comfort and so sailed on up the Chesapeake, the Patapico, and into the Baltimore harbor, and here I had reached terra cognita, a place I had often before visited, and which I last left two years and four months ago. And I at once sought my old oilcloth customers to learn from them what they might know about my Lansingburgh friends, from whom I had not heard since their letters written about two years before, that I found at Oahu. And I found that they still dealt there and were alive and well. And on from there I went by railroad to Philadelphia and New York. Oh! what a change had come over this part of the world since I left. Railroads from city to city and propelled by locos. And how, too, these cities had grown. And then I went by steamer, as of yore, up to Hudson, and by stage to Lansingburgh, where I took my friends by surprise indeed, for they had not heard from me since I wrote from Fort Vancouver, a year and a half before, and thought me still there.

All my friends and acquaintances showed a deep interest at seeing me again, and a great curiosity to learn from me, personal experiences and what I had seen. And I was like happy in meeting them and learning of their welfare, and after a short visit at Lansingburgh went to New Hampshire to visit my connections and friends there. My father had died about the time I was off Cape Horn, at the age of 82, my mother still living in tolerable health, my oldest brother, Nathaniel, quite feeble in health, and the others with their families pretty well. And oh! they were all as glad to see me as though I had come from the grave, for they did not think it an equal chance that they ever should see me again, and supposed me in Oregon. After visiting all and talking over their and my experiences I returned to the State of New York.

What Next to Be Done?

And now came up strongly the question, "What next is to be done?" I had up to this time rather expected and wished to return to the Sandwich Islands, and received a schedule of goods fitted for that market from the Mr. Brinsmade I met there, by the mail from Valparaiso over to Buenos Aires and so on. But my friends would not aid me in that project, and I gave it up. As to means I brought none back with me, but instead had to economize severely to get around, and all I had was about $400, due me from the avails of the sales of cloth at the factory made before I left, my one-third.

I became discontented and half disheartened, felt little inclined or fitted after my wild wanderings to sit down to any business. Went to New York on some vague idea that I could get goods for the Pacific market, or do something else. I, in fact, wanted still to roam. Thought I would ship to Europe, working my way and wander there.

My friends urged me to make a book of my travels. That struck me as absurd, for I did not feel at all fitted to act the author. I did communicate a short article to Professor Silliman to correct some mistakes in my letters to Professor Eaton that had been published in that Journal here and also in Europe, being translated into different languages and read, it would seem. And he asked me for more, but got from me but little. But all he did get from me was published in the first number of the *American Journal of Science,* of 1835.

I was asked to address meetings on those things I had seen, and that I at first declined. And it seems strange to me now that I was so reluctant to write or lecture, for I was ever free to converse with friends and strangers and tell them what I had seen, for there was then little, very little, generally known of the parts I had visited, and deep interest to know more.

Had the lecture business for pay then been in vogue, as illy fitted as I was for it, had I undertaken it with determination, I should have succeeded and made a small fortune. As it was, the next winter a new formed society then in Troy did induce me to give two lectures in the large court room in the court house, and the notice filled the room to overflowing. The members of the State Legislature and others came up from Albany to attend, and though I spoke with much fear and trembling to such an audience, they were well received, seeming to give great satisfaction.

Law Business in Troy

But before that, finding nothing else to do, I had gone into my old business of law in Troy, being offered a partnership with an old practitioner, Esquire Wilson, as he was always called. His office in the basement of the court house. I continued with him one year, and then opened an office alone on Congress Street, opposite the Mrs. Willard's Female Seminary, but I could not so compete with the old practitioners as to get very much business. And of society I was rather shy, and as I was situated, had but little claim on it. Continued my acquaintance and intercourse with my old friends in Lansingburgh and Troy, and found but few new ones. An old bachelor in life and ways and no thought of being anything else till I could have a supporting business.

Most of my particular friends were of the then Whig party in politics, but I adhered to my old preference, being a Jackson man. And as to church matters, I was not with them there, for I had no particular one, as most of them had. I was advised one time by a friend to take a seat in the Second Presbyterian Church, as it would aid my business, but it was always repulsive to me to mingle sacred and secular things. I boarded at a hotel called the Mansion House, and there were many boarders, one of whom is now my neighbor, Mr. Ransom E. Wood, but of the renewal of our acquaintance I will speak hereafter.

BOOK THE THIRD
Michigan in the Making
1836 - 1857

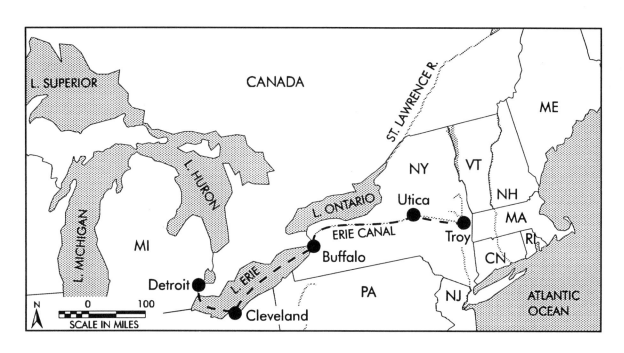

John Ball's Travels
To Michigan, 1836

SPECULATING IN GOVERNMENT LANDS
CHAPTER I

It is but little that one can recollect, or say of himself, when living a life, the daily routine of which is the same. My friend, Dr. T. C. Brinsmade, was now living in Troy, and of course, I often saw him. And he, Dr. Leonard, of Lansingburgh, J. E. Whipple, my sister Powers' partner, and a Mr. Webster proposed to me, as my business was not lucrative, to furnish me with some means to go west and operate in lands, there being then much doing in that line. It was the great year of speculation and I have always thought strange that so sober men as those should have yielded to the mania that so pervaded the country.

When they proposed the project, I fell in with it, for I was glad of an excuse for a change of life. Anything lawful, that would give me occupation, and a possible chance for making something for myself, though my expectations were not as high as theirs. So the agreement was this: that I should take such amount of money as they should furnish from time to time, the amount not limited; go anywhere West, north of the slave states, and operate in real estate, wild Government lands, second hand, village or city. Anything and everything that should promise a safe investment, and probably quick and good and great return. Buy and sell in my own name, as though the money was all my own, and have one-fourth the profits. Though I had none, not even enough to meet expenses.

One Week from Troy to Detroit

And I first started out on the 27th of July, 1836; just about two years from my return from the Pacific. I went with a Mr. Mann, who had before been West. Went by railroad to Utica, which was as far as I had ever been in that direction. Then we traveled by canal to Buffalo, giving me the opportunity to see the villages and country along the same. The great New York State Canal had then been in full operation twelve years, and had wonderfully aided the trade and growth of all this western part of the same, and states and territories farther west. We went by steamboat by Cleveland to Detroit. The first of my sailing on our great lakes. Sailing was no great novelty to me, except that waters so broad, were fresh. Cleveland was then but a village, and Detroit, though of older look, also of but a very limited extent. One week from Troy to Detroit.

Finding corner lots too high in price here to promise the needed advance, we took steamboat for Monroe, where I delivered a letter of introduction from the Hon. Job Pierson of Troy to the Hon. Austin E. Wing, delegate from the Territory of Michigan; and he, Mr. Pierson, a member from the county of Rensselaer. Monroe claimed then to be the business place for all the south part of the state, and its prospects for growth very great. But we, thinking Toledo more promising, sailed for that new and pretentious village. We found its population quite low, but the prices of its lots and blocks, as we thought, enormously high. and we went up the river to Maumee and Perrysburgh, and returned to Toledo and Monroe, and had made no purchases. Nor had I found anything in all those promising villages that I deemed at all an object to purchase. And thus passed another week.

Still I was unwilling to give up the finding of something that I could risk to buy. And there being a United States Land Office in Monroe then, for a district of land comprising that southern part of the state, and unsold lands out in Hillsdale County, I made up my mind to see what might be found in the way of wild lands. So I procured at the office maps designating the unsold land, and started out for an exploration of the same. And alone, for my friend, Mr. Mann, who had been with me till this time, became sick and was unable to accompany me. And this trip gave me an opportunity to see some of the country and the lay thereof, which I found in the interior quite diversified with hills and dales, rippling brooks and rills, quite unlike that on the Detroit and Maumee rivers and along Lake Erie.

Gains Experience in Land Looking

I went out by the way of Tecumseh to Macon, Clinton and to Jonesville by stage or other ways, as I could get the chance. There were then but few buildings in any of those villages, and the country but little settled. I found a man experienced in land looking and went horseback to the last settlers in the direction of the land, and then, of course, footed it about the woods. I remember we passed the present site of Jonesville, where there was then one house and they were building a sawmill. It was in Townships 7 and 8 south of range 3 west, that we explored for unsold United States lands, and I found

some of so good a quality I made up my mind they were worth purchasing. Though the lands in those parts had been thoroughly culled, I soon learned from my guide the whole mystery of land looking. A business I pursued much for the following six or seven years.

After some ten days absence I returned to Monroe, but to find my friend, Mr. Mann, gone, and I could by no means find where. The landlord of the house at which he stopped said he left a memorandum for me, but he could or would not, find it. And I went to the land office to buy the lands I had found, and that was closed, and as they said, by the order of the Government. So I seemed destined to disappointment in finding my friend and getting the wild land. But what was worse, my new made acquaintance, Mr. Wing, induced me to purchase some of his out-town marsh lands, that proved a losing concern. Went back to Detroit, and then down the lake to Buffalo. From there by stage through Canandaigua, Seneca, etc., being a different route, and so back to Troy, September 1st, feeling that I had made but a poor trip, as to business, but had to my interest and pleasure, seen some of the country.

A tow boat on the Erie Canal, part of John Ball's route west to Michigan in 1836. [Collections of the Library of Congress, #LC USZ62-32150] ·

Starts for the Grand River Valley

F. N. Mann, Esq., of Troy, informed me that he had heard from his brother William, whom I could not find. That he had got better and had gone to Ionia, where they were about to open an office for a new land district, the same that received the name of the Grand River land district. And that he expected me to follow him there. My friends not being at all disheartened in the matter furnished me with more funds, and on the 25th of September 1836, I started out again, and with the intention of going to the Grand River country. So I traveled by railroad to Utica and then by stage, traveling day and night for three days to reach Buffalo, it being very muddy. Then by steamboat to Conneaut, Ohio, and by boat to Detroit, arriving there the first day of October.

I met at Detroit an acquaintance, a Mr. Fake, with whom I advised, he being acquainted as to the best means of getting into the country, and he advised, by all means to purchase a horse, as horseback was the only convenient way, the roads were so bad, for traveling. So bought a horse and saddle and saddle bags, and transferred to the latter from my trunk things most necessary, but omitted to take along a brace of pistols I had purchased in Troy to please my friends, they thinking that I was going into not only a wild, but a wicked country. But having before seen a good deal of voyageurs and pioneers, I did not deem them particularly necessary. Such tools are usually more needed in the city than country.

Horseback on the Territorial Road

Well, I mounted my nag and struck out on what was then called the Territorial Road, built by Government from Detroit to St. Joseph, on Lake Michigan. And, Oh! what deep traveling. The mud so deep I did not trot a step till my horse had waded to Ypsilanti. Still I reached the first day the village of Ann Arbor, where I stopped. There was no University there then, and not very much else. And here I met two or three Rensselaer County acquaintances, who were also going westward for the same purpose as myself. So the next day we traveled on together. And as we traveled on we got in company on matters of education. We stopped at Jackson, at the only hotel, kept by a Mr. Ring, and then traveled on to Marshall, and there I found some acquaintances, a Mr. Charles Smith and wife, a Miss Dougery, both their parents lived in Lansingburgh. Just out in the country where Judge Hickock and daughter, Mrs. I. E. Crary,[17] whom I also knew. The judge had sold his

valuable farm on the Hudson, just above and opposite Waterford, to go to Michigan to be with this daughter, his only child. He had lately bought of the Government 1,000 acres of land, much of it marsh above a stream, just north of Marshall, that had been left by other purchasers and settlers, as being waste lands. But he said they had left just what he preferred, as being the more valuable. And I have often observed that the first purchasers failed to select the best lands.

To show how strangely people will meet in distant parts of the world, I will mention a case. I was returning into Marshall over a part of the road which was very muddy, when I met a young girl with a child whom she was trying to carry, on account of the mud, and being a humane man, I told her I would help her about the child. So I took it on my horse and traveled back and carried it to better ground, where I met a man, whom I asked to take down the child, which he did and spoke to me by name. I did not recognize him, and asked him where he had known me. He answered, at Lansingburgh, but the last time he had seen me was aboard a City of Hudson whale ship, to which he belonged, at the Sandwich Islands.

Calhoun County

I noted the beautiful country in Calhoun County thus far and so on to Kalamazoo, that even then a beautiful village. They had left the native forest on their lots and in the streets and had protected the same and planted others, and having no bad grading to disfigure the natural fine shape of the land, it had from its foundation always been most beautiful. The next day I proposed to continue my journey north to the Grand River and urged my Rensselaer friends to accompany me, when they answered in a way that sounded quite ridiculous to me (having myself gone so much deeper into the woods and come out safely) that they would not risk their lives and health to go any farther. So I mounted my horse and journeyed northward alone, without the least fear or trembling, crossed the beautiful Gull Prairie, its native smoothness then having only been disturbed by two or three settlers and then no house until I reached Yankee Springs, where a Mr. Lewis had a log cabin. And it being a day's journey to any other place, or at least it was a half-way place, he of course kept tavern, so I stopped with him for the night.

In early times this Yankee Springs became quite a celebrated stopping place for the travelers and as

---

[17] *Wife of Isaac E. Crary, first Michigan representative to the U.S. House of Representatives.*

business increased Yankee Lewis, as he called, added another story to the cabin and so one after another till his premises were some four or five stories long. And Oh! what splendid big wood fires he would have of a cold evening in his huge fireplaces, and his lady would get up a supper that beat in excellence any that city supplies. But I could stop but one night so next day went on my way stopping for lunch at a Mr. Leonard's at the fording place of the Thornapple River.

Indian Trail

The next house was that of a Mr. Marsac, an Indian trader on the south side of Grand River, opposite the mouth of the Flat River, the present site of Lowell. The route was on an Indian trail from the crossing of the Little Thornapple, where it left the Grand Rapids road, by the way then traveled, keeping east of that river to its mouth. And none of the roads in the country were at all worked. But the white man generally followed the track of the Indian, as long acquaintance had made him familiar with the most passable grounds and the fording places across the streams.

The next day I went on a like road to Ionia, a village then of half a dozen houses all told. So few

that there was but poor accommodation for the great numbers who then visited the land office business. I stopped at a Mr. Yeoman's at his farmhouse a little below the offices. But here, as I expected, I did not find Mr. William Mann. He had left for parts unknown. His brother had sent to him by me some 1,000 dollars or so to invest on certain terms, which he afterwards requested me to do on the same terms, that resulted quite to my advantage.

And now I procured at the office maps of unsold lands and prepared to go forth to look up the same. And now I left my funds behind, for I had made thus far my journeying with some $1,000 in gold and drafts, I do not remember to what amount, in my saddle bags, but had not been robbed nor did I hear of anything of the kind during all those times of wild speculation. Everyone knowing that each one he met whether on the byroads or in the lone cabins, had money. But in this speculative deal in corner lots and broad wild acres, there was not the same circumspection. No scruples as to exaggerated representation. If one bought today and gave the full value, he had no scruple in taking for the same tomorrow five or ten times the amount from you, his dupe, and all seemed deluded.

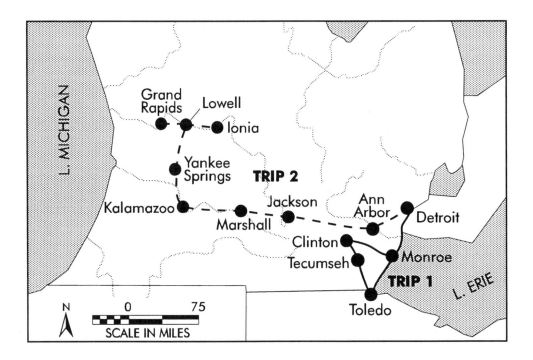

John Ball's Travels
In Michigan, 1836

LAND LOOKING IN WESTERN MICHIGAN
CHAPTER II

I was first at Grand Rapids on the 18th of October, 1836, but little thought that I should make it or any other one place so long my home. Seeing it had great natural advantages I inquired the price of property and found the village lots, whether corner ones or others, were fabulously high in price. I met Judge Almy[18] at his office on Bridge Street. And he informed me that lots on Canal and Kent Streets were 50 dollars per foot front, making the 50-foot lots $2,500 per lot. And on the Campau plat proportionally high.

Grand Rapids in 1836

The Eagle House, a much smaller building than now, was the only tavern in the place, and was kept by Mr. Godfroy. And there were so many travelers it was much overcrowded. Difficult for him to keep a supply of provisions and as to bedding, the narrow Indian blankets but poorly covered the two sleepers in one bed. There was the frame of the Bridge Street House up and fitted for use the next summer. Mr. Coggeshall was then living in his partly finished house on the next corner. All above Bronson Street

---

[18] *John Almy was president of the Grand Rapids village board of trustees in 1840, and president of the first bank in Grand Rapids, the Grand River Bank, founded in 1838.*

The Eagle Hotel, built in 1834, was originally a story-and-a-half building. It served as John Ball's first lodging place when he arrived in Grand Rapids in 1836. [Grand Rapids Public Library, Fitch Collection, #1909]

89

was deep mud and the stumps still unremoved. Few buildings except some temporary shanties north of Monroe Street, not over eight or ten of all kinds. Mr. Louis Campau's, now a part of the second and third stories of the Rathbone house and Mr. Richard Godfroy's on the Catholic Church lot, the best.[19] And about the same number on Waterloo, including some two or three warehouses on the river for they had to get all their supplies by water from Buffalo and Cleveland and by Mackinaw and the river. For there was not anything raised in the county, or all the country about, except in Ionia County, and they had not a supply for their own consumption.

Half of the population of Grand Rapids was then French, people who had followed Mr. Louis Campau, who had been here as an Indian trader ten years, many of them mechanics, but most of the rest of the white population were here to make their living, like myself, by their wits. And all were full of life and hope as though it were a sure thing. Seeing it was no place for me I stopped but a day and then out again for the woods and looked some lands out in the northeast part of Allegan and western part of Barry and purchased the same.

The rush for Government lands was so great and the soundness of the state banks, the bills of which was the main currency, so doubtful that the Government issued an order that specie only should be received in payment for United States lands. For which President Jackson was much abused; but time showed that that was a much needed measure. Still the purchases went rapidly on and the specie paid in for the same much or mostly in silver. And soon they received at Ionia, the amount of Mr. Hutchinson's bail, $150,000, and his orders were to deposit the same in one of the territorial banks in Detroit; for Michigan was not yet a state. And his only means of transporting the same was by wagon over the unworked roads with an ox team.

Pine Lands in Ottawa County

While they were carting the specie to Detroit the land office at Ionia was closed as to making sales on land, so there being nothing to do there a Mr. Anderson, a fellow boarder at Mr. Yeoman's proposed to me that we should take an excursion down into Ottawa County to look at some pine lands of which he had a memorandum, but how he came by such he did not know. And as pine lands were deemed the

Louis and Sophie Campau came to Grand Rapids ten years before John Ball did, and like him dreamed of an important city along the Grand River. [Grand Rapids Public Library, Fitch Collection, #1963]

most valuable we mounted our horses and started out to see what we could in that line. Stopping over night at Grand Rapids at the Eagle, we went on to Grandville the next morning before breakfast. And when we got there we found no tavern, but a Mr. Charles Oaks said he could put up and feed and keep our horses, but had no feed for us, not even a breakfast. Still after some urging as to our hungry condition, his wife, a half-breed lady, gave us some coffee and a quite good though not very bountiful breakfast. But as for anything in the way of food for us to take into the woods they protested that they or their few neighbors had nothing. But they said a Mr. Ketchum, who was building a sawmill down a mile below on the Rush Creek, could supply us. So we left our horses to be cared for and went on down to where the mill was building, and there found a Mr. Nathan Boynton, keeping house for the workmen, but Mrs. Boynton had no cooked provisions not even bread, and then seeing no better way we stopped until she could bake us an unleavened loaf, which we took with some raw beef, and packed for our woods' supplies. This made it late in the morning to start out.

---

[19] *Louis Campau, a fur trader, arrived in 1826 and is usually credited with being the founder of Grand Rapids. Richard Godfroy came to Grand Rapids in 1832, engaging in the fur trade business and later operated a mercantile store. George Coggeshall was Grand Rapids' second village president. He held numerous other public offices in the course of his life. The mechanics Ball refers to is the term generally used for laborers.*

There being no settlers beyond, we struck due west keeping our reckoning by the surveyed lines and got on to the ground described by his memorandum, as night came on being on section 33, township 6, north of range 14 west, and which is now the organized township of Blendon.

Government Surveys

And here perhaps I ought to describe the manner of Government surveys. In Michigan all the lands reckon from one point, the intersection of a due east and west and north and south line. These lines intersect on the north line of Jackson County. A township

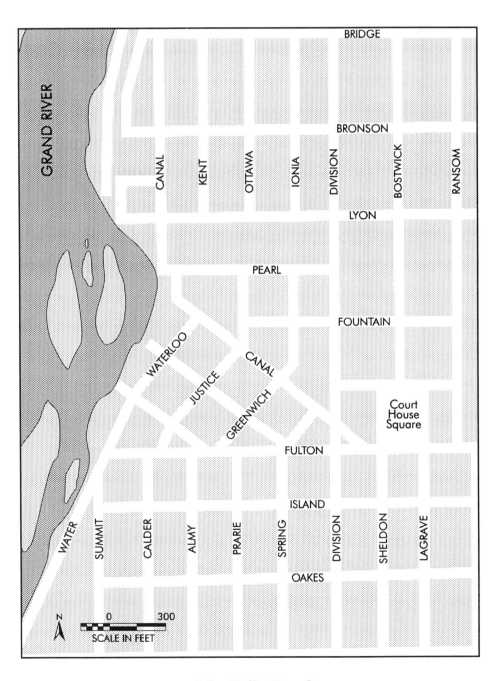

John Ball's Travels
Grand Rapids, Michigan, 1836

is six miles square making thirty-six square miles. Reckoning north and south from this first east and west line is called 1, 2 and so on, town N. or S. and from the meridional, or N. and S. line they say range 1, 2 and etc., W. or E. So all this Grand River country reckons north and west. And each township is sub-divided into square miles. So each way are lines marked by the surveyor cutting off a chip from each side of trees along the course. And at the mile intersections of these lines, mark on trees with just the initials of the township, range and section. So the land looker, if he knows he is in the state of Michigan thus knows in just what part.

And I shall be the more particular as this was the first of encamping out in Michigan, being November 4th, 1836. We stopped for the night, not among pines, but in the regular hardwood beech and maple, and on a small creek, which we saw by our map was a branch of what is now called the Black River falling into the Lake at Holland.

Prospecting in the Snow

So we built us a fire and broiled some of our steak, took supper, rapped ourselves in the blankets we had packed along for the purpose, and slept as well as the tramping deer and howling wolves would let us, they being probably attracted by our fire. In the morning, though we had not found the pine land where we expected, we concluded to look some farther, and did find a small tract. And when we had determined by the surveyed lines its precise locality and extent, we turned to get out before night, as we had taken but one day's rations.

But taking the route more to the north than the one on which had gone in, we had not gone far before we came into a dense forest of pines, and, to learn its extent we turned west on the section line and finding the timber of the finest quality, it enticed us on in the same direction till night overtook us. When without supper, to leave the morsel we had left for a breakfast, we wrapped around us our blankets and laid down for sleep, making the protecting root of a pine tree our pillow. And thus and then at the south-west corner of section 14, T. 6 N. R. 14 W. soundly slept until morning, when awakening we found ourselves covered with an inch or two of snow. After eating our scant supply we were so desirous of seeing the extent of pine that we traveled in different directions for some time, till admonished by our failing strength that it was time to leave the woods to get some food.

Supposing that there was some kind of road from

As one of several investors in public lands, John Ball contributed to the bustling business at the White Pigeon land office. [Robert Thom painting, Michigan Bell Telephone Company Collection]

Grandville to Grand Haven on that side of the river, we put out in that direction to find it. And did find an Indian trail but no other road, and following that it brought us to the river where we found some Indians. We offered them the silver dollars to take us up to Grandville in their canoes. They declined the offer saying, as we understood by signs, that they were going hunting. So we pushed on over broken ground, as we could pick our way, up and near the river till night again overtook us in the forest. And our last match lighting our fire we laid us down to sleep. But before sleep came we heard a cow-bell, an indication that a house was near, but in the darkness we did not seek the same and slept it out.

The next morning, missing the house where the cow belonged, for there was one in those parts, we made our way out to Grandville in rather a dilapidated condition, having been three or rather the third day on the one day's allowance. I had before been longer without food, but was then traveling on horseback, not as now on foot.

Securing the Prize

This time the Grandville folks readily gave us a breakfast, after taking which, and settling our bills, mounted our horses for Grand Rapids and next day to Ionia. We felt that we had found a valuable prize, but just the position and extent of the pine we did not yet understand with sufficient certainty to make the purchase. So in a few days after we started out again to re-look the same, and this time a son of Mr. Anderson accompanied us, and we furnished ourselves with a tent and an ample supply of food. Though the weather was very bad, rain and snow, we made a thorough exploration of the lands, finding some 2,500 acres of good pine almost in a body, on a part of which there was also some good white oak. One oak tree was seven feet in diameter with a clear body say of seventy feet high and a fine spreading top, the largest tree I ever saw in Michigan. It was sawed and sent east for navy purposes.

Ionia

And returning to the land office at Ionia, the question arose as to the division of these lands we had together found. And after some negotiation on the subject the Messrs. Anderson sold me their right in the same, for a few lots I had before bought in Allegan County. I think they were induced to do so from their want of funds. So I made the purchase of the whole tract in my own name. In exploring the Ottawa land the last time we were in the woods about a week, and coming out we stopped at Ezra Chubb's, on his farm in a log cabin between Grandville and Grand Rapids, on whose place near

the Grand River are some Indian mounds as well defined as I have ever seen.

I continued my explorations about the country, stopping when not so engaged mostly at Ionia, and there was, all the fall, a great crowd of land lookers coming there to make purchases and often a greater number than could be well accommodated. A Mr. Spencer kept a kind of hotel in a one-story house with three small rooms, and a chamber or garret over the same, as a general sleeping room, and in which were as many beds as could well stand, and, of course, two usually in each bed. As all came horseback with their saddle bags and valises, these, often containing money, were thrown promiscuously under the bed and there left perhaps for days.

Detroit by Way of Marshall

On the 8th of December, wishing to go to Detroit by the way of Marshall, instead of going as I had up to that time thought the only way, by Yankee Springs at Gull Prairie, we were told that there was a trail, and possibility of going through with our horses, direct to Marshall as the swamps were then so frozen to bear up our horses. It was then all a dense timbered beech and maple forest except the swamps

Indian mounds along the Grand River fascinated John Ball when he first came to Grand Rapids. His belief in their antiquity was confirmed when later archaeological investigations unearthed objects such as the copper axe, shell dipper, and pottery pictured here. [Grand Rapids Public Library, Oversized Photograph Collection]

Sketch of the village of Grand Rapids in 1838, facing northeast, showing a flatboat and a small steamer on the river. [Grand Rapids Public Library, Fitch Collection, #18-2-2]

from near the Grand River to Calhoun County, with only the settlement of three families on the Thornapple at what was called the Vermont Colony until you got to Bellvue on the south border of Eaton County and ten the only settlement in that country. The same elder Mr. Anderson was to accompany me. So we started out crossing the Grand River on the ice and struck off on the trail which for a time was quite pleasant. We were expecting to reach the colony by night, but from delay in finding ice on which to cross Grand River and other hindrances, night came on long before we got there and the trail so dim that we had to walk by turns to keep the trail. But finally to our great delight we saw a light. We were welcomed in the first log cabin and told they could give us a supper, but for our horses they had neither hay nor oats, and did not think that there was at the other houses. But one of their neighbors had gone out south for oats, and on going there we found that he had just got home with some, so horses and men were fed.

The next day we continued on our journey out to Marshall and so I continued my journey on by the usual route to Detroit where I arrived on the 15th. We did not travel then at railroad speed. Receiving my funds by draft, I had to go to Detroit to get the exchange into land office funds. I stopped there some days and then went to Monroe, I hardly know for what purpose. But there I got, by giving quite a boot, a better horse, on whom I could travel with greater speed. Returned to Detroit and there stayed to the assembly of the State Legislature, the first day of January, 1837.

Return by Shiawassee

This time I returned to the Grand River by what was called the northern route, the first day to Kensington, next to Williams on the Shiawassee, next Scots on the Looking Glass, these being then the only residents in Shiawassee and Clinton Counties and the next to Ionia. When I soon went down the river again.

I stopped at Edward Robinsons'[20] who lived in a log house a mile below Ada. He had a big family, a baker's dozen, he told me. And then as usual in all stopping places in those times men, women and children slept in one common garret. And from there next day to Grandville, where by this time they had a tavern, kept by Messrs. Blake and Osgood. There happened to be there at the time some Grand Haven men who were going home down the river on the ice, for it happened then to be well frozen over all the way. And for means of travel they had one horse and a cutter. Still they invited me to share the same, so we all slid down to Grand Haven.

Grand Haven

And when we reached there, there being no tavern, I stopped at the private house of a Mr. Luke White. He had there a brother Thomas, Rev. Mr. [William] Ferry[21] and family, a Mr. Throop, T. B. Gilbert, and in all, say one-half dozen families. Mr. Ferry had been a missionary at Mackinac, but came early to Grand Haven to operate in lands. Still as occasion required he preached. Then, as everywhere in those times I formed an acquaintance with the residents. With all of whom while living and now living I have continued a very pleasant friendship.

---

[20] *Early settler of the Thornapple River basin, whose brother, Rix, was an agent of the American Fur Company.*
[21] *Founder of Grand Haven and Ferrysburg, for whom the latter is named.*

But an object on my part at that time was to go into the woods from there south of the river to take another look for pine lands, thinking probably there were others further west as good as I had before found. I employed to go with me a half-breed man, raised at Mackinac and used to the woods, and in his fur business, to encamping at all seasons of the year. So we took our blankets and some provisions and put out southeast till we struck the Pigeon River. The snow was about knee deep, making it hard traveling so as night approached I told him I thought it time to encamp, but he answered "Not here." "Any why?" "There are no beech stubs." "What of beech stubs?" "They make a good fire and break in falling and save chopping." For, of course, we had an axe along, and soon we came where there were beech stubs and prepared for encamping.

It would seem to one unused to a camp life, that the chance for comfort would be small, but selecting a smooth spot on the lee of a fallen tree to break off the wind we scraped away the snow as well as we could, gathered a large pile of wood for the night, and built a fire from part of it, cut hemlock boughs or limbs with their green savoury leaves to sit and lie on, and spread them before our fire. Wrung out our wet socks, and moccasins and hung by the fire, the latter far better for the snow than boots. Cooked our supper, consisting mainly of broiled pork and bread and laid us down to sleep. And never in all my life did I sleep more sweetly or soundly. And so we tramped and encamped for four or five days, but found no land that I thought worth purchasing. So quit and came out at the mouth of Bass River and footed it up the Grand River on the ice to Grandville.

The next day I went south into what is now Byron, Town 6 N., Range 12 west, to look at its beech and maple lands to see if they were worth purchasing. A Mr. Nathan Boynton was the only man with a family then residing there. His brothers, Jerry and William were boarding with him. Near his place I found good lands which I bought, and out of part of which I after made a farm. Doing my business at Ionia, I soon again went to Detroit, and this time by Portland, stopping at Mr. Moore's and so to Scots, Williams, and so on.

Fellow Boarders in Detroit

When in Detroit that winter I stopped at the American, the same house that was Gov. [William] Hull's[22] before he surrendered the place to the British. Among the boarders were Gov. [Stevens T.] Mason,[23] unmarried, and Mr. [Henry R.] Schoolcraft,[24] whose wife was a half-breed of the Johnson family. She did not often appear at the table, though well educated in England and a real lady in her manners. When she found herself cut by some of the white ladies when at Washington, she could never get over it, but rather retired from company. I now became well acquainted with some of the members of the Legislature from different parts of the state, territory I should say, and the Detroit people and travelers whom I again met. But, just about this time, it was declared a state by an act of Congress, for the Toledo war,[25] for Toledo and the six mile trip, had passed and Michigan had consented to take the Upper Peninsula. And when the news reached Detroit it was celebrated by discharge of cannon, etc.

Going along Jefferson Avenue I noticed two boys ahead of me talking earnestly, but all that I understood, one said to the other, immediately after the discharge of a cannon, "Now Michigan is a state."

I had no particular place of residence that winter of 1837 so traveled much about the state, and always on my horse, just as business or fancy seemed to dictate, the winter being mild, but little snow. Went to Detroit and returned by different routes to Monroe and Toledo. And all were waiting for the opening of spring that men might again come up the Lake as years before on the business of speculation to buy their corner lots in the settled villages and blocks in the prospective towns in the woods. And many such were planned and platted, and some sold at high rates that are still forest or at best but farms.

Muskegon

In the spring Horace Gray, then of Grand Rapids, now of Grosse Isle, and myself, went down the Grand River on a keel boat sailed or rather poled by Captain Sibley and his men. Then from Grand Haven we footed it down the lake beach to Muskegon, where we then found residing two Indian traders, Mr. Lasley whose wife was an Indian, and a Mr. Troutier, a half-breed, and I suppose a full-blood wife. To whom, (Mr. Troutier), the now millionaire Mr. Martin Ryerson[26] was a clerk at the wages of eight dollars per month, and they the only people,

---

[22] *First governor of the Michigan Territory.*
[23] *First governor of the state of Michigan.*
[24] *Ethnographer and geologist and influential leader in early Michigan history.*
[25] *A dispute between Michigan and Ohio in 1835 over the control of the so-called "Toledo Strip."*
[26] *Grand Rapids pioneer who provided funds to build the Ryerson Library in downtown Grand Rapids in 1904.*

except Indians, there. We paddled ourselves up the Grand River in a very small log canoe with some discomfort, to a Mr. Yeoman's, the only settler on the river below Grandville, and stopped over night. The next day in preference to rowing, footed back on the direct trail to Grand Rapids.

In the spring I took up my residence at Grand Rapids and boarded at the Eagle Tavern, then kept by the late Mr. Louis Moran. Provisions were so scarce and dear that our living was not luxurious. I recollect the Messrs. Nelson, who were also boarders and who had a store opposite, used to bring over the cane sugar for their coffee, not exactly liking the maple made by the Indians, being rather dirty. It was said that they sometimes boiled the rabbits and other game in the sap they were boiling down to sugar. The people at Grand Rapids who held property were as full of hope and expectation as elsewhere, little dreaming what a change was near at hand, and when it came, they did not seem to realize it as in Detroit.

For about the first of June I was in Detroit, and Oh! what a collapse, and instead of high hopes it was all despair. The bubble had burst.[27] The New York banks and those of other states had failed or suspended specie payment by an act of their legislatures, and all speculation was up and over. Big fortunes had dwindled then, a hundred per cent in an hour. Instead of the walls of the hotels and public places being covered with village plats and lands for sale, as the month before, they were all bare, and sadness was on all faces.

Wildcat Banking

Governor Mason was pressed at once to call a special term of the Legislature to have a law passed as in New York to authorize the banks to suspend. And they convened and did pass such a law, and strangely they made it to apply to such banks as should go into operation under a general banking law just passed at the late session. And this made the wildcat banking, for specie carted from place to place started off many. And I ought perhaps to say more about the wildcat banking. At the regular session of 1837 the Legislature, the same that passed the law for making a state loan of five million to construct three railroads and two canals across the state, passed also a general banking law authorizing companies, by giving such mortgage securities as would be acceptable to the bank commissioners, and placing in their vault thirty per cent of the proposed

capital in specie, could perform all of the usual business of banking. Had it been left there few if any banks would have gone into operation under the law. But when at this extra session, they authorized the suspension of specie payment to extend also to such banks as should go into operation under this general law, for none yet had been organized, it presented a great temptation to go into the business. And it is said that some forty, as small as the population and business of the state was, were organized. The moment the specie had been counted by the commission to put one into operation, it could slyly be carted to the next for the same purpose, for it was not needed to redeem their issues.

Receiver of the Bank

We had our Grand River Bank at Grand Rapids of which Mr. A. L. Almy was president and Mr. Richmond, cashier, which was as good as the best of them. But Mr. Coggshall and some others wanted another, and they got up, to be, the People's Bank, of which they induced Uncle Louis Campau unwillingly to be president and Sim Johnson willingly to be cashier. But I am a little ahead of my journal in time, for this bank was not gotten up till the summer of 1838. They sent for D. N. Bell, bank commissioner, to come and put them in operation, but having on hand only six thousand in specie instead of thirty thousand, as required, he being an honest man, did no such thing. But put what they had into the hands of a receiver to redeem the bills they had already put into circulation and paid depositors. And I with much reluctance, being strongly urged by the commissioner, was appointed said receiver.

One of two "wildcat" banks, the Grand River Bank served Grand Rapids in the 1830s. [Grand Rapids Public Library, Porter Collection, #42-2-8]

[27] *The nationwide Panic of 1837.*

STATE REPRESENTATIVE
CHAPTER III

From my frequent journeying about the country, and stopping at any and every place where I could find feed for myself and horse, I became quite well acquainted on every road leading out of the then Grand River woods. And wherever I stopped I sought to make the acquaintance of those I met, and they with me, for often the settlers were so far from neighbors they were glad to see strangers. And from this free intercourse it was soon learned that in politics I was a Jackson man, or Democrat, and that being at the time the predominant party in the state, especially in the Grand River country, they soon noticed me in that direction. They first sent me in July to a state convention at Ann Arbor, where we nominated for second term Stevens T. Mason for governor, and then they sent me to Schoolcraft to a senatorial convention, I think.

And more strangely, considering my short residence in the country, they nominated me representative to the state legislature to represent an extensive woodland district, for under the first state constitution, in apportioning the representatives, about fifty in all, they gave, as they expressed it, to the unorganized counties of Ottawa, Kent, Ionia and Clinton one representative. And there was nobody farther north to be represented, for Muskegon lake and vicinity was then in Ottawa, and Clinton county had but Mr. Scot as an inhabitant. Each organized county had its representatives, no matter how small its population, other counties were attached to them often for legislative and judicial purposes. Barry was attached to Kalamazoo and Eaton to Calhoun and so on.

Nomination

At the convention that made the nomination there was great unanimity in my favor, and the whole was gotten up and carried through almost without my knowledge. The convention met at the Bridge Street House, then got in operation, and I was quietly passing the evening at my boarding house, the Eagle. And who should arrive there and put up but the Hon. C. C. Trowbridge, the whig candidate for governor out on a canvassing tour. I was introduced to him, and on his inquiring for his political friends, Messrs. Bostwick, Henry and others, I showed him where they lived, all then at Mr. Henry's and introduced him to the ladies, the gentlemen being out. And let me say the ladies were Mrs. Bostwick, Mrs. Henry, Mrs. Stoddard and daughter, Miss Henry and Miss Bridge, after Mrs. Nelson. On meeting Mr. Trowbridge the next morning he expressed great surprise, as well he might, to meet here a circle of so fine ladies, and, on learning of my nomination on the other side ticket, at my civility to himself.

Mr. Stoddard was the Whig candidate, a fit and very worthy man, and during the campaign there was maintained the most friendly relations between us as ever after. Later, he went and lived at Charlotte, Eaton County, named for Mrs. Bostwick.

When the election came on the first of November, out of about five hundred votes I had over four hundred. There were but five places of holding the poll in the four counties, there being but that number of townships organized. Ottawa had none, and the voters, some seventy came up on the steamboat and marched in line to the polls. In Kent county, Byron and Kent; in Ionia, Ionia and Maple; and Clinton all one town DeWitt, but which I think gave no votes.

Third Representative

I was the third representative from the district after the organization of the state government. Maj.

Briton of Grandville first, then Judge Almy of Grand Rapids. And now being elected, I began to think of my coming duties with some anxiety, as they would, to me, be all new, and would bring me in association with men, as I anticipated, of much more experience if not wisdom than myself. But of cares to leave behind at my new home, I had but few, for my operations in lands either in buying or selling were but few. My Troy friends advanced no more money to buy, and of purchasers there were none.

So on the 15th day of December, I packed my saddle bags and mounted my horse and started for Detroit, that then being the seat of government, and the sessions held in the old Territorial Hall. I stopped the first night at Ada and the next morning had much difficulty in crossing the Thornapple for there had been very heavy rains which had raised the streams, and there was much running ice in the river. Got over and journeyed on in my usual slow way, and reached Detroit the 23rd, the going being very bad.

At the Capitol

On arriving there I put up at the National Hotel, which was on the site or a part of what is now the Russell House and where many other members as they came in also took lodging till it was filled. I had a room to myself at first, but was soon informed by Mr. Bingham that a Mr. Barry of the Senate wished to come to the National, and that there was no place for him unless I would take him in with me. Said that he was not very well liked, but that he thought I could get along with him. He did come in with me and I got along with him first rate, and felt myself much honored and instructed by being thus associated with him.

The first of January, 1838, came and the Legislature met in their respective rooms and organized. The House elected K. S. Bingham, speaker, who was then a most decided Democrat in his views, as was a large majority of both houses. S. T. Mason re-elected for Governor, qualified and made his speech to the joint houses. There were many with us that winter who have since held high political positions. In the Senate Governors Barry and Trowbridge, in the House Governors Bingham and McClelland, Senator J. M. Howard, Representative Buell of Detroit and many others that I could mention who were perhaps as well fitted for such places as they, had they chanced to get them.

Liberal Views

The previous Legislature held an adjourned session in the fall to pass a revision of the laws, but

Stevens T. Mason, Michigan's first elected governor, presided over the state when John Ball took his seat in the state legislature. [Michigan State Archives]

failed to complete them. So that duty fell on us, and I recollect we had a hard contest on the chapter on witnesses and evidences, especially as to the rejection of witnesses on account of their belief. Mr. Bingham, in committee of the whole, myself and some others arguing that the subject of religious belief should not be raised; that the witness that had the honesty and boldness to say that he disbelieved what was the common or popular belief was much more deserving of belief than one who, for the sake of being a witness or the fear of unpopularity, would or might belie his true belief. Still it passed with the old restriction, but the very next winter it was repealed, and placed as it now stands.

The routes of the railroads and canal had been surveyed and it took much time to settle the contesting claims of aspiring villages on the different lines, Tecumseh and Adrian on the Southern, Owosso and Corunna on the Northern, and so along on all the routes. And then the appropriation of a portion of the five million loan on these different state works was a matter of great moment and took up time. The north and south had to combine, or the center counties, as the tier through which the Central railroad runs, would have monopolized the whole on that road. The result was that there was something appropriated on each of the three railroads, two canals; and thirty thousand to improve the navigation of the Grand and Maple Rivers. And the other works were to be commenced on the east end, and they so far had constructed the Central that we, the members were invited to take a ride on it to Ypsilanti, but on our return we got aground and some mile or two out of Detroit and had to foot it in.

Educational Committee

Then all minor matters had to come before the Legislature, like the organizing of townships and villages, and there were any number of these done up. In my district the number of townships was quadrupled, I should think, all of which had to be on petition presented, and these matters kept me quite busy. As to petitions I recollect of presenting one, at the request of Mr. Cooper, Senator from Jackson County, to change the name of the village of Jacksonburg to Jackson, and so on. I was on the committee on Education, and there were many petitions for sectarian colleges and schools, all of which I opposed on the ground that the state had then its universal common school system, its University and its branches, and all for all without any sectarian bias. I thought as far as the state was concerned it should have nothing to do with religious sectarianism. Our high schools have taken the intended plan of the branch universities.

Toward spring we had a strange experience at our hotel in the breaking out among the boarders and all, of the smallpox or varioloid. A traveler was taken sick and they put him into a room in the garret and his sickness proved to be the smallpox. And all unknown to the boarders, until many were taken with the disease, which showed itself in all forms, the slightest symptoms to one fatal case of a Miss Kellogg, who was there with her father, a member from Allegan. The funeral was indeed a sad one, the alarm was so great that only the father, clergyman, landlord, Mr. Bingham and myself attended the same.

That winter commenced early but there came a thaw in January that lasted some weeks, and it was as warm as summer. A steamboat came up the lake from Buffalo and I recollect General Scott came on it on business connected with the Canadian Patriot war that was then passing. It was the same breakup that the ice came down the Grand River and so dammed it up on the rapids as to throw all the water out of its channel and came sweeping down through Canal Street, but most of it swept down through the low lands on the west side, coming in again down by the Eagle Mills.

Returns in a Wagon

We had a protracted session, not adjourning till the 7th of April. And on the 16th, having sold my horse, I took passage home in a wagon, with Mrs. Watson, Mrs. O'Flynn, a Lucy Genereau, the late Mrs. John Godfroy, fellow passengers. And we had a slow passage but social time, taking six days. I was welcomed home by my constituents who seemed well satisfied with my doings, and here I whiled away my time, making some journeys about the country, one of which was to Port Sheldon, where some Philadelphians, had started a town that was to surpass Grand Haven as a lake harbor.

Now, as there was nothing to be done in a land way except to take care of what I had purchased and pay taxes on the same, I began to think it time to look out for permanent business and I did not see what I could better do than to go back to Troy and tell my friends the state of matters, and to get my law library and try to do something in that line. But as I was about to leave for that purpose, there came up that People's Bank business so I attended to that for a time but in September, as soon as I could be released from that, I went back to New York and I think to New Hampshire, and was gone some six weeks and brought back my library, that I found scattered in nearly all of the offices in the city of Troy. For when I left I expected so soon to return as to find it on the shelves.

Attorney Charles P. Calkins, like John Ball, came to Grand Rapids in 1836. [Grand Rapids Public Library, Oversized Photograph Collection]

Ottawa Avenue, between Monroe Avenue and Fountain Street, in 1840. Charles P. Calkins' law office is the center building. [Grand Rapids Public Library, Porter Collection, #42-2-8]

HARD TIMES
CHAPTER IV

The people at Grand Rapids seemed surprised to see me, saying that they were informed that I had left for good, for if they had known that I was coming back to stay I should have been again nominated for Legislature. This shows how careless I was on the subject. Colonel Finney had been nominated and I turned in and aided to elect him.

No Money

So I now held myself out as a lawyer, but got but little business for there was none to be done in that line. A deader country than this was, these years, never was. A few settlers too far from anywhere to do business and nothing to do it with. The money that many had brought they had mostly used up to subsist. No money or anything to buy with it; for when the few farmers raised something to spare, it brought little as the village was the only market. The few settlers who came, squatted as it was called on the newly purchased lands on the north side of the river. It was all barter. If a mechanic built a house, his pay was in village lots or wild lands.

The lands north of the Grand River were surveyed and brought into market in August, 1839. The settlers on those lands were most of them entirely unable to pay for their claims, as they called them, and were in great consternation for fear speculators would bid them off and they would thus lose their improvements. But their fears were not realized; for as great as the inducement was, there were none bought on speculation and comparatively few for settlement. A perfect blight seemed to have come over Michigan.

No New Settlers

All immigration passed by her to what was deemed far better lands. To show the dearth of money, the settlers paid Mr. Richmond, who had some money from Governor Hunt in New York to loan, one hundred per cent. And in this way the lands were bid off in their names, he paid the price on their giving him a mortgage on the same for twice the amount payable in two of five years, as they could agree, with interest.

I had a small amount of money belonging to my Troy friend, F. N. Mann, and the man on the N. W. ¼ of Sec. 35, Town 7 N., Range 12 West, a Mr. Tilton, had no money and was in great trouble about it, as it was just below the town on Grand River, for fear someone would buy it. But there was no danger for there had been appointed in each town a committee to settle the quantity each settler might call his claim, and no one presumed to covet or interfere with a settler's rights. For settlers, they were so few, were almost sacred persons. He told me I might buy the whole tract, 150 acres, if I would give him the N. W. 40 on which he lived. And I did so, and afterwards gave him 80 acres on the back part of Walker for his 40. And I bought of Mr. Mann his right, and still own said lands.

In the fall of this year came on the hard cider campaign, as it was called by the Democrats, when General Harrison was the Whig candidate for president. Henry P. Bridge, now of Detroit, was the Whig candidate for state senator and I the Democratic. The district then, besides all this northern country, included Kalamazoo and Calhoun counties, and come to the election, though I got a large majority in the Grand River county, he got so much greater in those that he was elected. I recollect that when the returns were coming in and the result uncertain Colonel Finney said to me one day, "Oh, Ball, how can you keep so cool!" Well I did keep cool and have ever since, as to matters of office. To be sure when the county had become so populous that Grand Rapids made a representative district, they nominated me, and the Republicans, a clothing merchant by the name of Porter, who was elected over me by a very small majority. But this bringing him out had been the means to him of a fortune and wide renown. And I think I was again defeated, that being my luck, as a candidate for state land commissioner.

Law Partnership

In 1840 I formed a law partnership with A. D. Rathbone, Esq. and our office was on the side hill on Lyon Street opposite the now county building. He was postmaster and I aided at times as clerk, but oh, how few then called for letters, more in an hour now than a week then. I knew all callers. We had some business and some of our clients consulted only with Mr. Rathbone, such for instance, as Mr. Geo. M. Mills. When the year came round neither of us seemed anxious to continue the connection, so we dissolved the partnership. But little business followed me. I had an office then on Ottawa Street where Ledyard's new block[28] now is, and a Mr. Reed was for a time with me.

The schoolhouse in which we used to hold our debates was on the same block. The greatest debaters were Rev. Mr. Ballard, C. E. Walker now of Detroit, Dr. Finney, C. H. Taylor and some lesser lights. There was no small ability shown on these occasions. We had then probably as large a ratio of that ability as since.

And as for myself, though then as deficient in speech as before and since, I recollect delivering in the same schoolhouse the first agricultural address ever delivered in Kent County. But it happened in this way. A Mr. Bridge, a young and promising lawyer, had been appointed, but he falling sick, I took his place, and believe performed with satisfaction. I told the farmers to respect themselves, that this looking up to priests, lawyers and doctors, or what was called learned professions, as their superiors, was a mistake; that, as farming was indispensable to life and sustenance, it should be reverenced. And the farmer be number one, and next to him the mechanic, mason and carpenter, who erected the structures that sheltered us from rain and cold.

Pleasant Sociabilities

The whole city, village rather and country about was as one family, all knew all, and associated mainly on equal terms, pecuniary considerations were out of the question, but moral not. All were poor, so in that alike, and there was not, I can truly say, any lack of general good morals. And as poor as we were, we did not forego some amusements. We had our hops as they were called, and as they were gotten up with little formality and at little expense, they were the more enjoyed. John Ellis, worthy man, made our music, and we met in the ballroom of the National Hotel and had social times in other ways, sleighrides and parties from house to house, also informal. Mr. Ballard, who then for a time lived on and cultivated a farm out in Paris, one autumn invited out all the citizens to husk his corn. The young people stopped in the evening, and led off by his wife's sister, Miss Hinsdill, then a young lady, we had a grand time in the sports of whirling the plate, and all those that resulted in a forfeit, to be redeemed by a kiss or be kissed all around, and we had a wild, pleasant time of it. But, if dancing was bad, as Mr. Ballard rather claimed to say, I could not see that this was much better, and to these doings he was an approving spectator. But this disapproval of dancing he probably brought from New England, for I well remember that it was there deemed sinful.

It was at an earlier time I think that there was a gay and interesting wedding party at the house of Mr. Richard Godfroy, Mr. H. P. Bridge married to a young widow by the name of Fay, a sister to Mrs. Godfroy. They were sisters of the celebrated Tom Lewis, the most inveterate wag I ever knew. No consequence could deter him from his fun. At this wedding was a circle of fine young ladies, their sister Fan, the two Misses Mccambs, three Misses Page, the two Misses Taylor, Miss Bridge, and others, and all our matrons and men and some strangers. Mrs. O'Flynn was there, and Mrs. James Watson played the piano, and she played, "The monkey he married the baboon's sister, he smacked his lips, and then he kissed her."

Indian Payments

The Indians did not join the grown whites in their amusements, but they gave them the best trade they had, for it was cash received from their annual payments. But the white and Indian children mated. Mr. Godfroy could fluently talk English and Indian, as

---

[28] *Corner of Pearl Street and Ottawa Avenue. Named for W.B. Ledyard, who in 1860 founded a private bank together with M.V. Aldrich.*

well as French. The Indians as I have said sold their land to the government in the spring of 1836, but did not receive full payment but only a small part. The balance they were to have in equal yearly payments for twenty years. And these payments, or a great portion of them, were to be made to them at Grand Rapids. They were made in the fall and of the time, the Indians received due notice, and all assembled here. And when all were duly numbered, the amount to be paid was duly divided, each man, woman and child receiving the same amount. The payments were made in silver coin, usually in half dollar pieces, and they often got trusted by the traders in advance of these payments and when not, they usually made purchases to the extent of their means. So our merchants provided themselves with such goods as they purchased, and soon the Indian's money changed hands, and I fear sometimes wrongfully.

Discouraged Settlers

Some, who came early here, found business so poor, or for some other cause, did not stop long. There was Mr. Jas. Watson, a merchant and Counsellor O'Flynn. Watson built Esq. Moore's house and O'Flynn mine, the first built south of Bronson Street. A Mr. Higgison, also a merchant, built a house where Mrs. Sorel Wood's now stands, moved off by Mr. Wood and now occupied by Mr. Baars. Tom Lewis built a house where R. Sinclair now lives, which long after burned down. John Wendell kept the yellow store on the corner of Luce's block, he was afterwards a merchant in New York.

This Mr. Wendell got embarrassed in his business and turned over all his claims and means to his brother-in-law, Robert B. Mintern of the then firm of Grinnell & Mintern of New York, and placed the whole in my hand for collection. This was quite a windfall to me in those lean times. Aside from his claims to be collected, there was the Lewis house and a large tract of wild land, located in this county for speculation in 1835 by Grinnell & Mintern. There being in these parts, after the lands that it was a long time before there was any demand for these. They finally sold on time at ten dollars per acre, twenty or thirty years after purchase, proving no great speculation after taking taxes and interest into account. Wendell married one of the Macomb girls, step-daughters of Lewis. That accounted for the house being among his concerns. This I rented, and at the time it was burned it was occupied by Judge Mundy, and I sold the lot and saved remnants of the house to a Mr. Allen, Mrs. Sinclair's father.

Governor John S. Barry appointed John Ball to select federal lands granted to Michigan to be sold for internal improvements. [Michigan State Archives]

LOCATING SCHOOL LANDS
CHAPTER V

Before much of this took place I was occupied in other, than office business. At the session of 1841, Congress granted to each of the new states, in which there was government land, 500,000 acres for internal improvement, a log rolling business probably. The state accepted the grant at its next session and authorized the Governor, then Mr. [John S.] Barry,[29] to procure the selection of the same, as authorized in the grant. In the session of 1837 and 1838, Barry was so conservative, opposing the five million loan and the building of so many railroads that he was very unpopular, but the marked change of time showed that he was right, and the electors showed their appreciation by electing him governor. And a more faithful public officer I never knew, and I had some opportunity to know, being with him while in the senate and now dealing with him as you will see, when governor.

Appointment by Governor Barry

Knowing that I was a woodsman and further that the best chance for the selection of good lands would be in this region, he wrote to me asking if I would be willing to make the selection of those lands. Not having much business on hand and liking the woods I answered him that I would, but wished for his advice as to where I had best make the selections, to make them near the settlements or down the lake, whether pine or farming lands. He answered much to my disgust that he should leave that entirely to my own judgment, still I concluded to undertake it. And Frederick Hall of Ionia, expressing a wish to go with me, I employed him to do

so at twelve shillings per day. I was boarding with Judge Lyon at the Bridge Street House, and his son James wanted to go as camp keeper, so I purchased an Indian pony for a pack horse, procured a tent, blankets, and the necessary camp apparatus and such provisions as we could best pack, and put into the north woods.

In the Woods Again

On our first trip we explored most of the east part of Ottawa County, north of the Grand River. For there were then no settlers in that country except a few along the river, so the whole was owned by Government and subject to my selections. I found most of it first-class beech and maple, heavily timbered land of beautiful undulating surface and good soil and well watered. Then we made a trip to the Muskegon River to see the prairies near Croton, but found them only miserable pine plains. Then struck through to the Flat River and found, about where Greenville now is, some fine opening lands and above on the river, fair pine timber. Luther Lincoln was then the only inhabitant of Montcalm County.

Before I reported my selection I also made a journey down the lake shore as far as the mouth of the Pere Marquette River, going out on the Indian trail to Muskegon Lake, where there was then but one sawmill and a half dozen houses. Swimming the pony across at the head of the lake after our boat, and the White Lake the same, where Mr. Charles Mears was the only settler, we struck the lake shore at the Clay Banks, and there found Indian planting grounds, where they raised corn, potatoes, pumpkin, etc., and

---

[29] *Governor of Michigan from 1842 to 1845.*

so on down the shore. Then we returned from Pentwater inland to the Clay Banks, finding a good country. Then on the beach, fording the mouth of the White River on the bar, packing our clothing to keep them dry on our pony. We expected to find means to cross the mouth of the Muskegon, so as to reach Grand Haven, and then home by steamboat. But finding no one there we had to back out, encamp and the next day found some Indians, who crossed us over to Muskegon, and so returned home on the trail on which we went out, making the hardest trip of the season.

After much thought on the subject I made up my mind that it would not be best to take any of these, more distant lands but take the good ones nearest the settlement. Some opposed it, saying the state would hold the lands high and it would impede settlement. My own reasoning was that as the state indebtedness was so widely diffused among its inhabitants, there would be brought to bear on the Legislature so strong a pressure to put the lands on the market in a way soonest to meet that indebtedness. And the results proved me right.

So I explored the county all the way from the Crockery Creek to the Flat River country on the north side, and the unsold lands in the south part of this county, Ottawa and the north part of Allegan. And, from time to time, as I settled on what to select, reported the same to the Governor and the land office as required. I having gone out the 20th or March, kept out till the 4th of July.

Severe Winter of 1842-43

Again in the fall I continued explorations with, however, only a camp boy, Michael Thorne, till caught in a snowstorm on the 18th of November, in what is now the township of Bowne. That was so unusual a storm I will speak of it more particularly. The previous day had been so cloudy and dark, with a little fall of snow, that I had stayed in camp. Near night the wind came on to blow hard from the southwest and we heard some trees fall, and although I felt there might be some danger, I did not see how we could move camp so as to get where there was less. I slept, but Michael kept a good fire for he expected a tree on him. In the morning the icicles were hanging down the pony's sides, and all looked so forbidding for a continuance of the business that I gave it up. We packed our effects and left the woods. It came on to snow hard, and so hard that by the time we had gotten to Ada, where we put up, it was two feet deep. And it kept cold and snowing, excepting a short time

in January, until the next April. The hogs were in the woods living on acorns, but never got out of the snow. And human feed, hog and cattle feed came so short that many of the animals out of the woods died.

On the first day of April the thermometer stood at zero, and the snow was four feet deep. The river here broke up on the 11th, but teams below went on the ice till about the 20th. But the grass was green and gave good feed as soon as the snow was gone, and it proved a productive season, but all old settlers well recollect the cold winter of 1842 and 43.

As to these selected of those Internal Improvement lands, it resulted as I anticipated. The Legislature this winter, 1843, passed a law, putting the price at ten shillings per acre, payable in state dues, which at first could be bought at forty cents on the dollar. And the settlers, who were afraid I would select their lands, now came to me to do so, that they might get them at 50 cents instead of at $1.25, and I willingly did so for they much needed the advantage. For with most of them their means were very limited.

Pay in State Warrants

For my services in selecting those lands I charged three dollars per day, for which I expected cash. But instead I had to take state warrants, worth but forty cents. I told Governor Barry it was rather hard and he admitted it. But said the law provided only the same funds for that purpose, and as I knew the lands, I must indemnify myself by making some good purchases with said funds. And further said that I should have noticed the provision of the law before, still would try and make out from the five per cent on the United States Government sales of lands in the state, money enough to meet my disbursements, which he did, all showing his strict observance of the law.

These lands were first offered for sale in August 1843 at the state land office then at Marshall, and D. N. Bell, I think, was commissioner. I attended and bought in some lands for such settlers as furnished the means, and strangely there were few sales besides. As cheap as the lands were none were purchased on speculation. When all had been offered and the sale was over, I made entry of a few lots with the funds I had for my services in selecting. I sold these when I could get some moderate advance, then bought again with the avails and sold those and so on, as one would buy and sell goods. And it was in that way I suppose I got a little start in the world.

THE SETTLING OF SELECTED LANDS
CHAPTER VI

Helping Farmers

The knowledge of these lands brought to me the business in aiding the settlers in looking and buying up the same. Up to that time all the immigration was going by Michigan to Illinois and Wisconsin, and the first who came to me to look at these lands said they were going farther west, but on hearing of selected lands that could be had so cheap they concluded to come and see what they were, not however, expecting to be satisfied with them. But it proved quite otherwise for they were so well satisfied that they not only purchased themselves but gave so good a report that soon they came in throngs.

I kept a run of these lands, informed myself of all sales at the land office, by having the plats often corrected, that they used when looking them up. So when a man wanted to look at a lot, I gave him a plat showing the lands and directed him to some settler to aid him in finding the same. And when he had made his selection, he would also want my aid in buying the funds and making the purchase at the office. For all this I charged him what some of my neighbors said was too small a fee. But the first thought with me was to secure them as settlers, for we had lived long enough in a country without inhabitants.

Besides, their means were very small, hardly a man having five hundred dollars. And most of them only enough to pay for their land and erect their log cabin and subsist the first year, till they could clear a patch and raise something. And when their money fell short, I often gave them time on my fees, or something more to enable them to secure their farms. Or, if considerable lack, I would take the land in my own name as security, give them a receipt for the amount they paid on it, and when they paid the balance assigned over the land. And these hardy, resolute men who thus first settled our woods, I found always punctual in the fulfillment of their engagements and there grew up between me and them a mutual confidence and respect that will only end with land's disuse.

Almost without exception these people, for the women too played well their part, after a few years of privation and hardship, found themselves in possession of farms, houses, cattle and barns, giving them all the independence and comfort incident to that most honorable profession. For who is honorable if not he who gains his livelihood in this original way. The little means they used in procuring their necessaries in the town greatly helped the poverty stricken villagers, for such we were.

Fortunately for the immediate settlement of the country, the lands mostly were bought by settlers, who soon came onto the same. Mr. Bostwick purchased for Mr. LeGrand Cannon of Troy a few thousand acres of these lands on speculation, but even this did not much delay their settlement, for these soon fell into my hands to be sold at three dollars per acre, payable on time.

Renewal of Business

The next year, 1844, S. L. Withey, Esq., now Judge, having read law with Martin & Johnson, had been admitted to the bar, came into partnership with me on equal shares in the law business, but having no part in my land matters. Our office was for a time in an office building on Monroe Street, opposite the new Aldrich and Godfrey block, and after in rooms in a house built for a dwelling where Luce's block now is. And after two years, George Martin, Esq. came in with us as third legal partner. He was after

Judge Martin. In two years after he went out and a Mr. Sargeant came in with us. We had quite a large amount of collecting business for New York merchants and others, some chancery business and some hard contested matters. Some that at the time were of a good deal of interest to the community.

Our worthy citizen, Mr. Williams, long since deceased, was the owner of the steamboat **Algoma** sailing on the river. He had mortgaged it to our Troy clients and under a spurious sale it was claimed by other parties, and an attempt was made to run away with it. But Mr. Williams, faithful to his creditors, prevented it, by the removal of the throttle valve of the engine. So when the steam was let on it escaped without propelling the boat. This same Mr. Williams was for a time engaged in the plaster business, down where it was first started on the Plaster Creek. The first plaster known in this country showed itself in the bed of said creek, giving it its name. It was a short distance above the present George White mill.

Religious Revival

In that tremendous hard winter of 1843, Mr. Ballard got up a protracted revival meeting, called in those times a forty days' meeting. And they were held day and night, and people came in from all about the country, and I fear sometimes left their poor cattle to suffer. There was much praying, exhorting and confession of private sins in a public manner.

I did not go to the meetings and one day Mr. Ballard called at my office, west of the National Hotel, to talk with me on the matter. He spoke of their interesting meetings, and said that he had not seen me there, and also asked me if I did not believe in a God. I told him that probably I did not believe in his god, a partial Jewish god, that it was too vast and deep a subject for me to form any definite idea upon. That I had a kind of feeling that there existed an overruling power of the vast universe about us.

I said, "You and your people talk of such a Being and of a heaven and a hell and all that; you all use words but do you all have the same ideas and pictures in your minds when you use them?" I told him I presumed not, perhaps no two alike. One's god was like a minister in the pulpit, another's like a king on a throne, etc. The heaven where the saints were assembled, a big meeting house or palace, and a city-like and earthly one, others one of green fields and flowers. If he would but gain their confidence, so that each would answer freely and truly, he would find that each had his own god and heaven, unlike all the others. Something that they had formed in their child's mind, when they first heard the words,

Solomon L. Withey was John Ball's law partner from 1843 to 1851. Later, he served as U.S. district judge for the Western District of Michigan. [Grand Rapids Public Library, Photograph Collection, #54-37-49]

George Martin, future chief justice of the Michigan Supreme Court, joined the Ball and Withey law partnership in 1846. [Grand Rapids Public Library Photograph Collection, #54-30-58]

and have ever retained, not thinking but that it was the very thing, and that all others had the same image in their minds.

Dancing Parties

That same winter of 1843 I boarded at the National kept by Canton Smith, whose skillful wife gave us a good table. And we used then and during many of those early winters in our place, where there were so few newcomers, that all well knew each other, to associate freely and informally as if one family. And we often had our hops, as we called them, in the National ballroom, and John Ellis was the ever ready man with his fiddle at a moderate charge; seldom had suppers, and our then young ladies, now our old settler matrons, would turn out without any very special preparation on an hour's notice.

We would begin and end the evening at early hours, have pleasant times and feel all the better for it the next day. Mr. Ballard preached against dancing, but we did not feel it any great sin, so kept it up, and had our sleigh rides too. And the boys used to call on me to take a leading part in these matters for they said the mothers would always let the girls go on my invitation. And I made it a point that none should be neglected who ought to share, and on the floor I got up the young misses and called out the diffident, and I was deemed a friend by all the children in town. And we old settlers often now refer to those good old times.

Settling of Holland

The settlers continued to come onto the state lands, but the population and business of the city increased but slowly. And when there arose a talk of a great Holland colony coming to the state, there was much interest felt to have them settle in these parts. And Mr. [Dr. Albertus] Van Raalte,[30] the leader of the colony, came here to see the country. He brought a letter from someone to me as a land man. And on his making inquiry for a good place for his settlers, and saying his people liked to be on or near the water, (quite natural I thought that they should), I told Mr. Van Raalte that I did not see, that he could find a better place, than our Grand River, that here was a navigable stream and all along below us to its mouth there were but few settlers, the lands cheap and unoccupied. He answered that he wished to have his people settled by themselves and there were too many other settlers on the Grand River.

Then I told him that there was the Muskegon country, on which there were the same as no settlers, and that the Government yet owned all that country. But then, he said, there would be only the wolves beyond them, and spoke of the Black River country, where they settled, as having the Grand River settlement between them and the wolves. A Mr. Kellogg of Allegan, who had some interest there, was with him, and had already, I found, gotten his mind rather fixed on that locality.

Well, his settlers came and located there in a dense forest. For them a new scene and situation indeed, for the people of the almost treeless lands of Holland, they knew not how to fell a tree. And in the attempt to clear off the lands, they would chop the tree on all sides so it would fall as it happened to lean. So when they got the trees down, they lay helter, skelter in all directions so that our skilled woodsmen said, they would rather had they the land to clear, take the trees standing. And they finally got some experienced choppers to give them some instruction in the matter, so by their indomitable industry, they eventually got on quite well. Still their reverend leader could not keep them compact and entirely out of harm's way. Many came here for employment, and, as this was their main place to get their supplies, their guilders much helped our village.

Purchase of a Home

The first houses built south of Fulton Street were Esq. Moore's on the corner of that and Division Street, by a Mr. James Watson, and mine by Counsellor O'Flynn, the former a merchant and the latter a lawyer. They came from Detroit and after pursuing their business here for a few years returned to that place. O'Flynn had so far finished his house that he lived in it, though not but partially completed inside. He had purchased the two and a half acres from Mr. Bostwick, and given him a mortgage in part payment.

Mr. Bostwick built the house west of mine, now occupied by Mr. McConnell. But when completed, he sold it with five acres to Mr. Louis Campau in exchange for sixty acres, on part of which is Wenham's Addition, 350 acres of wild lands in Allegan County and some village lots. A Mr. David Briswell worked on the Campau house for Mr. Bostwick, who turned out to him in payment O'Flynn's mortgage on my lot. Briswell left the place going west, and finally to New Orleans, leaving his

---

[30] *The founder of a colony of Dutch settlers in Holland, Ottawa County, in 1847.*

John Ball built his home at 458 E. Fulton in 1838 and added to it numerous times in subsequent years. [Baxter, History of Grand Rapids, Michigan, p. 72]

This photograph of John Ball's homestead was taken in 1869. [Reprinted from Autobiography of John Ball, p. 170]

John Ball's home had taken on a derelict look by 1965, shortly before it was demolished. [Grand Rapids Public Library Real Estate Listing Card Collection]

claims with me for collection, among which was the mortgage on this place. After a time he wrote me to sell the mortgage for any amount I could get for it. I could find no purchaser, so made him an offer of two hundred dollars for it, being not more than half its face, and he unexpectedly accepted the offer; which I met though my means were so limited, it was with much difficulty I raised that small amount. I afterwards paid fifty dollars for the original title. Then got Mr. Burnett to look at the house and see what it was worth, and to my surprise his estimate was six or seven hundred dollars and I had gotten it for four hundred. I had him finish it off, made many changes and improvements, under the advice of Rev. Dr. Cuming then living opposite.

I first rented the house, when finished, to Mr. Peasley brother-in-law to Lieut. Gunnison, who was killed on the mountains of Utah by the Indians or Mormons. But they did not stay long. I was agent for the New York owners of a good two story house and half the block opposite to National Hotel, now Morton, and being instructed to sell it for what I could get, I found a purchaser in said Lieut. Gunnison, who paid one thousand for it, and he moved his friend, Mr. Peasley, there.

I then rented my house to a Mr. English and boarded with them some two years, and his kind and accomplished wife made my home very pleasant. He soon after died and his body lies in my cemetery lot. She returned to her friends in the state of New York, and did not long survive him.

The first journey east after our marriage[31] we called to see her, then near her departure. I passed one winter sleeping in my house alone and boarding with Mr. Kingsbury down town. I then rented to Mr. Sargeant, who at the time was of our firm, Ball, Withey & Sargeant, and had with them a pleasant home.

Better Business

We had a fair legal business in our office, and I had other land agency business, after the sale of the state lands, so that I began to accumulate something. I operated in wild lands, commencing with the pay for my services for selecting those lands, selling at low rates when opportunity presented, knowing where I could reinvest to advantage. At one time joined Esquire Chubb in the purchase of some three thousand acres of pine land of the assignee, a Mr. Brown of Chicago, of the Michigan Lumbering Company, who had built a mill at the mouth of the Rush Creek below Grandville, where they made lumber for the Chicago market, but in those down times, made a failure. The lands were along down the country below, and paying but one dollar per acre, we did well with it.

Then came on the Mexican War, resulting in our acquisition of Upper California, giving us that splendid bay, that I felt when there, would some day be ours. Oh! what modest set, we United States people are, individually and governmentally. We only take from the Indians and our other neighbors what we want — not what we need. This pushing — enterprising, I should, you know call it — of ours, has its beneficial effect doubtless in other directions. It opens a wide world for the European emigrant, the German and Celt, people more progressive than they.

Looking east up Monroe Avenue from Pearl Street in 1844, showing a busy assemblage of wooden and river stone buildings. [Grand Rapids Public Library, Fitch Collection, #1945]

---

[31] *John Ball married Mary T. Webster of Plymouth, New Hampshire, on December 31, 1849.*

For nearly 20 years, from 1849 to 1867, this building at the northwest corner of Ransom and Lyon was Grand Rapids' public school. [Grand Rapids Public Library, Fitch Collection, #1905]

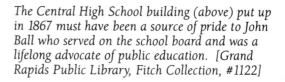

The Central High School building (above) put up in 1867 must have been a source of pride to John Ball who served on the school board and was a lifelong advocate of public education. [Grand Rapids Public Library, Fitch Collection, #1122]

One room at Central High School (left) served as home for the natural history collections of the Kent Scientific Institute, successor to the Grand Rapids Lyceum of Natural History, which John Ball helped organize in 1854. [Grand Rapids Public Library, Merrill Collection, #86-54]

GRAND RAPIDS SCHOOLS AND OTHER MATTERS
CHAPTER VII

Our village gained some in population and business, and some of us began to look about to see what were our schools, and found that the provision was very deficient. So about 1848 we agitated the subject, and after several trials effected a junction of the two districts on the east side of the river, into our Union district, as called, for then there were no school houses. The one on Fulton Street had been burned down, and the schools we had, poorly kept part of the year, in private houses.

We got a place for a house and against much opposition succeeded in raising the sum of two thousand five hundred dollars to purchase a site and build a house. For a site we pitched upon the present one of the High School building. It was then all woods back of there, not a house, we paid six hundred for the land and contracted with David Burnett to erect the Old Stone Schoolhouse, which all older citizens will remember, for $2,700. I gave to help on the enterprise one hundred dollars.

The school opened in November 1849, with six teachers and two rooms, but we soon made the basement into another to supply the want.

Securing Teachers

A Mr. Johnson was the principal and Miss Hollister and Miss Thirza Moore his assistant; in the secondary or primary department, Miss Mary T. Webster, now my wife, and Miss White and Miss Hinsdill, her assistants. There was much interest taken at the opening of the school, and a number of the citizens came in to see its opening. The principal made quite a long prayer on the occasion, at which some of the citizens, the Catholics, took alarm, and

complained of it. At which the trustees, six in all, of which I was one, considered the matter, and wishing our school should prove what it was intended for, the place and means of instruction to all the children of the village, we unanimously adopted this rule, "That all teachers in opening the schools should only read or rehearse the Lord's Prayer." It proved satisfactory and all went on smoothly, and so many

Thirza Moore was one of Mary Webster's fellow teachers. [Grand Rapids Public Library, Keeney Collection]

applied for admission that we at once went to work to fit up the basement of the building for another, a primary department. And the next quarter that too was also filled. At the end of the first quarter Mr. Johnson resigned, and the Rev. Mr. Ballard employed to fill his place.

My Wife

At the holiday vacation there was another resignation, Miss Mary T. Webster, who on the New Year's Eve of 1850 exchanged her tutorship of a full room of young girls and boys for one old boy, myself. And as I never liked much ceremony and much noise about individual matters, no one suspected the intention, till we called on Esquire Henry at his house to perform the ceremony. And you may well think that as I made my usual New Year's calls the next day, when the news had got abroad, I was much rallied, especially by my other young lady acquaintances.

Mr. Kingsbury's folks were living in my house and I was boarding with them. And when she came, being sent by my acquaintances in New York, to whom I had applied, to send us a good teacher, she also became a boarder with us. And so, though not personally acquainted with her, I had so well known her friends that it did not take long to appreciate her also. I knew much of her father's people and of her mother's, the Powers, personally, back to her great-grandparents.

A few months after, Geo. S. Seymour of Laporte, Ind., married my wife's sister Lydia. And the following summer they and we made a pleasant journey east, going down the lakes from Chicago to Buffalo, visiting all our connections in New York and New England; Seymour's living in Connecticut, the wives' parents living in New Hampshire.

But to be more particular about the way my wife came here. She was raised in Plymouth, New Hampshire; I, in Hebron, and her mother's family ancestors, in Groton. Her great-grandfather was in the battle of Bennington, and her grandmother's name was Thompson, where she gets her Mary T. My youngest sister Deborah married her oldest uncle, William Powers 3rd, who lived at Lansingburgh, New York. He died in 1829 leaving two sons, Albert and Nathaniel. And when in 1849 I was seeking teachers for our new school, I wrote to my nephew Albert Powers to look up and send on one or more. And my wife was then visiting them, and he induced her to come on, and in that way seek her fortune.

Withey and Sargeant left me when the former had been partner some eight years, and I kept office alone for about a year when James H. McKee came in, as they, to share equally in the law business of the

John and Mary Ball from an old daguerreotype taken soon after their marriage. [Reprinted from Autobiography of John Ball, *p. 176]*

office. But after the first year, I told him that we would share alike in all the office business. And we then kept on hand the Mexican bounty land warrants for the immigrants who came to buy government lands, and had quite a business in that direction and were agents too for a number of eastern land owners.

Coming of Old Acquaintances

When living in Troy and boarding at the Mansion House, a young man by the name of Ransom E. Wood, a clerk to Day O. Kellogg, was also a boarder, and about the time I came to Michigan he went to the city of New York. For a time a clerk, then in business, and it had passed on thirteen years that we had not met or heard of each other, till in the bustle of a business street of that care-for-nobody city, he recognized me, so we renewed the acquaintance. In 1852 he closed business, came west and though he did not think much of Michigan, he called to see me and inquire after some investment I had made for him, and on looking about concluded to invest further. The next winter his brother Sorel came with a letter from him to me and made our office his stopping place, to gain information about the chances and invested in lands to the extent of his means and credit. He said to me one day, "Ball, why don't you operate, you would make more in that way, with your knowledge of the country, in one year, than in all your life in this office business," I answered that I did operate to the extent of my means.

The next spring Mr. Ransom Wood also came with his family and soon many followed them from New York and Connecticut where they had acquaintances. The settlement and business of the village and country had improved, but real estate not yet. I sold Ransom over three acres of land, but on condition he should build on it, for five hundred dollars. And as agent, to Sorel, five acres and quite a good frame house on it for $1,200. In a year after, the adjoining lands sold for one thousand dollars per acre. In selling so low for others I of course, followed instructions.

I was five years here, before I saw here anyone I had previously known. But after a time my old acquaintances began to come and others followed them, so I can justly claim that I have aided the settlement of the country in that way and, in my manner of aiding the immigrants, to a large extent — Morris Ball and his father, William T. Powers and his father's family, etc., but if they have benefitted themselves and the place I am paid.

With the law and land, our office business was fair, and as I got the means in that way, or by the sales of lands, I purchased more, mostly Government pine and other lands. And so went on to the extent of my means till my acres amounted to some ten thousand. But when the tremendous check of 1857 came it put so sudden a stop to sales that I soon had to borrow money to pay taxes. And when times so improved that I could again sell I did so, though at small profit. Sold sometimes at rates that time has shown I should have done much better to have held on longer.

Market Street west from Monroe Avenue in 1857. The Eagle Hotel is the second building on the right. [Grand Rapids Public Library, Fitch Collection, #53]

This photograph of Campau Square taken 16 years after John Ball's arrival shows a city that is still made up of wooden and stone buildings and dirt streets. In the distance is the Bridge Street covered bridge. [Grand Rapids Public Library, Fitch Collection, #101]

VARIOUS INVESTMENTS AND JOURNEYS
CHAPTER VIII

And one investment turned out quite poorly. A young man of our place, Thomas Cuming, whose father was the Episcopal clergyman here, was appointed the Secretary of the Nebraska Territory when first organized. And in fact he was the first acting governor and put the territorial government into operation on account of the death of the governor appointed. On his representations of the prospects of the place, a Mr. Wells, a banker here, and myself were induced to advance to him some $1,500 each on which to operate for us. And though I have no doubt he acted in good faith, it proved disastrous, and instead of a great gain, as was expected, the title of the purchase he made so failed that we lost nearly all. Before the result was known, and while I thought the prospect was fair, and to again see something of the west I made the journey out there. It was in 1855.

West Again

I traveled by railroad to Rock Island, crossed over to Davenport, which was then not a large village, took stage from there to Muskatine, which is also on the river. From there to Iowa City, and from there on the old trail of the Mormons, stopping a day at Des Moines, not yet the state capital, but a new village of a dozen buildings.

Down the river where they were quarrying the lime rock I could see on its surface scratches and a worn surface, showing that a drift had been swept over the same. And from there we staged on, often almost entirely out of sight of land, that is forest. A fine rolling country with very few settlers, and if their fences crossed our road we turned aside and went around, for there was no laid out or worked road, and the travel was over the most feasible ground. And in this way on the sixth day from Davenport we arrived at Council Bluffs. The next day crossing the Missouri I found Omaha on a beautiful site, but its buildings few, being in fact less than a year old. Found the only hotel, owned by our old citizen George M. Mills. Found Cuming full of high expectations of wealth for us and himself. Michigan's first Lieut. Governor, Richardson was there. Our William Clancy was the first settler they said, and there was still standing his shanty, sodded up on the sides to keep out the cold. They were getting together material on that beautiful hill for the Territorial Capital.

Mouth of the Platte River

And the Governor and others induced me to take a horseback ride down to the mouth of the Platte River, to see the site of the future great city, as they claimed, of Plattsmouth. A very pleasant ride, but the being induced to take some stock in their prospective city did not prove so very pleasant. It was overflown grounds of the Missouri, and no city was ever built there. It seemed like the meeting of an old friend to again see the river alone whose shore I had rode so many days, and at night encamped on its banks and quenched my thirst from its turbid waters. I even broke away from my company to ride for a time along up its waters.

I also went above Omaha to the old winter quarters of the Mormons, for they on leaving Nauvoo, all or a part of them, stopped over here long enough to raise a crop of corn to feed them on their wearisome journey over the plains to Salt Lake. Oh! how persecution adds to the force and perseverance of character. But after all I do not know but this patient endurance of the persecuted is any very certain proof of the truth of their belief, others, as well as Mormons.

In returning, instead of by land, I descended the river by steamboat, giving me a fine opportunity to see its turbid waters and its effect in washing away the banks on one side, and at the same time forming new lands on the other. And on which the young cotton wood pippins immediately spring up and by which one could see the one, two or more year's growths, and thus determine how old this new land is. The river is constantly changing its course in this way. In some places it is ten miles between its lime rock bluffs. Still over all this wide bottom land the river had ranged, and now is sometimes sweeping along the bluff on one side, then around it curves till it sweeps the other, a crook a mile across and fifteen miles around, and has now broke through and taken form, and given to Iowa the peninsula. And one could see how the sawyers and snags were formed. Where the river turns onto a bank and is wearing it away it is the deepest channel, and it soon undermines the bank so the trees drop down root first into this deep water, and as the water wears further on the land the falling earth covers the roots of these slumped trees. But the river current bends them down stream, so they do not stand erect, and the moving ice strips off the limbs and tops. So the down bound boat slides over them, but going up its bow goes butt on their down pointing end that often butts a hole. For these snags are often planted all across the river, making it difficult to find a passage.

This washing away of the shore, as we saw, had made terrible havoc of St. Joseph, Missouri, where we stopped. It stood on a high earth bank, not lime rock like Kansas City. And the river had taken a lurch on the city and worn it to the extent of the whole width of the river, so that the made land on the other side was over ground on which had stood parts of the town. It would undermine brick blocks, so that first they would know, they would drop into deep water. At Independence we came where I had before seen the Missouri. And at its junction with the Mississippi, I again noticed the mingling of its turbid waters with the clear waters of the same. I found that a great change indeed had come over St. Louis since I saw it the spring of 1832.

Eastern Trip

From St. Louis I took boat up the river to Alton, and then railroad to Chicago. From there instead of coming home I went East to bring my wife, going to Toledo, Buffalo and Troy. Visited my friends at Lansingburgh, then went on to Plymouth, New Hampshire to my wife's father, by the way of Nashua. Then to Haverhill and visited our Uncle Joseph Powers, then sheriff and keeping the jail. A fit man for the place, being so kind and sensible in his treatment of his prisoners that they became much attached to him, and listened to his good counsel.

Then down the Connecticut to the White River, up the valley of that and down the Onion, enjoying the Vermont mountain scenery, to St. Albans. Then crossed over to Rouse's Point and to Ogdensburgh and up Lake Ontario to Lewiston, by land to Buffalo, boat to Detroit and so home. Gone some five weeks, leaving on the 4th of June and getting home the 10th of July, 1855.

Plaster Mines

Mr. [Richard E.] Butterworth[32] had explored in the bluff on the west side of the Grand River and found that there was plaster on that side, the Eagle Mill concern, as well as on Plaster Creek. And he opened a quarry, erected a little mill on the creek this side, and ground some land plaster, and tried to make stucco. A Mr. Barnard Courtney worked in his quarry and lived in an old log house of mine on the north side of the road, the Carroll house. And he came to me one day and wanted I should enter a 40 acres of Normal School land for him, lying back of Butterworth's land. I sent, as for others, to the State Land Office and entered the land for him, but I little thought at the time to what extent that purchase of his would influence my life and business. It has pursued me these twenty and more years past, and is not yet ended.

Courtney soon after told me he did not enter that land for farming so much as under the belief that there was plaster, and wished much to explore and see of such was not the fact. and he induced me to loan him a little money to enable him to explore and see if such was not the case. And he soon found that there was plaster, and then he wanted more money to get some out and join in some arrangement to have it manufactured. And we got a mill at Grand Rapids to grind for a time, and then I was induced to go further and erect a mill on the ground. And after we had made land plaster for a time we must join with it what would be more profitable, the stucco manufacture.

---

[32] *Born in Jamaica, and trained as an engineer in England, Richard Butterworth came to Grand Rapids in 1843 and engaged in such enterprises as gypsum mining, salt wells, oil wells, and the Grand Rapids Iron Works.*

Making of Stucco

They had first made stucco from our plaster in potash kettles, and had tried to get up heaters, but they would leak badly. And when I determined to go into its manufacture I wished to do so understandingly, so I made a journey to the city of New York partly on that account, to learn how it was done there. I found my friend, A. E. Powers there and he volunteered to aid me. We could not get into the works in the city, but in Jersey City a heavy manufacturer gave us access to his works freely. His supply of rock was from Nova Scotia, and his heaters were made with a bottom in segments and liable to leak.

Near one of the establishments in New York we saw what we inferred was a kettle bottom in one entire piece, turned up at the edge and raised in the center so as not to break by the expansion and contraction. From this hint Albert made out a drawing, from which when I got home, a heater bottom was cast that is now the one in use by all in these parts, and that, though thousands of dollars have been expended to try to get something better. We at once put our heater in operation.

But after I had advance money for the erection of the mill, I had taken an assignment of Courtney's certificate of the land for my security but kept a strict account of all advances and receipts for sales and he had a stated pay for his services. The building of this mill was some of Mr. W. A. Berkey's first work in this place. So men go up from small beginnings. Our Mr. [Charles C.] Comstock[33] is another.

And so Courtney and I went on for a time, but neither well satisfied, so, as the title of the assignment was in me, I deeded it over to him, on his giving me a mortgage for my claims on the property, and he ran the concern on his own account. He called it the Emmet Mill.

Messrs. Stewart and McReynolds purchased out his interest and gave me a mortgage for my claim on the same, and all the plaster concerns went into a company called the "Grand Rapids Plaster Company." But Stewart and McReynolds did not pay my mortgage, and the company broke up, and I foreclosed my mortgage. And there being no other bidders I bought in the mill. And after it stood idle a year or so I sold it to C. H. Taylor and McReynolds, young McReynolds, for $20,500.

Glen Haven

My wife had long been feeble, and to recruit her health had gone to Glen Haven at the head of Seneca Lake, some ten miles west of Homer, to a famous water cure establishment, under the charge of a Dr. Jackson. She took with her our two children, Frank and Kate. So in June 1857, I went there and stopped with them for some weeks, and lived as the patients did, entirely on vegetable food without salt or anything that had been near an animal except milk. As I had on the mountains tried a meat diet, I had now the opportunity to live without it. And I found this too, very good living. One feels a change, and perhaps some inconvenience from the change, from one kind of food to another quite unlike. But if healthy of its kind it is as often beneficial, as detrimental, and the privation should not be mentioned so it be you have a good supply.

I found the Glen a most beautiful and romantic place, on the lake under a high hill sheltering it from the west winds, and all its sides beautifully wooded, and footpaths leading up the same, and also down the lake shore where the patients could take their walks. And they also had boats to row on the lake. All the ladies were required to dress in bloomer costume, and loose and easy; to take exercise in the open air according to their strength, live socially and pleasantly, and forget their ails as far as possible. Indeed it seemed quite a good place for patients.

Philadelphia

After a time, for a change, we left the children with a trusty girl and journeyed to Philadelphia, going to Homer, then by rail to Binghamton, down the Erie railroad a piece and then turning off into Pennsylvania to Scranton and on, where we overlooked a great extent of country, the Blue Ridge Mountains with its wind gap, and so down onto the Delaware River, and through the romantic water gap, and so on to the Quaker City. My wife wore her bloomer dress, so attracted some notice, and as far as remarks were made, they were in commendation. When we got to the city we met Dr. Hemphill and his worthy lady. And, to go about the city, she loaned my wife a different style of dress. We passed some days there, visiting the Girard College and other places of interest, always accompanied most kindly by our friend, Mrs. Hemphill, a person I have always deemed, from my first acquaintance in 1836, a most accomplished and kind hearted lady.

---

[33] *Mayor of Grand Rapids, 1863-64, who later served in the U.S. Congress.*

In returning we took the road to Allenstown and up the wild valley of the Lehigh by Mauch Chunk, and so through the coal country and over the mountains, partly by stage, as the travel then was, to an inclined plan railroad by steam power down the steep mountain side into the beautiful historic valley of Wyoming to Wilkesbarre. This broad valley skirted thus by mountains, with the grand river Susquehanna meandering through the same, is one of the finest in our country. We looked about the place, crossed over to the monument, entered some of the coal mines, and then took rail up the river to Pittston, and Scranton, where we came onto our down track, and so returned to Glen Haven.

And after spending some more time there we left for home, going around the lake by stage and taking the railroad at Auburn. And thus for me, at least, I passed some two months very pleasantly. The children seemed to enjoy their stay there right well. Frank old enough to row himself on the lake and my wife evidently much improved in health.

BOOK THE FOURTH
Civil War, Travels at Home and Abroad, Later Life

❧

~

REFLECTIONS ON THE CIVIL WAR
CHAPTER I

From my first coming to the state, when at home, I kept a rough meteoric journal, noting the temperature two or three times in the day, the course of the wind and aspect of the heavens, whether clear, cloudy or storm, and when traveling did the same as far as convenient. But to my regret, I noted little else on my journeys or at home. So having now nothing in referring to my past life, whether at home or abroad, I have to depend almost entirely on my memory of the occurrences, persons met and conversations and doings. And in this attempt to say something of the past I may commit some mistakes, and may omit what it would be quite as important to record, as what I shall here mention.

From 1857 I began to feel much interest and some concern for the peace of the Union. The warm discussions and active measures of the Abolitionists and others at the North against slavery, I saw had aroused the opposition of the South, and that yearly an increased antagonistic feeling was fast growing; that it had apparently destroyed the prior wish and effort of many of the people of the border states to take the necessary steps for the gradual emancipation of the slaves in those states – the way it seemed to me the safest and best on all hands to get rid of the dire incubus.

Desire for Compromise

The northern Democrats no better liked the institution than others but felt bound by the terms of the constitution to sustain it while the states in which it existed saw fit to retain it. This gave the southern politicians a preference for that party, giving a pretext for their opponents to charge them, the Democrats, with favoring the institution. And the breach grew wider and wider, nursed rather than allayed the northern and southern antipathies.

And when the Whigs and Abolitionists joined hands and adopted the name of Republican the prospect of conciliation seemed much further removed. And when this new party had gained the ascendancy in the national government the sky seemed more to darken. Still I had hopes that there would be some peaceful way out of the difficulty. And up to the last, to the day the mad people of Charleston fired on Fort Sumter, I continued to hope for a peaceful adjustment. Though I saw that many of the northern men were as unwilling to accede anything as the worst at the South, still all the masses and the better statesmen of the North, and at least some at the South, sought, prayed and worked earnestly for compromise. But their honest and patriotic efforts were unheeded, both by the ultra politicians, North as well as South. No doubt in my mind now many of the North even were at least willing that a collision should take place, if begun by the South.

Meeting at Luce's Hall

But when it did come the people of the North were united and aroused, and felt to say, "You have commenced it by striking the first blow and you must abide the consequences." On the very day the news of the attack on Fort Sumter reached Grand Rapids, a mass meeting was called in Luce's Hall, and when filled the meeting appointed me chairman, and I felt and said that now the South had passed the Rubicon, they must account to the Union for their rash act; that the attack of United States property was a defiance of the Union. Still little did we think, that small beginning would lead on to seas of blood and all the mighty consequences that have followed. As bad as was the road I trust the result will prove the nation's good. Is war a civilizer?

Michigan was so far from the active scenes of this terrible conflict that we did not see or feel its horrors as those who were in its midst, or even those who were nearer its operations. We only saw the mustering of our soldiers to be marched away to the scenes to active war. We saw them depart, and many of them never returned. The greater portion, who went, did so from true patriotic motives, especially those who entered the ranks, while perhaps some of the officers were influenced by ambitious motives. And very many of the outside men who neither risked life or even comfort, if honest in their doings, worked for gain, and too many for a dishonest gain. The last I more despise than the rebels themselves, and even some of our politicians were influenced by motives about on par with the shady contractors. They nursed the strife and cared not for the ruin, could they but wreak their unholy vengeance on political opponents.

Political Leaders

The southern political leaders were as bad at heart but I do not see, as worse and the great mass of the southern people also, from their point of view, acted from patriotic motives. When their states went out they felt it their duty to fight for the state against the Union. There were southern men who viewed it rightly and came to the North or kept out of the contest as best they could. And a few northern men served the South, and as to the negro, he acted his nature, kept clear of risk and trouble till his liberation found him, working to maintain his master in rebellion till freedom came.

Except at the Bull Run fight, when the Union army ran back to Washington, and where the Rebels invaded Pennsylvania, we people at the North seemed to feel that we should soon put down the South and all come right. Received the news of battles and the progress of the war as coolly to appearance as though it was a war with a foreign country. This was the look, but there was a deep and anxious feeling in the minds of all thoughtful persons, a grief at the passing events, and fears for

John Ball's Grand Rapids, 1859. Looking west down Monroe Avenue, as John Ball saw it on countless occasions. The large building on the left is the Luce Block, and farthest to the west is Daniel Ball's Bank, later the site of Sweets Hotel, and in 1915, the Pantlind. [Grand Rapids Public Library, Fitch Collection, #1801]

the result. Fears that it would be the end of the Union, as it had been. If not severed in fact, worse severed in feeling, than ever heretofore.

Visits our Army

The war little influenced my personal pursuits. I pursued my business at home, or journeyed as I had occasion to do so. In June of 1861 made a journey to New York and New Hampshire. Reviewed the places of my former residences, and in the winter of 1864, February 22nd, left Grand Rapids with Mr. Henry Whipple for Washington. Went by Detroit, Cleveland, Pittsburgh, Harrisburgh and so to Washington. First day to Detroit, next Cleveland, next Harrisburgh and February 25th arrived at Washington. The next day visited the camp near the city. Went to the Smithsonian Institute, which had lately been partly destroyed by fire with a great amount of valuable material. Still much left that I found of great interest. Next day went to Georgetown and looked about the grounds opposite the White House, and the day following crossed the river and visited the Freedman's camp.

March 1, 1864 I went to the frontier of our army on and along the river Rapidan, and as I passed through Alexandria I bethought me of the fact that when at Washington, before going West, I went over to Alexandria on this same day of the month, 1832,

making just 32 years. How changed since then was all the world and its inhabitants. A new race of men, with other opinions, and their result. Little then did I expect to live to see our country in a civil war, and myself going out on the same road to see its hostile armies, and now the travel was by railroad. And when we got in the neighborhood of where our army lay, and in fact to the end of where it was used by the Union folks, for just beyond, the same road was used by the Rebels to communicate with Richmond, I went to the camp of the Michigan regiments.

In Camp With the Michigan 3rd

In the camp of the Michigan 3rd Regiment I found a number of acquaintances, by whom I was treated in the most civil manner, and shown what was to be seen, and stayed with them two or three days. One day took a ride horseback, accompanied by an officer, all along a little north of the river, down by the celebrated Germania Ford, but more so after the crossing there of our army. We kept along the line of our guards, and in plain sight of the rebel guards on the other side of the river. We stopped at the house of a clergyman known to my guide, residing there quietly on his own premises in his comfortable house. He received us courteously and conversed freely, and seemed Union in feeling. When I left the third some accompanied me to the camping

The Third Michigan Infantry in camp outside Washington, D.C. John Ball visited the Third in 1864. [Grand Rapids Public Museum, Photograph Collection, #H2.11]

grounds of another of our regiments lying some two or three miles west of the railroad. And we passed near a house that they pointed out as the headquarters of General Grant. And we returned to Fairfax and to Washington on the fourth. This seeing the armies thus watching each other in the winter of 1864 deeply interested me. But little did I or they know of the hard fighting they were doomed to pass through so soon between there and Richmond and Petersburgh.

I should have mentioned the difficulty I had to get a pass to the frontier, for at the time the orders were very strict on the subject. A Dr. Bliss, an acquaintance told me could get one, but failing I spoke to the representative to Congress from our district, Mr. Kellogg. He at once took me to headquarters in the War Department, and being a staunch war man it was at once granted on the asking. And he then introduced me to some of the officials. But the person I best recollect was Dr. Mary Walker in her bloomers.[34] I left for home on the seventh by way of Harrisburgh, Cleveland and Toledo, arriving home on the ninth I think.

Changes in New England

The next summer I made a journey East to New York and New Hampshire to visit friends, and oh! what change the years bring in those New England lands and the dwellers therein. The lands always of hard tillage, most of them, and now I found all the hilly parts barren and to a great extent deserted. Many less inhabitants than formerly, and those how changed! Matrons and mothers instead of childhood and youth. I visited the few connections and friends left. Enjoyed it well, still an attended sadness.

And the sad and bloody Civil War went on, bravely fought on both sides, and sad to think, its end seemed to recede, instead of anything indicating a close. But when the next year came it looked more as though the Union arms would prevail. The South, except its leaders, wanted an end, and all the better people of the North under the lead of the good hearted Lincoln, longed for an end of the sad conflict on reasonable terms to the rebels. And finally peace came.

---

[34] *Dr. Mary Edwards Walker (b. 1831, d. 1919) was commissioned assistant surgeon in the U.S. Army, the first woman to hold such a post. She wore both the bloomer costume and male attire.*

~

TRAVELS SOUTH WITH T.D. GILBERT IN THE WINTER OF 1866
CHAPTER II

Wishing to see the southern states, where I had traveled but little, and especially so soon after the close of the war, the winter of 1866 I fell into conversation on the subject with Mr. Thos. D. Gilbert,[35] my old acquaintance, whom I first met at Grand Haven in the winter of 1837. And we soon arranged to perform the journey together. So on the 29th of January we took stage to Kalamazoo and railroad from there to Chicago. The next day, he having business, I took the opportunity to look quite generally about the city to see its vast growth, and with the rest, went north to the cemeteries and wooded openings — noticing the ridges and swales parallel to the lake, showing that its shore was once further inland, and had from time to time receded.

In the evening we took the Illinois Central railroad for Cairo. It was a beautiful moonshine night, so we could look out on the interminable level prairie lands and see their character as well as by day. I marked that they were less improved near the city than one would have expected, but they are wet to a great extent and not easy to put under improvement, and answer, as they are, for a pasture and hay. But when morning came I saw at once a change had come over the face of the country. The land was rolling, dryer, and much of it under good cultivation. And as we passed on, it became more uneven, and finally some timber and lime rock. At one part of the journey, many shaft trucks for coal, which they find, but some 40 or 50 feet from the surface. Was much surprised as we approached Cairo to find the country even more broken, hills, rocks, timber, fine oaks, valleys and swamps. Cairo, rather a hard looking place, in a hard locality for a town as far as its swampy site in concerned; commercially it is good.

Memphis
On the first day of February took steamboat for Memphis, a beautiful, mild, sunny day, and with the turbid, swift flowing current of the mighty river and the steam, we are swept along at a swift rate down the same. Something grand and interesting to be thus carried along winding right and left between its wooded shores. For the extensive bottom lands were not much yet improved. It is said some are still owned by the government. Passed New Madrid, and thought that there the John Ordway, who crossed the mountains with Lewis and Clark, settled and died. At one place where we stopped to wood, the man who supplied the wood said that he had in his employ as choppers men who had fought in both the Rebel and Union armies, chopping, eating and sleeping in a friendly manner together. Arrived at Memphis at night, late.

The next day explored the town and talked with the people. They seemed to think the condition of the negro would be but little, if at all, improved by his liberation. Were glad the war was ended and wished it had been sooner. But the leaders would keep trying as long as there was any possible hope of success. They felt a great relief from not having the care of their slaves, for they used to not only have to

---

[35] *Opposed Comstock in the campaign for mayor in 1863. Gilbert was active in many local business ventures and was president of the Grand Rapids Light Company after 1890.*

127

set them to work and feed them, but even think for them. We saw a sample of the grand leading product of the country in the immense piles of cotton bales, numbering at the time some 26,000 bales.

Havoc of War

Left Memphis by Tennessee and Mississippi railroad for Jackson, and first saw the war's doings at the village of Grenada. The country all along rolling, except the bottom lands on the streams, and that mixture of clay and sand that as soon as cleared washes badly, the side hill showing deep gullies. And the look of the soil and the crops would not indicate great fertility. Still it produces the cotton and the timber oak. We had much conversation with some of the passengers on the train. They conversed most freely of the war, the part they took, and the reasons for their doings, and described their present condition and that of the country in general. A man who lived near Holly Springs, by the name of Lyon, said that before the war he thought himself pretty well off, but during the contest in that part of the country, one army and then the other swept across his plantation, and what one did not destroy or devour the other did. His slaves left with the Union army, for they must, to get anything to eat. His wife and self for weeks had nothing on which to live except some corn meal. He wished to again work his lands, but having neither money, men nor teams he did not know how he was to do it. Another man, who lived between the railroad and the river, told us he was opposed to the war, and they threatened to imprison him because he would not join their armies, but having a sawmill and they wanting lumber they let him run his mill. Still he lost much besides his slaves. These men expressed the opinion that the whites when they, by time, had got things shaped to meet the change of the situation, would be better off without their slaves. But as to them, the slaves, they would be in a worse condition. So great a sameness in the country, I did not feel my usual regret at traveling at night, for we did not reach Jackson till the next day, and such a scene of devastation I never witnessed. Of course, I had not; but now and hence forward I was to see enough of the effects of this civilizing Christian practice of war.

Jackson, Mississippi

Jackson is situated on a high, beautiful plain, and must have had a good look before it was half destroyed by bombardment and flame, but now it presented anything else — the remains of blackened walls and ruined dwellings, piles of ruined railroad rails and rolling stock. And then we left the scene for

Vicksburg and soon came to where there was the hill and valley, and the beautiful forest, so unlike any of ours at the North — the pride of India, the holly, magnolia, cane brakes and palmettoes. As the railroad bridge over the big Black River had been burned we crossed on a temporary pontoon one, and as we approached Vicksburg were much surprised to find the bluffs on the back as well as the river side of the city. The country had a better soil on the way than north of Jackson, but had been but little cultivated for two or three years. So the land, buildings, destroyed railroad and everything, looked hard.

Vicksburg

February 5th, when we went out this morning at Vicksburg, found it had turned cold and that the trees were covered with ice. Strange to see a town here, on the Mississippi, built up the sides and on the tops of so high hills. It gives a ready look onto and across the river, with its boats at the shore and sailing up and down. We took a ride out and back to the fortifications, and the monument to Grant and Pemberton's capitulation. On the way the streets and road were muddy and cut through bluffs into which we saw many holes and caverns dug, where the citizens lived safely sheltered during the bombardment of the town. The earth being of solid clay they could dig out from the perpendicular sides of the streets, residences of any size or form to their liking.

New Orleans

At night we took boat for New Orleans. Found the next morning, as we sailed on, the banks mostly low and timbered, though occasionally plantations in view, and bluffs again coming to the river before reaching Natchez. All we saw of this showed but a narrow village under a bluff, which they said had a fine town on level lands above. But the boat did not stop long enough for us to go back and see. And so we sailed on, passing Baton Rouge at night, and when morning came we were down among the sugar plantations, of which we could get a full view from the deck of our boat. For recollect, we were floating on a river as high, or higher than the adjoining lands, an interesting sight, level extending plains with the sugar houses, with their steam power, and other buildings, like little villages, and the timbered swamps in the distance, to which is the drainage from these plantations.

As we approach the city we find village-like establishments on its side, and quite a town on the other sides, and, on arriving and landing on the broad levee, the sight presented was indeed a strange one. We were as high as many of the buildings, and the streets down below, with the water in the gutters running swiftly away, instead of towards the river. And so it is, the whole city is drained back into Lake Ponchartrain. The streets are paved with square blocks of basalt from the Palisades of the Hudson River, and the better buildings, including the part-finished custom house, are of Massachusetts or New Hampshire granite. This big custom house of stone about 60 paces square, we found or were informed, was erected on a foundation of wood. They had dug down into the bottomless soil, or mud, and then placed big timbers horizontally in these trenches and built up on said timbers, relying on their durability from being always kept wet.

Stopping at the St. Charles, we went onto its roof, from which we got a full view of the city and its surroundings. I was surprised at its extent and magnificence, far exceeding my expectations. We went up and down the streets in their street railroad cars with no conductor but the driver. Each passenger on entering drops a fare into a box so arranged that as it falls down he can see that it is right. And on looking about one of the strangest things we noticed was their cemeteries all built up with mason work, with niches or vaults for the dead, for if put under the ground they would be under the water, the land is so low.

Mobile

On the evening of the 8th, on taking a street car for Lake Ponchartrain, to ship for Mobile, we found all swamp by the time we had got half way to the lake. Oh! what a watery country to build a city in. And the mighty Mississippi flowing above your level so high that just remove the levees and you are drowned. Before we had got out of the bay, or lake, of Ponchartrain, night came on and continued till we were entering the Mobile Bay. So we did not see the connecting passage of the so-called lake with the Gulf of Mexico.

Found Mobile, too, a much finer city than I expected — good docks and buildings, what were left after that awful explosion of the magazine, all still lying much as left when it took place. It was on the outskirts of the town, but prostrated blocks of buildings almost to its center, or damaged them by bursting in or out the windows and doors — cannon balls, bricks, and all things thrown around. They told us that two walking together, one was killed, the other not injured, a woman stripped of her clothes and not killed, 70 killed, strange so few. A deep hole now in the ground where the explosion took place.[36] Mobile stands on rising ground, so it is easily drained, and the pine forest, near the city, stretches off far to the west. And all about in and out of the city, and in the harbor, are the military defences to be seen. Here we met Mr. [Francis W.] Kellogg, now the collector of the port, the same man who, the last term, was our representative to Congress, and two years ago procured for me a pass at Washington to the Rapidan. I was happy to see his kindly ways, in employing in his office a wounded rebel soldier. That is christian, and I have noticed that where Union and Rebel men meet they are usually friendly and keep up the old grudge when apart. I found that this was what the people we conversed with most complained of. They asked, "Why can you not take us at our word? We have given it all up, and glad it is ended. We consider ourselves in the Union and wish and expect to remain n the Union as good citizens, and we want you of the North to believe us."

Montgomery

Left on the evening of the 9th to ascend the river to Montgomery, and all the next day on the same, steaming up against the current. The river is not very wide, still it seems well fitted for navigation, usually ranging along bluffs on one side and extending bottoms on the other. And often seen in the bluffs was what they called soap stone, a kind of lime rock, as it looked to me. The plantations we saw along the river looked rather dilapidated, not having been much worked of late. We met a Monroe, Michigan man, and another who had come there to work plantations. And they seemed much encouraged with their prospects. We heard an Alabama man talking with his friends on the boat. he said he had $30,000 and he put that into the war, and then, like a fool, put himself in. That if he had not done so he might have done something for himself, but here you see "I have not a red." Poor man, he had my sympathy, and also that of my friend, Gilbert too. I think, though when we saw their losses in a thousand ways, he would sometimes say it was serving them right. But we agreed in this, as to our man who had put in $30,000 and then himself, that he was a representative man of those parts. Everything showed that all had been put into the lost cause.

---

[36] *Mobile had been the last Confederate city to surrender to Union forces, on April 12, 1865, three days after Lee's surrender at Appomattox Court House. On May 25, twenty tons of captured powder exploded in a warehouse being used as an arsenal. Boats at the dock, warehouses, and other buildings were left in ruins. An estimated 300 people were casualties, and property loss was put at $5 million.*

Selma

We stopped at Selma long enough for us to look about and see what was left after its bombardment and burning. The remains of the burned foundry buildings and works for casting their cannon, and other war matters were of an extent that much surprised us. The material still on the ground was of a great amount, all there lying apparently as the fire left them.

We learned that when we arrived at Selma they took a smallpox negro ashore from the boat. And we were also informed that the negroes were dying by the thousands from that disease, especially in the villages and cities all about. The course they took when informed that they were freed, served widely to spread the disease. They said to each other on the plantations, "How do we know that we are free?" So to test the matter, they said, "If we can go away it will prove we are free." So from plantation, or wherever their homes, they would start out and all go to the first town, station, or landing on boats, or railroads, without ceremony or paying fare. And then they would meet others from all directions, have a good time of it while they could get something to eat and keep well. Then they would abandon the sick to die and go back to their old homes, or where they could get something to eat, thoughtless on all these matters as so many children. We were told of cases where mothers had been known to abandon their young children in their desperate condition, to perish and even throw the infant from their arms, and that few of the children born, now that they had not the care of their mistress, lived. All the result of the sudden change in condition and the poverty of the country. The old masters were not unkind to their former slaves, but having no longer the control of them, what could they do? They still fed them if they had anything, but naturally first fed their own children. This liberating them so, all at once, was indeed a terrible war measure.

As we ascended the river from Selma we found less sameness than below. We could see some hilly country back, there being more cultivation along the river, or rather there had been, though little of late. They had raised little cotton but some grain from necessity, not having the avails of the cotton to buy with, nor facility in war times to get their usual supplies from Illinois and the northwest country. We found Montgomery very beautifully situated on hilly lands bordering the river, well laid out, many fine buildings and beautiful public grounds. From the state capitol we got a splendid view of the city and the fertile, well cultivated country around, and we attended the Legislature in session then. It was now the 13th of February and the weather quite spring-like, flowers blooming brightly.

Atlanta

We left next morning by railroad for Atlanta, and arrived there in the evening, giving us a good opportunity to see the country. The country was hilly and did not seem very fertile, being of the same red or yellow sand and clay. At Columbus on the Chattahoochee there was fine water power from the fall over the extreme edge of the granite rock. At West Point, saw Wilson's destruction of property. But before he had reached Macon, Lee had surrendered. It had been warm and rained, but at night turned very cold all over the country. And there next morning, the 15th, down to nine. Atlanta beautifully located high in a hilly country, and some mountains in sight. But, oh! how destroyed by war. It must be seen to appreciate it. Still business seemed quite active, and they had commenced building up, but not such good buildings as those destroyed. Same account here of the negroes dying off. A Mr. Cook, of Macon, a planter, said he was an Ohio man and came there about the breaking out of the war. His negroes left him and many died. A Mr. McCrath from Grand Rapids, now in business there, whom we were glad to meet, also spoke discouragingly of their character and prospects. Had much changed his opinion of the race since becoming acquainted with them.

Augusta

Next day we left Atlanta by railroad for Augusta. The country was the same red clay, sand soil, and seemed not fertile till we got onto the headwaters of the Oconee and Ockmulgee where it looked better. The old fields, however, were more in weeds than crops. Everywhere was that look of neglect of not only fields, but fences and buildings. If you had not occasionally seen people as you passed you might well think they had long since died. Passed stone mountains of naked granite on the left, a very marked feature in the landscape, and often along saw not only bowlders, but the rock in places. On reaching Augusta it presented the pleasing sight of not having suffered by the war. Our armies in going to the sea passed it by, and why I know not for it was as guilty in its manufacture of cotton shirting for their armies as Selma in the casting of cannon. Found Augusta a very handsome, well laid out and situated place, on a plain rising gradually back to the distant hills with good public and other buildings. Three or four cotton factories built of granite from a quarry some six miles above were lighted with gas and warmed with steam. There were also flour and other mills, propelled all by water brought in a race from the falls some six or seven miles above. And the same race is used for a canal connecting the navigation down with some 200 miles of navigation above. We visited their cemetery and found all beautifully ordered, and some fine monuments. And we went into the Freedman's bureau court held by a Judge Davis of Augusta, and found that he spoke rather encouragingly of the conduct and prospects of the freedmen. Glad to hear one thus speak.

Savannah

On the 18th we took railroad for Savannah, going south to Millen, but before we reached there, and all along and often we saw Sherman's doings, especially the destruction of the railroads and all that pertained thereto. Roads were torn up, the ties used to build fires, to so heat the rails that they could be bent and twisted as to not be again laid, often wound around trees, and all now lying where then left. For where roads were in use they were of new rails and reconstructed. After leaving the river bottoms we came into the usual poor pine and swamp lands, and at places high bluffs, quite broken. When we had reached the bottom lands of the Ogushee there were seen better plantations and here, arriving in the city, I found myself in the same Savannah that I had seen in the year 1823, and all of the handsomest places in the Union, one-fourth left as public grounds. Oh! that there could be an improvement in this bungling manner of platting new towns. There as everywhere, I noticed the change that had come over the general look and bearing of the negro from what it was when I knew him here, and at Darien, in said year of 1823; then he was a thoughtless, joyous creature. He showed his freedom from care, for he was cared for by his master. Usually he was joyous. Now they all look thoughtful and more sober, look kind of puzzled, as though they did not know what had happened to them. No wonder, for it is indeed a new and strange condition for them.

After looking about for a time seeing the Pulaski monument and the city generally, we took boat for Charleston. And in descending the river, noticed Fort Pulaski and others, Tybee light and the Keadan, and so out to sea. It proved decidedly rough, and our boat accommodations were but poor for comfort. I still enjoyed it well, not being seasick, and it brought up the recollection of the time I was sailing the same Atlantic coming up from Cape Horn. From which time I had not been at sea till now. Friend Gilbert did not so well enjoy it, looking a little skittish.

Charleston

As we entered the Charleston bay they pointed out the place where the cannon were planted to bombard the city. And then passed Forts Moultrie and Sumter, which we after visited, and so landed in the renowned city of Charleston. And on going out and about what a sight of devastation was presented. The accidental fire of 1861, which burned a third of the compact part of the city, showed all its work as when it ceased, for there had during the war been no rebuilding, and then the subsequent fires and bombardments all as plainly shown, was to us a sad and awful sight. War spared nothing; churches riddled by the balls and shells; cemetery enclosures and monuments knocked down and into fragments, monuments of worthy and Union historic names. We went into a church where a shell had come down through the roof and burst at a point to stave to pieces the organ. Another church, away five miles from the place of discharge, one ball only had struck, doing but little damage. As many as twenty struck the Mills Hotel. But no use to particularize, for there seemed no end to the war's doings.

We visited the Freedman's school kept in the State Normal school building. At its head was a New England lady with 200 pupils of all ages, sex and might say colors. Noticed a little girl that had none of the look of the negro, but following the condition of the mother, she was probably a slave. The assistants in the school were mulattoes who had been educated there. And there was a higher department of a few pupils that were taught by mulatto, educated in England. I was mistaken in saying we visited Sumter. We went out in a United States steamer, used to carry out supplies, to Sullivan Island, saw the strong walls of Fort Moultrie and big guns. Sailed to Sumter, but from some cause were not allowed to land.

Having spent two days at Charleston, on the 23rd we took rail for Columbia. The lands for a long distance level, and pine and swamp and few good plantations till we got to Branchville. Then better and some hilly till we reached Kingsville. From there to Columbia level and extensive plantations. Through all the South extensive plains usually extend along the rivers. To cross the river Congaree was a bridge and trellis work for a long distance, the water high and yellow in color.

Columbia

Columbia is a well laid out town on a plain high above the river, broad streets at right angles, and must have been a good looking place before burned. The fire too had destroyed the mulberry and other beautiful trees that shaded the streets, to show the extent of the burning, which they ascribed to intent not accident, for which they still cursed Sherman. We visited the partly built state capitol, started and partly completed before the war, nothing done since, 300 feet long and 70 feet high, built of granite and marble, immense blocks of granite brought from the river two miles below, some 33 feet in length and weighing 51 tons.

Railroad not rebuilt, so we had to travel by stage, on starting out north from Columbia and for the 22 miles till we reached the end of the Charlotte Railroad up and among hills, poor pine lands and grubs. When we had reached a station we had to take our lodgings in a car till morning, when we went on to Charlotte through a better country. It appeared a pretty village, mostly on one street, and here is a United States mint.

Started early next morning, the 26th, for Greensborough. Found the country rolling and well fitted for grain and grass. Passed the prison town of Salisbury, quite a large town and situated on a hill, as seems usual in this country. On leaving, found the best looking farms and buildings we had seen. But beyond Greensborough not so good, more like our openings, and still the red soil and granite rock.

Raleigh and Richmond

We reached Raleigh of a moonshine evening, and looked about it some. We went to see their Legislature, which was in session. The capitol built on the top of the hill, on which the town stands, and seems not much of a city. Left Raleigh before light for Richmond. Had a fine, pleasant day. country undulating and granite stones. Came to the Roanoke River and crossed it by boat, the railroad bridge being out of repair. To my surprise found that this river was not navigable. From there the ground level and some good plantations, then swamps and poor looking lands and much second growth pine. As we approached Petersburgh we saw the entrenchments, forts, towers, etc., of the late war. We so hurried through Petersburgh that we saw but little of it, seemed a compact and well built town. Crossing the Rappahannock River we continued on over a very hilly, untilled, bushy country to Richmond.

Now the last day of February and a spring-like day for the looking about of the renowned city of Richmond. Stopped at the Exchange, a good house every way. Splendid water power on the James River there, in all 50 foot fall, one lock with a lift of 20 feet. And though we saw the ruins of the mills and other property, to a great extent burned at the time of the evacuation, we went into a seven-story mill that had forty run of stones. The mills and warehouses were along the banks of the river, but most of the city, on high lands back, reached by a steep ascent. Noticed the celebrated Libby prison building, and saw the house where President Davis lived, now occupied by General Sems. The capitol building nothing very remarkable, but beautifully located on an open square. The Legislature was in session and debating the matter of the confederate indebtedness. And there stood General Jackson's equestrian monument in a position to be seen far all around. And oh! how often I thought, had he been at the head, or his like, at the needed time, that Civil War, whose effects we so plainly see hereabouts, would never have happened.

March 1st we left Richmond by railroad for the North. Saw something of the defences on that side. The country not very good and but few improvements, except on some bottom lands on a creek of a long name. The house where Stonewall Jackson died was pointed out to us, and the fortifications about Fredericksburgh showed how Lee arranged to draw our army into a pocket. He had the hill a little out southwest of the town, well fortified, so it made for the Union army a bad battle. From Fredericksburgh to Acquia Creek very hilly and poor. Saw some military ruins, but very few improvements, and on arriving at Acquia Creek took steamboat on, here, the broad Potomac. And we sailed pleasantly up the same till we got against Mount Vernon, where, as their custom is, they tolled the boat's bell for the priceless, though so long ago dead. And there the river narrows, and as we passed along we had a view of Fort Washington and Alexandria, but it being a foggy day and chilly not a good time to enjoy the trip. And on arriving at Washington we put up at the National Hotel, the same where I stopped when there in 1832.

The Capitol

Next day went to the capitol and to the navy yard, and there at the yard we saw four or five monitors, the *Stonewall* and another taken from the rebels, the bursted cannon, the old Tripoli and a Mexican brass cannon — all worth seeing. Then the day following went to the Smithsonian Institute and looked at its interesting materials. And in the evening Mr. Ferry, our representative, proposed that, as we had come from the South, we should call on Mr. Boutwell of the Freedmen's committee, which we did. Still, though thus introduced, he did not use the civility to make any talk of any kind, but kept about his business as though we had not been present, and of course we left the gentleman.

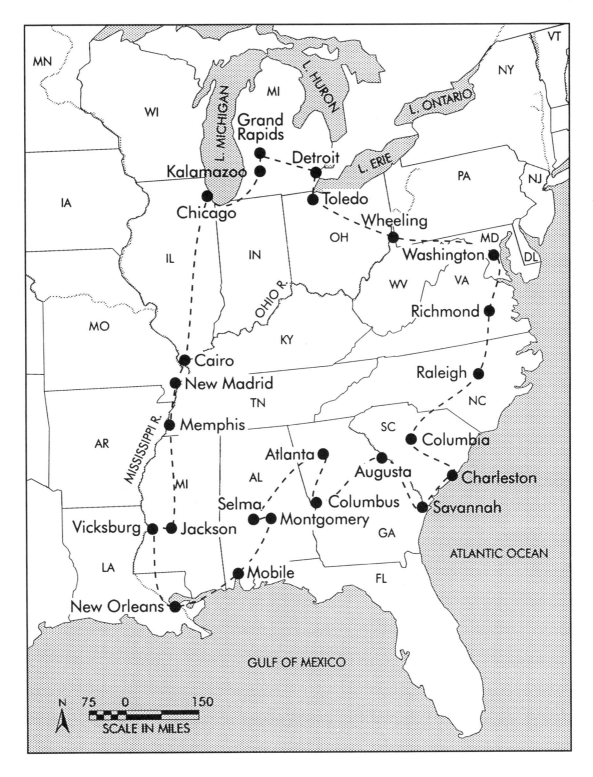

John Ball's Travels
Southern U.S., 1866

Then Sunday we heard a Mr. Boynton preach a decidedly fanatical sermon, not worth repeating. The next day, the 5th, visited the Treasury Department and went much over its massive building. Called on a Mr. Burch of our place, in the pay department. From the Secretary got permit to go through all the greenback and fractional currency rooms, and see all the machinery, and the 100 girls counting and packing the fractionals. Of course during the days we spent here we visited the House of Congress and listened to debates, but I have said enough of Washington.

And I stayed long enough there, so bought a railroad ticket for Detroit, and the next morning left to return straight home. But when at the junction of the Baltimore & Ohio Railroad, with the one from Washington, my traveling companion, Mr. Gilbert, and myself parted, he going east to Massachusetts to visit friends. And on turning off passing by Elliott's Mill, and so on to Frederick, there was brought back strongly to my mind the time I passed over this same road by horse power, in the spring of 1832. What a change this world of ours has passed through since that time. The railroad then a strange and new institution, and now universal. And the telegraph then not known, and all things gone on with railroad speed. And so I swept on and on over and through the Allegheny and Cumberland mountains, with all their wild scenery, and through a new state, that of West Virginia, and to the Ohio River at Wheeling. This new state seems to have come into and continues as a state in the Union, rather informally. It has been a puzzle to me. So crossed over into and wound along through Ohio and Toledo, to Detroit, and so home having enjoyed my journey well and felt well paid, and glad to be again at home.

EAST AND SOUTH AGAIN
WITH MRS. BALL
CHAPTER III

My wife and Flora having spent the summer of this year, 1866, at Wentworth, New Hampshire, with my niece, Mrs. Dean, on the third of September I left home for them. And though President Johnson was, at the time I passed there in Detroit, instead of stopping, as perhaps I should to see him, I kept on my journey. I thought well of Johnson then, and still more of him after the attempt to impeach him – to impeach him for not entertaining the narrow prejudice and bitter feelings toward the people of the South, whom I saw when there, wished to be considered in and of the Union. And I was glad that his worth, before his death was generally appreciated and allowed. The next day arrived at Lansingburgh, where I of course, stopped to see my sister, Mrs. Powers, and my old friends. For that place ever seemed home-like to me, having passed so many years there in a varied way, but as satisfactorily as most part of my life. Saw my old life-long friend, Dr. Brinsmade, and others with whom I had so long been connected in Michigan in matters of land business.

New Hampshire

Mrs. Powers concluded to go to New Hampshire with me, so on the 7th we left for there by the way of Lowell, and, stopping there to see our nephew, Artemus Brooks, continued our journey up to Wentworth. And there I had the pleasure of meeting my wife in tolerable health and the other friends. Went also to Haverhill to visit my old friend, Joseph Powers and family. And went also to Hebron to again see the scenes of my childhood and the few friends left. And stopped with my old neighbor, Col. Isaac Crosby. Returned through Groton, Dorchester and

Rumney to Wentworth. Oh! on these old roads that I used to travel, no change but for the worse. Few new improvements and the old ones, buildings and all, going down.

On the 13th, to see more of the world and to visit some friends at Portland, we started for home, not to be sure by the most direct way, to that place and then by sea. Took railroad down through Plymouth, my wife's native place, but her people having gone west too, did not stop, but kept on, having a splendid view of the country and the distant mountains, to Wiers Landing on Lake Winnepesaukee and from there crossed over the lake by boat to Center Harbour. Next day took steamboat down the beautiful lake, the largest in all that part of country, and surrounded by very varied scenery and the distant mountains, even the White ones, in sight. On arriving at the foot of the lake took rail for Dover. There we stopped long enough to take a ride about the place, and also look into their calico-dyeing establishment. The cloth was carried over circular blocks, so arranged as to the dye that they could roll off and stamp one color in a minute on a whole piece, and when dry apply another color. A swift process compared with what I saw near Hudson in 1830, and such is the progress of the arts.

Portland

In the afternoon we took rail for Portland, but in the evening there came on a most tremendous thunder shower, which interfered with our getting much idea of the country. But a thunder storm seems somehow doubly impressive when traveling on a railroad. On going out the next morning saw the ocean and the beautiful lay of the city on its harbor.

But there had lately been a fire that had burned nearly one-half of the town. Was told that the heat was so great that three-story brick buildings were consumed in ten minutes. On going about the city found it wonderfully variegated, by surface of land and inlets of water. But not finding our friends we left the same evening by sea for New York.

By Boat to New York City

It was a beautiful September evening, the 15th, that we embarked. It gave us the best of an opportunity to enjoy a view of the town, harbor, the sea and coast for a time before the night obscured the same. The ocean to me was an old acquaintance, while to my wife and Flora it was all a new scene, and they of course experienced the enjoyment that novelty, especially of things grand, brings. The next day also beautifully clear and calm, so it made our voyage very agreeable. Saw in the distance Cape Cod and Nantucket, etc. and all the while some ten or twenty vessels in sight, schooners, brigs and ships, all shapes and sizes that sail the seas. And then another night at sea, and the next morning we could see lying low off on the right, Long Island on the right and the Quarantine station with the telegraph signals on the left, and then Governors Island and its forts and New York harbor.

On going ashore from our good boat, *Franconia*, put up at the Astor. We found our old friend, Dr. John Ellis, and he and wife visited us at the hotel, and looked some about the city to see its growth and wonders — how much, do not now recollect. Next morning crossed over the Hudson and took our seats in an Erie railroad car for Elmira. And out we started through the Palisades and then wound our way up the winding valley of the Delaware. Passed over the fine picturesque country to Binghamton, and up the fertile valley of the Chemung, and the mountains and valleys to Elmira. The next day went on to Cleveland, noticing all the varied scenery, and from there took the night boat to Detroit, expecting to reach there in time to take the morning train home, but too late, so did not get there till the next day, 21st. Glad after our long journeyings and longer absence of my wife to all be again at our home.

The Following Year

And a year passed around in my usual humdrum office and home life, the particular doings of which I do not now recollect. In the fall of 1867, to give my wife a journey for her health and pleasure, and for myself, that I might see a portion of our country that I had not yet visited, on the 5th of October we left home to go southwardly. The precise route not

exactly determined. Stopped at Detroit over Sunday, and in the forenoon heard the Reverend Mr. Duffield preach one of his orthodox sermons, and in the afternoon went out to the cemetery and some about the city. And how beautifully Detroit is situated on ground rising so conveniently up from that noble river, and how much it has grown in build and extent since I first saw it — then only 7,000 inhabitants in 1836.

Ohio

Then to Cleveland by boat, and on looking about the same and noticing how finely shaded, we concluded the appellation of Forest City justly applied. Went out to the water cure establishment and to Woodland Cemetery, and so looked about the place. From there took railroad for Columbus, where we stopped long enough to note its splendid location on such a high ground with the state capitol at the summit. And hereabouts and most of that we had passed through in the state, of good soil and under good cultivation. But everywhere they had cut away too much of the original fine beech and maple forest. Everywhere in the fully settled parts of our country I am led to say with the poet, "Axman spare that tree" etc. And then on we went to Cincinnati and found the country more diversified with hills and river plains than expected, and almost mountainous as you approach the Ohio River. The city on a plane, so almost surrounded, except on the river side, by those high bluffs, and these we climbed to the observatory from which we could look down and out on the whole city.

Clay's Home

On the 11th we crossed the Ohio River, on that grand suspension bridge, took rail for Lexington. On leaving the river soon found the country very hilly, even broken, and from the looks of the buildings, few negroes and from the looks of what crops there were, I inferred the soil was also poor. But as we approached Lexington we noticed an improvement every way. A fine, high undulating country and good farms, and the city most beautifully located and well built. Looked about, went to the cemetery, where we noticed many fine monuments. Rode out and looked over the beautiful buildings and grounds of Ashland, all now dedicated to the glorious cause of education. The chancellor of the university showed us in [Henry] Clay's old dwelling, some pictures, among others one of himself, Clay, delivering, what was so much spoken of at the time, his compromise speech in Congress on the trouble between the North and South.

Next took rail for Louisville, passing through Frankfort, the capital of the state, without stopping. The country all the way beautifully diversified with hills, plains, and streams. Next day went to church and heard a good orthodox discourse. Went across the river to New Albany, in Indiana. Quite a town, some 18,000 or 20,000 inhabitants. A courthouse built of a singular looking rock, the Bedford rock or marble. Noticed the rushing of the Ohio waters over the rough lime rock making the falls. And they were erecting a bridge for a railroad over the same. Traveled about the city on the street railroad and found in every way a well situated and well built city. And from here took rail for the nearest station to the Mammoth Cave, which was one of the things to be seen. Though the country rather level, is somewhat rocky. and from the railroad had to travel some eight miles by stage to the cave.

Mammoth Cave

On the 15th went into the cave as far as my wife thought her strength would allow, then looked about and observed what the guide pointed out as the most interesting parts and objects, the Star Chamber, etc. But I will not particularize, as the same has been so often well described. Only a half-mile below the mouth of the cave flows the Green River, winding among hills and cliffs, and 300 feet below the cave, showing how mountainous is the country. This cavernous lime rock is a marked feature of the surface and the underground of this region. More underground streams than on the surface probably, as the river in the cave. The very bowlders often have their little caves. And we returned over this rough, rocky country to the railroad and took train to the South for Nashville. The country about Bowling Green is quite level and seems fertile, but as we cross into Tennessee more hilly. Crossed the Cumberland with its deep channel, as are most of the courses of the streams in this lime rock country.

Hermitage

Nashville is a most beautiful city, as to its high locality and build. The capitol building built of mottled marble, and all the country about quite hilly and very pleasant in its aspect. Could not forego the pleasure of visiting the Hermitage,[37] so we took carriage and it being a pleasant day had a fine ride. It is some eight miles out. On the way saw them picking cotton, and went into a marble quarry. At Ashland

went into the old house where the hero once lived, quite plain in its structure. And went to his tomb and about the grounds, pilgrim-like, and then returned to Nashville, and the next day left for Chattanooga. A beautiful and warm day. Found the country after a time less knobby, and about Murfreesboro good. Saw the site of Stone Run Battle and the graves of the slain, sad mementoes of war's doings. We then ascended and traveled along a tableland, and through a mountain tunnel, and down to the Tennessee river, at a point in the state of Alabama. And then turned up that river at an acute angle, and kept near the same, at one place touching the state of Georgia, and so wound in and out among the precipitous mountains and came out to Chattanooga village, situated on a plain.

The river being navigable for boating and with the railroad, this seems quite a business village, in a quite an extended fertile valley, but in view the abrupt mountains near, and the extended ranges more distant.

Lookout Mountain

And of course we must visit Lookout Mountain, at the battle of which one of my wife's brothers took an active part (the Missionary Ridge one). And our team wound around and around and up the side of the same, ascending six hundred feet to its summit, from which it is said seven, I think only five, states can be seen. We are there just on the line of Georgia, and near Alabama. And looking away up the Tennessee valley one probably can see Kentucky, and the mountains of North Carolina, and perhaps South Carolina. The north point of Lookout Mountain looks right down almost perpendicularly into the river, and a little off to the right is the village. A short distance back it spreads out into a tableland, extending off into Georgia and Alabama, where there are farms. And near by it a female seminary of much celebrity, where the girls from the lower and less healthy homes of all these states can come and breathe the pure mountain air and receive the needed instruction. We called at the school and all seemed very well arranged for the purpose. Then descended to our quarters extremely well pleased with our visit to Lookout Mountain.

On the 20th we find ourselves at Knoxville, in the midst of the 50 miles in width valley of East Tennessee. The Allegheny and Cumberland ranges in full view. Generally, as we came, noticed that the soil of a red or yellow color seemed productive, but there

---

[37] *President Andrew Jackson's estate in Tennessee.*

were occasional ridges within the valley, and hard flinty stones about. Since the war the city seemed much improving, and as there were many less slaves in these parts than most of the country, the change from their liberation was much less felt. But as we passed through the country we could but notice the very small number of animals. The war had left so few, for the armies of both North and South had so fed on them that there had not yet been time for their increase.

Virginia

Next day we left Knoxville for Bristol, in Virginia. Kept up the valley of the Holston, one of the great branches of the Tennessee. A very diversified interesting country, as to its scenery. It was interesting also to see the place of residence, Greenville, of the late, much abused President Johnson. He having now gone to his final rest, his enemies will cease their malice, I trust, that he would not do their unreasonable, spiteful bidding. At all events he was never charged, even by them, with the prevailing sin of these later times, Government peculation. Stopped over at Bristol, and the next day continued on to Lynchburg. All along the route over the Alleghenies a good grazing country, not being at all broken, but a high tableland, till you come down into the valley of the new river, the main branch of the Great Kanhawa. The height at Airy, a station, 1,700 feet, more broken as you pass through the Blue Ridge and come onto the waters of the Roanoke. Saw Otter Peak, highest mountain in Virginia.

On the 23rd stopped over at Lynchburg and looked about that old, set up on edge, city. For its site is very hilly and ridgy and on the James River. The weather up to this time had been warm and mostly pleasant, but today cooler. A place of some 12,000 inhabitants of rather a hard look, as far as I had opportunity to see. But it being with them their election day, perhaps it was not a good time to see them rightly. Saw a man they called General Wilcox.

Washington

The 24th went on to Washington, clear and the Blue Ridge Mountains all day in view on the left. The country to Orange County rolling and well watered, and then to the Rappanhannock level and undulating. Then level and less fertile till in region of Bull Run, and so on to Alexandria rather broken. And so crossed the Potomac River to Washington, of which one gets a fine view as it is approached.

Next day, on looking about Washington, saw that it had much grown and improved since there in the winter of 1864. Visited the Patent Office, went to Georgetown, the Washington and Jackson squares and grounds about the White House. Saw Mr. Lawrence and wife and some other acquaintances, and the following day went again to the Patent Office, and to the Agricultural Building, where we saw the wonders of the vegetable world. And to the Smithsonian Institute and to see more of the city on the street railroad, north and south. And the day following, the 27th, took a ride on the street car to the Navy Yard, and crossed the grounds of the Capitol. Next day it rained so hard we did nothing except to visit the Capitol and look about the same. The 29th we visited Arlington Heights and looked about its grounds and the cemetery, a sad memorial of the fratricidal war. And called on Major Bird, and our townsman, Chas. H. Holden.

October 30th, we thinking it about time to be getting home, started out in earnest and traveled 178 miles to Sunderland, in Pennsylvania, passing right through Baltimore and Harrisburgh without a stop. I do not remember why we stopped so long in Washington, and passed by these places unlooked at. But on the way noticed the hilly lay of the land about Baltimore and its bay, and the better looking country as we came into Pennsylvania, and the lay of the same about Harrisburgh and the Susquehanna region, and as we get further north the mountains begin to loom up. And the next day right on to Rochester. From Williamsport, mountainous, and in the state of New York, rolling varied, and of course all the while the view was very interesting, that is, so to me, for I never tire in looking out on this world's face. Something always of beauty or interest. The artificial also as well as the natural has its interest for it is of man and for his use — the long coal trains on the railroads, buildings, and the farming improvements.

Niagara Falls

Then on the 1st of November went on to Niagara. Visited the Falls, went onto Goats Island and looked all about to see the wonders of this wonderous fall. And then we took a ride down the river to what is called the Mountain. The great offset above Lake Ontario, where the Niagara River begins to cut its channel through the rock till it has not got half way up to Lake Erie. Next day came on to Detroit and stopped at Mr. Edward Lyon's Exchange, and met him, pleasant as heretofore and so on home. And having safely arrived and feeling well and benefited by our journey, and finding all well at home too, we felt very well paid by the trip, and ever to be remembered with much pleasure.

MONTREAL AND THE WHITE MOUNTAINS AFTER FIFTY YEARS AND OTHER JAUNTS
CHAPTER IV

To pass over again to the 24th of August, 1868, on which day I started on a visit to see my friends in New Hampshire, and New York by the way of Montreal and the White Mountains. Went to Detroit, that is to the junction of the Detroit and Milwaukee railroad and the Grand Trunk, and then by that to Port Huron. Seldom one travels so far over so perfectly level country. Crossed over the St. Clair River, with its great sweep of water from Lakes Superior, Michigan and Huron, in view of the outlet of the latter, to Port Sarnia. And then on and on over the rich, rolling, well cultivated country, to Toronto, that fine city on the Ontario, of which one gets a view before reaching there. Then down along said lake to Kingston, and so along and along, sometimes in view of the mighty rushing St. Lawrence to Montreal.

And here I am fifty years from the time, and only time, I was ever in Montreal before. And from anything I see, except the mighty broad rushing river and the mountains, and beautifully rising of the land from the river, I should not mistrust I had ever before seen the place. Now, instead of the dingy stone two-story buildings along a few narrow streets, European like, and the whole of no great extent, now I see a splendid Americanized city of great extent, and not behind our best towns, and better evidently in the respect to stability of build — in that ahead of ours. I went up onto the mountain and up onto an observatory, from which I got a most splendid view, not only down on the whole city and river and the country beyond, but back and all around. Never have I seen anything of the kind to surpass it. One feature quite marked, other knobs like the one on which you stand off in the distance.

Descending from the mountain into the city I stepped into a street railroad car to go to another part of the same. And who should I find in it but my townsman and lady, the Rev. Dr. Tustin, and quite to our mutual surprise and pleasure. They had left home the next day after myself, and had descended the St. Lawrence. And on enquiring whither bound, they as well as myself, to the White Mountains. So we started out and over or rather through the wonderful and renowned tubular iron bridge, over the broad St. Lawrence, and then over the level, well-tilled lands, all lotted out by the French occupants into small, long, right angular fields — just as you see in Germany, France and other countries on the continent. And then rolling lands and less cultivation with some high lands ahead. Passed the junction of the Quebec road, and I rather wanted to take it. And passed through a corner of Vermont, then the Connecticut River into New Hampshire. This boundary river here comparatively but a creek or brook. And traveled on, winding among the surrounding hills and mountains to Gorham.

Mount Washington

And here we leave the railroad and take a stage for the Glen House, in a valley at the foot of Mount Washington, on the east side. Dr. Tustin wished to ascend the mountain and have his wife accompany him, but she rather declined, and so I had to leave them and ascend without their company. I think he after went up alone. They had carriages, open wagons and strong horses for the service. So I took a seat with some half dozen others and started off on the eight-mile ride drawn by six horses to the Tip-Top House. The direct distance is not half that, but I soon found that we were traveling a winding zigzag road at all points of the compass, like those of the Alps, and like those cut into and formed from the solid rocks, and this smoothed up with earth, but theirs with pounded rock.

Tip-Top House

As we ascended we had a fine prospect for a time, but before we had reached the summit, as very often happens, we were enveloped in a chilling, dense fog. On reaching the top put up at the very comfortable Tip-Top House, and was quite struck at its manner of build. The mountain is not of solid ledge, but made up of broken and cleft rocks and stones of all shapes and sizes, from one pound weight to thousands of tons. And out of these stones they built up a thick wall of one story, leaving space for one door and a few windows, all rough as any stone wall on the outside but plastered and papered the inside. On this wall is built a framed and bordered, rather steep roof. And in this garret are fitted up their sleeping rooms.

And in the west one of these chambers I was assigned, and oh! how the wind did whistle by and shake me that night. Winds half the days and nights the year around, that would blow the roof away, if not the walls down, if it were not chained down by a number of heavy chains being carried over the same and fastened to the big rocks at the foot of the side walls. There is another house and a stable, and each built on the same plan.

Fortunately on going out in the morning I found it gloriously bright, and no clouds to obscure the look out over all the grand mountain peaks around and in the distance, even as far as the Green Mountains of Vermont and detached summits in the other direction in Maine. Could look down southerly on Mounts Monroe, Pleasant and Clinton, up which I climbed fifty years before, when there was no track from any direction onto the mountains, and was driven back from reaching this spot by a driving snow storm.

They were then building the railroad up the mountain on the west side, and had got it made some half way up, and were daily bringing up the materials by the same to construct it further. And I was told that at noon a train would be up, by which I could go down, if down to that point called Jacob's Ladder. So I at the time went down to that point and waited their coming up, but to my regret they did not come, for I found it no easy thing to go down and down at an angle of say 40 degrees on rough and smooth rocks lying at all possible angles. Granite and gneiss and showing nothing of

rounding, so these heights must have been above the glacial grindings. No rocks even striated as I have often seen in other lower parts of that state.

And as I descended, part of the time from tie to tie on this road, I noticed its build. Timber stringers resting on the rocks and where depressions, for the mountain side is in all shapes, posts and braced to keep them in place, and usual railroad rails on the outer timbers, and on a broad central timber a kind of double rail with horizontal iron pins joining them, into which a cog wheel propelled by the steam meshed, so as to roll the engine and the car up the mountain. With brakes to well arranged that they could command it with safety.

And, oh! how lame my legs felt before I reached the base of the mountain where the road commences. And there I found a tavern where I got a dinner and a team going out some seven miles through the woods, over a good road constructed by the same company that is building the mountain road. And so came out onto the old road at the Fabian place where may be seen the ruins of the old burned house. And so I went on to the Washington House, a well kept house and main stopping place for the visitors to these parts.

Back to Native Hills

From there the next morning I took stage for Littleton and then by railroad to Haverhill, where I stopped to visit my old friend, Joseph Powers, my wife's uncle. And they gave me some ointment for my lame legs that much relieved them. And then I went on to Wentworth to visit my niece, Mary M. Dean, the only child of my oldest brother, Nathaniel, and her aged mother. And this niece took a ride with me over to visit our old native hill in Hebron, and much did we enjoy the ride and the look about the old grounds, for she was born on an adjoining farm to my own native one. Great changes had come over the lands and their inhabitants. Still to see the few old acquaintances left, and look out on our childhood scenes, the lakes and the mountains was a melancholy pleasure.

And then I visited my connections, the Ladd family at Alexandria and Bristol, and took rail to Franklin in hopes to there see my old classmate, Judge Nesmith, but did not find him at home. Finding it would be about as direct a way as I could reach Lansingburgh, where I wished also to visit, I took the railroad to the White River junction on the Connecticut. Had a pleasant day and passed on over the hills and tablelands, and looked out on the other side of the granite Cardigan Mountain upon the opposite side from which in all my childhood I had looked. When I got to the White River junction, finding no train soon going down the Connecticut, but one immediately going to Burlington, I took that and so wound up the valley of the White River that so many years ago I had traveled by stage, before railroads were thought of. And that most beautiful town of Burlington I had not since seen, now quite a city, then but a small village. But still the same wide and splendid view of the lake and mountains, a fit place for a seat of learning, which and much else also had grown.

From there took train for Lansingburgh. The first part of this route I had not before passed over, so enjoyed, as always, the seeing parts I had not before seen — the towering Green Mountains in the distance, on the left, and occasionally glimpses of the lake on the right. Visited my sister, Mrs. Powers, and other friends at Lansingburgh, and noted their continued prosperity in business. Ever a matter of much gratification that a concern that I had aided when under much embarrassment had so prospered. And though the old village had much grown and improved in looks, still there remained more old landmarks than usually seen in our towns. Enough of this journey, so home I go.

Trip with Horses and Carriage

In June, 1869, took wife, Flora and Lucy with my own team on a ride about our own country. Went out south on the plank road. Dined at Van Lew's and had much talk with him about the first settlement of the country and its progress. I thought of the times I traveled all these parts, about the south part of Kent and north part of Allegan in 1842, and on the 4th of July came in, following the same route of this plank road, by the surveyor's marks. The ride gave wife and children a good appetite, so did justice to the good dinner, and then went on to Wayland and stopped for the night. Next morning went on and got to Martin's Corners, and there stopped, and a rain coming on did not leave there till after supper. Then hitched up and went to the junction. And quite cold, though the 9th of June. Noticed the good quality of the lands in the towns of Martin and Gunn Plains, and that the crops were looking well. Went from Plainwell, on the east side of the river to Kalamazoo, and stopped at the Burdick House.

Kalamazoo

General Burdick, whom I well recollect, laid out this place and showed much good taste in the selection of the site, its plan, and leaving uncut the burr oak forest trees for ornament. We called on Mrs. Stone, the celebrated traveler, and had some

pleasant conversation with her. How this seeing the world and its ways liberalized the inquiring, well-minded person. Mrs. Stone is the aunt of our neighbor, Mrs. Judge Withey, and sister to C. E. Walker's wife. She was married at their house, the same, now Mr. Brown's on Fountain Street, and I attended her wedding. The next day went on through Galesburgh and along over those fine lands, now well improved, to Augusta, where we dined, and then to Battle Creek, ever a sensible and industrious village and now much improved. And the next day to Marshall, always a very fine place, but not the great one early predicted.

Reminiscences

Took a ride about Marshall to see the place, and stayed there the next day, it being Sunday. And on Monday went to Bellevue in Eaton County on the

John Ball with his little daughter, Mary Joanna, taken in 1867. [Reprinted from Autobiography of John Ball, *p. 224]*

Battle Creek River that falls into the Kalamazoo at Battle Creek. Though near the middle of June, cold and uncomfortable riding. All these parts, and the rest of our journey home, all new to my wife and the girls. And though I had been here before, its look was about as new to me as them, a great change having taken place since December, 1836, when I came through from Ionia, there being then only Vermont colony, and Bellevue between there and Marshall. Next day went winding through the hilly, still good country, to Hastings, all the while a changing scene that we much enjoyed. And the day following instead of taking the road to Grand Rapids, turned off on a by one that led north to Lowell, at the junction of the Flat River with the Grand River. Passed through Bowne, the southeast township in this county, where I was encamped when that tremendous snow storm of the 17th and 18th of November, 1842, came on and drove me out of the woods. At Lowell met a number of old acquaintances, Mr. Hooker and wife who used to live at Saranac, Mr. Hatch and Mr. Hine's people. And leaving my wife in the keeping of her old friend, Mrs. Hine, took the girls and came home, all well satisfied with our trip.

Looking west up Canal (now Monroe Avenue) in 1870. Horse-drawn streetcars travel down the center of the street, and poles for the recently installed telegraph system run along the left side of the street. [Grand Rapids Public Library, Fitch Collection, #1982]

~

TRIP ABROAD
CHAPTER V

This journal ends here, there is a later one recording the events of a trip to Europe. This journey was taken in the spring of 1871, when in company with his wife and two older children, Frank W. and Kate W. he sailed for Europe. They had expected to return in the fall but his wife's health prevented them from doing so. The son Frank was sent back for the two younger children, Flora and Lucy. The family then made Geneva their headquarters, and there was born the youngest member of the family, John Helvetaie, named for his father and the country of his birth.

While in Europe Mr. Ball traveled extensively through Germany, Austria, Switzerland, Italy, France and Spain. A journal was kept of these wanderings of two years and a half, but as there are many descriptive trips of European travel we thought best to make only such excerpts as would continue the story of Mr. Ball's life and that might be of some particular interest.

At the beginning of the voyage he writes:"*May 3, 1871.* I am bound across the Atlantic, a thing that has been in my mind ever since I came up the same from Cape Horn on my return from the Pacific in 1834, after that long voyage, it seemed only as the crossing a stream by ferry, to cross it from our side to Europe."

While traveling in Italy in June of the same year he met an old classmate of Dartmouth College in Florence, Mr. George P. Marsh, who was a United States minister and had a wide reputation as a scholar and writer. Of this meeting Mr. Ball writes in his journal:

Meeting G. P. Marsh

"*Florence, June 20.* Being tired I did not try to do much, but in the evening I called on my old classmate, G. P. Marsh, at his pleasant residence in the suburb of the city, and had an interesting, at least to me and apparently to him, an agreeable meeting after fifty years of separation. We were of the Dartmouth College Class of 1820. He referred to the great contrast in course of life. He, having been for many years in the Old World, while I had been in the new settlements or wilderness of America. He, having been some years minister to Turkey in Constantinople and traveling in Egypt and Syria and the past ten years minister to Sardinia and Italy. Found his wife, a second one, a very pleasant and intelligent lady, and they invited me to dinner the next day.

"*June 21.* Went to Powers' studio of sculpture and also Thomas Ball's and looked about their wonderful works in marble. Took a ride over the hill road among the villas on the south side of the river, where one gets a grand view of the city and country and returned by the upper bridge. And then dined, as engaged, with Mr. Marsh."

With the aid of Mr. Marsh, he engaged a commissionaire, an Italian, who knew English, to accompany him to Rome. Of this guide and this trip to Rome he speaks thus quaintly:

"*Rome, June 24.* The weather being pleasant favored our work. I put out with my commissionaire, Ferri, to see Rome, and knowing the ropes well, he led me a terrible round of sight-seeing. So much so, that at evening when I took up my memorandum book, I asked where we had been and what we had seen, for I did not know, and he gave me the names as follows:"

Then comes a most appalling list of objects visited during the day. It was with this untiring energy that Mr. Ball, though then seventy-seven years of age, saw all the principal places of Europe. His wife was seldom able to accompany him on account of her health, this was a great grief to him. But his older children when out of school took trips with him.

Mr. Martin Ryerson

I think the happiest moments of Mr. Ball's sojourn in Europe were these meetings with old friends. In Paris he met Mr. Martin Ryerson, an old Michigan friend. This Mr. Ryerson was the father of Martin A. Ryerson, the donor of the Ryerson Public Library and Campau Park in Grand Rapids.

Mr. Ball writes of this meeting:

"*Paris, June 21, 1872*. A beautiful, clear and comfortable day and friend Ryerson invited me to take a ride and see the destruction of the Communists. We rode down to the river, then up and along it to and through the Bois de Boulogne and so through the city back. Saw everywhere their work of destruction. Buildings entirely demolished, others partially, and ball marks on the buildings in every street. Some of them had been plastered over, but still showed their place. Private property had been rebuilt and re-paired to considerable extent, but public property not at all. From the look almost every street had been contested.

"We talked over Michigan matters, at our leisure, of old friends and acquaintances, alive and gone, of the woods, rivers, and lakes; of our first and frequent meetings, and our respective prior lives.

"He gave me more of an account of himself than I had known before. How at the age of sixteen in 1834 he had run away from his father at Paterson, N. Y. and went to Michigan and first into the employ of a Mr. Richard Godfroy, an Indian trader, and other employments as he could get them. And how and where we first met at Muskegon in the spring of 1837. He, then in the employ of an Indian trader, a Mr. Troutier, at $8.00 a month. How he after pursued the fur trade with the Indians, and tramped the woods on snow shoes to reach their camps and went through exposures and fatigues in pursuing that business for a time.

"And how he went into the lumber business, first in the employ of others, then in a small way on his own account. Ran a mill and then bought it, then bought land and got in his logs, sawed them, and after a time owned his vessel for shipping the lumber to Chicago. And four years ago, when his income from his share of the business amounted to over $100,000 per year, he made up his mind he could afford to stop hard work, so came to travel and reside this side. He had traveled last year going to Norway, Russia and to the Black Sea, returning by the North of Italy. His wife, a Miss Campau, was a Grand Rapids lady with whom I had been acquainted since a child."

Alabama Claim

It was while we were residing in Geneva that the meeting of the Alabama claim took place. The writer well remembers her father taking her sister and herself into the court of the Hotel de Ville and trying to explain to them the historical significance of the meeting going on inside. Thought it did not make much impression on them at the time, it was remembered in after years. He speaks of this event in his diary.

"Geneva, July 17, 1872. The Arbitration between England and the United States is in session here in Geneva. And, of course, a subject of much general interest and speculation as to the result. But persons here knew nothing more of their doings than the countries interested. For their sessions were always with closed doors. I casually saw the arbitrators and counsellors. And had I been more of an interviewing disposition I might, perhaps, have seen more of

Martin Ryerson had this photograph taken in France in 1872, at about the same time he met John Ball. [Grand Rapids Public Library Photograph Collection, #54-34-27]

them, but my curiosity is not very strong in that direction.

I have a great aversion to going beyond the bounds of my own business. Besides, the bare seeing or meeting the talented and titled adds but little to one's own intelligence or consequence.

Geneva seems to be a place, some way, to gain a good deal of historic notice, and the holding of this arbitration here has added another item. Their sessions were in the marriage room of the old Hotel de Ville."

The ensuing year was spent in making many trips either alone or in company with some of his children. The family was keeping house in Geneva where the two younger girls were in school while the older son and daughter were studying German and music in Hanover.

The new baby grew, and when able Mrs. Ball made some trips while Mr. Ball stayed home and looked after the family.

But finally the day came when they turned their faces homeward, the journal says:

Return Home

"On the 18th of June, 1873, left Geneva for good. It had long been our residence, all the time for some of us for almost two years. And there, as seems the usual lot of mortals, we had our joys and sorrows."

After some further travel, giving the entire family an opportunity to see the most interesting points in Europe, they left Liverpool, September 10 on the ***Egypt*** and sailed for New York. Mr. Ball and part of his family reached Grand Rapids the last of the month. He thus closes his diary:

"When we arrived on September 30 we were warmly greeted by our friends and glad again to be in Grand Rapids though so much changed we hardly knew it."

As these two photographs show, until 1873 when several buildings were removed, John Ball and other Grand Rapids residents had to deal with a sharp jog in Monroe Avenue at what is now known as Campau Square. [Grand Rapids Public Library, Fitch Collection, #2027 and #1923]

Grand Rapids' U.S. government building and post office, erected in 1879, near the end of John Ball's life. [Grand Rapids Public Library, Fitch Collection, #1784]

Looking toward the east end of Pearl Street in 1875. On the right is the tower of St. Mark's Church, and in the distance is Central High School. [Grand Rapids Public Library, Fitch Collection, #1783]

LAST YEARS
CHAPTER VI

After Mr. Ball's return from abroad he never went into very active business again though he made his daily trip to the office of Ball & McKee, neither did he renew his connection with the public schools, a connection that had lasted forty years prior to his trip to Europe.

On the occasion of his eightieth birthday, November 12, 1874, his family and some old friends arranged a surprise party, the general invitation was given through the newspapers. The following article was printed in the "Daily Eagle," of that date.

The Hon. John Ball — A Birthday Greeting

To the Editor of the Daily Eagle.

The **Daily Democrat** of this morning contains an invitation to the "friends and acquaintances" of the Hon. John Ball, to meet him at his home on Fulton Street tomorrow (Thursday) evening, the occasion being the eightieth anniversary of his birthday. Doubtless a large number of our citizens will respond to this invitation, for it may truly be said that there are few people of mature years in the city that cannot be claimed among his "friends and acquaintances." It is nearly forty years since Mr. Ball, then in the prime of life, made Grand Rapids his home, and thoroughly identified himself with the best interests of our city. From the days of the old stone school house to the present, he has been the one man above all others that has fully appreciated the importance and utility of our public schools, and by his intelligent and untiring care assisted in bringing them to their present efficient condition. Although he has attained an age when it is expected that interest in public affairs will cease, it cannot be said of our friend that he withholds his sympathy

Eighty-year-old John Ball posed for this photograph in 1875. [Grand Rapids Public Library, Photograph Collection, #54-22-30]

147

and support from anything that deserves it. In all that goes to make a man of pure and blameless life, and a good example to the young men of today, we can point to our venerable friend as worthy of a large following. Mr. Ball has never devoted himself to the acquisition of property, but it is gratifying to know that he has a competence upon which to rely, and is largely endowed with that greatest of all blessings, a good constitution, and such vigorous health that he has good reason to expect ten and perhaps twenty years longer lease of life. Let us all respond to the invitation of his children, and extend to him our hearty congratulations.

An Early Settler.

Passing of the Old Traveler

The ensuing years passed very quietly, varied only by an occasional trip East to visit his relatives. The last trip was taken the summer of 1883, when in company with his youngest daughter, he went to Lansingburgh, N. Y. and was joined there by his sister, Mrs. Deborah Powers, four years older than himself, and her son, Mr. A. E. Powers. The four visited the scenes of their childhood, the old farm on Tenney Hill and other familiar places in New Hampshire.

Mr. Ball's death came the 3rd of February 1884, after an illness of a week. He had retained to the last his unusual mental and physical vigor. Shortly before his death a neighbor seeing him run to catch the street car, remarked, "I am jealous of John Ball, here I am twenty years his junior and I could not run to save my life."

There were many tributes and resolutions to his memory by the bar, the courts and societies of Grand Rapids. I can do no better, however than select the following beautiful tribute given him by a fellow townsman, the Hon. At. S. White, in a paper delivered by him before the Grand River Valley Horticultural Society, January 1904. The paper refers to his gift to the city of Grand Rapids of the first forty acres that comprises its beautiful park known as John Ball Park.

Tribute by At. S. White

"I cannot close this brief and hurriedly written paper without referring to John Ball. He was one of the first to join the State Pomological Society and the first life member of the Grand River Valley Horticultural Society. He was a lover of the field and garden, and among the varied interests to which he devoted his time and means and during his life, horticulture was not the least. But the most notable act of his

Appropriately, a large granite bolder marks the last resting place of John Ball and Mary Webster Ball. [Michael Hoffman photograph]

long and useful life was the provision made in his last will and testament by which the City of Grand Rapids became possessed of the splendid tract of hillside, valley and plain, known as John Ball Park. His generosity and forethought in providing a place where thousands living and yet unborn, may study and enjoy the beauties of nature, freely and as often as they please, has endeared his memory to the people of our city and of our state. Men seek to perpetuate their names by providing for the erection of costly monuments over their remains in the cemeteries, but chiseled granite wears away and the names inscribed thereon are forgotten. If you would write your name on the scroll of the people's benefactors; if you would be regarded as one who loved his fellow men; purchase a suitable tract of ground and give it to the city for park purposes. A $100 monument would bear your name as long as one costing $1,000. A public pleasure ground would preserve your name forever. Remember that the rippling waters on the western hillside, the birds, the flowers, the sun glints and the zephyrs, whisper the name of John Ball, and if you should emulate his example, the same forces of nature and hundreds of thousands of grateful people, would whisper yours."

Tribute by His Daughters

To this we would like to add a word of the deep love and veneration his memory has been held in by his children. At the time of his death his widow called his five children together, and alluding to the very modest competence he had left his family, she spoke of how he had left them something far greater than wealth, "an honored name."

And to his children there was more than this, a memory of a kindly and most conscientious father, to whom no sacrifice was too great to make for their welfare.

We remember him when as little children he was always ready to put down his reading to read to us or to play, or to swing us; and later his care and painstaking anxiety for our education and health; and at all times, especially as we have grown older, are we conscious of his never failing love and goodness.

It has been indeed a wonderful legacy.

Kate Ball Powers
Flora Ball Hopkins
Lucy Ball

Descendants of John Ball posed around his three surviving daughters in Grand Rapids in the summer of 1924. Rear, left to right: Albert Powers Ball, Myron Hopkins, Waldo Ball, Harris Ball, Marshall Tipson Ball, John Rathbone Ball, Albert Ellis Ball. Front, left to right: Virginia Lee Ball, Gertrude Josephine Ball Brokaw, Flora Ball Hopkins, Kate Webster Ball Powers, Lucy Ball, Luie Hopkins Ball, Mary Jean Ball Watson. [Photograph courtesy of John M. Ball]

John Ball's statue remains a popular gathering place for children visiting Kent County's John Ball Park and Zoo.

APPENDIX
John Ball's Scientific Publications

THE

AMERICAN JOURNAL

OF

SCIENCE AND ARTS.

CONDUCTED BY

BENJAMIN SILLIMAN, M. D. LL. D.

Prof. Chem., Min., &c. in Yale Coll.; Cor. Mem. Soc. Arts, Man. and Com.; and For. Mem. Geol. Soc., London; Mem. Roy. Min. Soc., Dresden; Nat. Hist. Soc., Halle; Imp. Agric. Soc., Moscow; Hon. Mem. Lin. Soc., Paris; Nat. Hist. Soc. Belfast, Ire.; Phil. and Lit. Soc. Bristol, Eng.; Mem. of various Lit. and Scien. Soc. in America.

VOL. XXV.—JANUARY, 1834.

NEW HAVEN:

Published and Sold by HEZEKIAH HOWE & Co. and A. H. MALTBY.
Baltimore, E. J. COALE & Co.—*Philadelphia*, J. S. LITTELL and CAREY & HART.—*New York*, G. & C. & H. CARVILL.—*Boston*, HILLIARD, GRAY, LITTLE & WILKINS.

PRINTED BY HEZEKIAH HOWE & CO.

ART. I.—*Remarks upon the Geology, and physical features of the country west of the Rocky Mountains, with Miscellaneous facts*; *by* JOHN BALL, of Troy, N. Y.

I. GEOLOGY AND GEOGRAPHY.

Troy, November 27, 1834.

TO PROFESSOR SILLIMAN.

Dear Sir,—THE article, communicated by Prof. Eaton, and published in Vol. xxv, No. 2, of your Journal, as being founded on a letter he received from me, written on the Columbia river, is found, in some respects to, demand correction; to do which, (in the mean time taking the liberty of stating a few facts, observed during the journey across the continent and a residence in that country,) is the inducement to make this communication.

The route pursued was from Lexington in the State of Missouri, along the road of the Santa Fé traders, about thirty miles beyond the line of that State, thence N. W. to the Kanzas river at the government agency, up that river to the village of the Kanzas Indians, then across the country, encamping on the Blue Creek, to the river Platte against the Grand Island. Soon after leaving the State of Missouri, the country becomes comparatively barren, with little timber except along the streams, and the grass not of sufficient growth to carry fire over the undulating prairies. Sandstone and flinty limestone, both containing many shells were found in *place*, and granite, and red quartzose rock in *bowlders*. Ascending the Platte, over the bottoms of two or three miles in width, to its Forks, you pass no streams coming in from the sandy bluffs, and rolling barren country beyond. The river is very broad and shallow, unfit for any kind of navigation, and sweeps along its due proportion of sand and mud to the main Missouri. At the forks of the Platte were met the first buffaloes; in fact no animals deserving of notice had been seen before, for all appear to have been destroyed by the hunters, or to have fled from their pursuit. From this time buffalo meat was the principal, or rather only article of food, and much of the time it was eaten even without salt. Still from that cause little inconvenience was experienced.

Do carnivorous animals seek licks and salt springs, or herbivorous animals only, and would man live on vegetable food without that condiment, and not suffer in his health? It was now the first of June, and to this time there had been frequent rains, thunder showers coming from the N. E. and the thermometer ranging at noon from 50° to 80°.

Now crossing the South to the North branch of the Platte, our journey was continued up the south side of that river in a W. N. W. direction about three hundred miles, over a country, for the first two hundred miles, similar, in most respects, to that on the main river below. The river was shallow, rapid and muddy; it was about one mile wide with extensive bottoms on one or both sides, which were in many places, incrusted with salt, a mixture of muriate and sulphate of soda; prickly pears, (cactus) and a kind of shrub, called wild sage, were found very extensively over the prairies. The bluffs in our rear were of sandstone, often worn into the form of domes and columns, and the country back afforded so little water that the river rather increased than diminished in size, as we ascended towards the mountains. Thermometer from 75° to 80° at noon. For days, hardly a tree was to be seen, even along the river, but on the Black Hills, which we now reached, stretching at right angles to the course of the river across the country, a few stinted cedars were observed, from the dark appearance of which, probably proceeds the name of these heights. Here the country, for two or three days travelling becomes quite broken, affording refreshing streams and green herbage.

The rock is gray puddingstone, and red sandstone in strata, rising a little towards the west. Then the country becomes open on the north of the river, but mountains appear on the south, and probably continue on in that direction, till they join the Rocky Mountains at the place where they were seen by Major Long. Snow was seen in the higher parts of these mountains, at this time, being the middle of June.

The river tending S. W. we soon crossed it, and continued our journey about west, most of the time along a branch of the Platte, called the Sweetwater. On each side of this river, from a horizontal plain of sand and sandstone, rise ridges of naked granite rock, capped with snow, and to the west could be seen the Wind-river mountain towering high, as white as winter could make it. After continuing on over a country, first of sandstone then of mica slate, with very little timber, we arrived at the head waters of the Sweetwater, about one hundred miles from the place where we had fallen on to that branch, or four hundred from the Forks of the main Platte.

Two hours ride over a smooth prairie, and slight swell, now brought us on to water flowing into the Pacific Ocean; not however, as our Geographers would lead one to expect, upon the waters of the Columbia, but those of the Colorado, of the gulph of California.

In fact, after leaving the main Platte, there is, as far as it has fallen under my observation, no further reliance to be placed upon maps or accounts of the country. The Arkansaw and Lewis river, instead of rising together as has been represented, have not their sources within five hundred miles of each other, the waters from an extensive region flowing south into the Gulph of California.

Standing on the *dividing* ridge between the great Oceans, at an elevation, (judging from the temperature of boiling water,) of about ten thousand feet, you look down East upon the granite mountains already passed, and then to the N. W. upon the snowy Wind-river mountain, rising probably, five thousand feet above the place where you stand. To the South on the height of land, stretches an immense prairie, as far as the limits of vision, with little variation of surfaces, on which are feeding herds of buffaloes; and far to the West, extends north and south, a range of mountains of apparently great elevation. Our journey now lay, for about one hundred miles, in a N. W. direction, along the foot of the Wind-river mountain, across torrents flowing cold from the same, and at about the same elevation; the travelling is sometimes almost obstructed by the granite bowlders, which showed conclusively the character of that mountain. On this mountain are said to rise the Wind-river and other branches of the Yellow Stone, the Missouri, Lewis river and Colorado. It was now the first of July, and we occasionally met with drifts of snow, and frequently had frost at night, although at noon the thermometer ranged from 60° to 70°; the nights were always clear, and the days were, generally, so too, although sometimes attended by slight squalls of rain, snow or hail. In one of the snow squalls, on the 4th of July, we reached a brook flowing into the Lewis river, which we pursued through a

deep break in the mountains, observed some days before in the west. These were found to consist of sparry limestone, and sandstone. Continuing our journey still in a N. W. direction through a broken country, across a larger branch of the Lewis river, and over a mountain of rock similar to the one last mentioned, we came to a plain, open only to the north and surrounded by snowy mountains. The rounded stones and gravel observed here, were all compact gray sandstone. At this place, where we remained some days, we observed that thunder showers come uniformly from the S. W. and not from the W. and N. W. as on the Atlantic.

The last of July we left this place, travelled S. and recrossed the mountain and Lewis river, the country to a great extent being much broken. We met with limestone of different kinds, and with sandstone.

We saw, also, for the first time, nigh the river, at probably one hundred miles from its source, resting on pudding stone, *a stratum of dark porous rock, evidently of volcanic origin.*

Leaving the river and going S. W. over a mountain of sandstone and sparry limestone, arranged in strata, highly inclined to the horizon, we encamped on a creek with high bluffs, composed entirely of volcanic rock, of from fifty to a hundred feet in height, a truly novel and interesting sight! The rock in particular parts, presented somewhat regular columns with small pores, and then irregular masses, with pores often of a size to contain many gallons, the whole having a dark burnt aspect, the upper parts presenting a somewhat stratified appearance. The next day we travelled in the same direction over a high barren plain, *strewed with volcanic glass and sharp broken stones of similar origin,* having little other variety in its surface than the deep channels of the streams.

We continued our journey, for many days, in a leisurely manner, and by a zigzag route, but the general course tended S. W. for a direct distance of about four hundred miles, over ridges, and crossing streams falling into the Lewis River from the S. E.

The atmosphere was still extremely dry, as was indicated by the shrinkage of timber and by extreme thirst. Occasionally, a threatning cloud of small size was formed, attended by thunder, when the rain might be seen falling part of the way to the earth, but seldom did a drop reach its thirsty surface. The plains, along the creeks, were of volcanic rocks, similar to those before described, and most of the intervening mountain ridges were composed of the same limestone that has already been named; but in one instance, we met with a mountain of mica slate and variegated marble, unburnt, while bowlders of the same were strewed over the basaltic plains. In another place we saw a country, broken into granite peaks, which appeared to have undergone the action of fire in different degrees. In some parts, the rocks were crumbling into sand, in other places they were vitrified, so that the particles of quartz appeared like glass; again, the whole appeared to have been melted so far as to form an impure jasper, and again it was transformed into amygdaloid. Often in the streams and elsewhere, we found chalcedony and other silicious minerals, apparently of the same origin.

Against the American falls, we were in sight of the Lewis river, beyond which extended an immense open plain, with a snowy mountain beyond. There was also snow on some of the mountains about us and often frost at night, it being now August; still the temperature at noon was from 70° to 80°. It was said, we passed nigh a large salt lake on the left, into which, flow several fresh rivers. and from which there is no outlet to the ocean, as laid down in maps. And why need we suppose an outlet, since we know that similar lakes, are similarly situated in the center of other continents? And did such an outlet exist would it probably continue salt? The supply of aqueous vapor to the atmosphere, in situations remote from the ocean, appears insufficient for the promotion of vegetation, and thus are producing desert steppes and savannahs, and our own parched prairies of this central region.

The last of August we had reached a country open to the south, with the streams flowing that way, and which do not probably join the Columbia. Here twelve of us, neither of whom had before been west of the Alleganies, bade farewell to our trapping companions, with whom we had travelled for mutual protection, from the Black-foot Indians, whom we had now passed, but gained nothing on our journey as to the distance, to be travelled.

We now turned our course N. W. and set ourselves to seek our way as it were, by *instinct*. We soon reached the head waters of a creek, by pursuing which in a N. W. direction, about one hundred miles, we again fell in with the Lewis river. The first part of the way was through a broken country, of granite, mica slate, clay slate, marble, sparry limestone, (burnt and unburnt,) then over a plain of apparently burnt sandstone, broken only by the creeks, which flow, as it were through clefts, produced by the baking and shrinkage of those plains, at a depth of many hundred feet below their surface.

There are but few places where from the parched plain, on which little water is found, you can descend to the streams below; these places are marked by Indian trails. The stream being once gained, you look up and behold perpendicular bluffs of one hundred feet in height, then by offsets ascending still higher, composed of strata still showing in some places the appearance of grey and red sandstone, in others, strata partly melted down, and presenting the appearance of lava. On one part of this creek gushed out in great numbers, from the porous bluffs, *springs and small creeks of water, apparently pure, at the temperature of 100°.*

We here found the Lewis river, a beautiful stream abounding with salmon, now the main article of food, for long since, we had passed the range of the Buffaloes, which are never seen at a great distance this side of the mountains. Here, and in other places further down the river, were columns of basalt thirty feet high resting on sand, which seemed constantly undermining the rock, and precipitating it far below. The basaltic bluffs sometimes approach the river, and again recede, leaving fine bottoms, over which we travelled in a N. W. course, crossing some creeks coming from the S. W. Thus we continued our journey, passing slowly along, so as to permit our foot-sore horses to recruit. On the last of Sept., we came to the place where the river turns to the north and enters a mountainous country, which shuts it in, in a manner completely to obstruct travelling nigh its banks, but we found an Indian trail leading up a creek, which takes first a west and then a north west direction. through a very mountainous country, which mountains are composed principally of burnt rocks, presenting occasionally however, bowlders of granite and other primitive rocks.

After some days, we came into an oval plain crossed by some creeks; the plain was fifteen miles in diameter, of great fertility and apparently surrounded and enclosed by high mountains. On leaving this plain, our course still continuing north westerly; we ascended a high mountain and travelled along a ridge of the same on an Indian trail, when the whole country to the south and west presented similar ridges, partially clothed with fine timber. These are called the Blue mountains, and are also porous rock. Far in the west could be discerned a conical snowy mountain which proved to be Mount Hood. Two days of severe travelling, with only water at night, and some rose and thorn berries for food, brought us down on to a prairie extending without apparent limit before us. After travelling on this two more days, without even berries, being somewhat dubious as to the proper route on account of the crossing Indian paths, we met with some natives from whom we obtained food. The day following, we reached Fort Wallawalla, which is situated at the mouth of a creek of the same name, nine miles below the mouth of Lewis river.

We had now reached *Terra cognita*, a place inhabited by some half a dozen white men. Here we parted from our faithful horses,

some of which had accompanied us from Missouri, while others were purchased of Indians, who possess them in great numbers; we next hired a boat and guide, and embarked on the Columbia. On this part of the river, and for a long distance below, there is only drift timber, the country being sandy and gravelly, and as you descend, there may be seen on one, often on both shores, the " *High black rocks*," mentioned by Lewis and Clarke, presenting pentagonal columns of from one to five or six feet in diameter, composed of blocks of a slightly concave form, set into each other, till they are raised to a great height.

At the Great Falls commences scattering timber, which at the Cascades, the last rapids before you reach tide water, becomes a dense forest, although there are extensive prairies, still lower down. Here the country is crossed by another range of mountains similar to the Blue mountains, crossed before reaching Wallawalla, and here resting on pudding stone. We now experienced the first rain, in any quantity, since we left the Forks of the Platte, five months before. Descending the river about forty miles, through a low country, we reach Fort Vancouver, the principal depot of the Hudson Bay Co., the west side of the mountains, situated on the north side of the river, one hundred miles from the ocean and six above the mouth of the Wallamette. The country, for many miles about Vancouver, is uninterrupted by mountains, and is mostly wooded. Still, there are many extensive prairies of great fertility, especially along nigh the river. Some of these however, are subject to be flooded by the freshets which occur in June, when the river rises to a great height.

As you descend the river to within forty miles of the ocean, you again meet mountains similar to those at the cascades, in places underlaid by very friable sandstone, and clothed with a very heavy growth of timber.

The Wallamette, (Multnomah,) is of much less extent than has been supposed, not being more than two hundred miles in length. Along its spreading branches above its falls, to which the tide flows, about twenty miles from its mouth, extends a very beautiful valley, of interspersed prairie and woodland. West of this valley, are the mountains extending along the coast, and on the east the range stretches south from the cascades, in which rise Mounts Hood, Ida, and others; also on the north of the Columbia are St. Helen, and other mountains still further north, which are of a conical form, and of such height as always to be clothed with snow, while it seldom falls in the plains. These extinct volcanos, although probably not so high as the Rocky mountains, appear covered with snow at a less elevation, proving the truth of the suggestion, that constant congelation descends much lower on detached mountains, than on elevated plains in the same latitude.

By the following meteorological observations, it will be perceived, that the winters on the Columbia are remarkably mild, there being no snow, and the river being obstructed by ice but a few days during the first part of January. Grass remained in sufficient perfection to afford good feed; and garden vegetables, like turnips and carrots, were not destroyed, but no trees blossomed till March, except willows, alders, &c. Often a frost in clear nights, from Oct. till May.

The difference in temperature in winter, between the eastern and western sides of our continent is indeed very great; even more striking than between the Atlantic side and Europe. It now appears a settled fact, that the eastern sides of the two great continents are much colder in the same latitude than the western, and need we seek further for the cause, than the prevalence of westerly winds in the northern temperate zone, bringing the tempered air of the oceans over the land; and in winter, the wind from the same direction, bearing on the accumulating cold to the eastern sides of the continents.

A return from the Columbia river by water around Cape Horn, touching at the Sandwich and Society Islands gave some opportunity to observe the winds and other phenomena; but having said much already, only one thing more shall be added. · During three weeks stay at Tahite, the tide was observed to rise about one foot, and always highest at twelve o'clock, noon and midnight, and I was informed that this is always the case.

II. METEOROLOGICAL OBSERVATIONS, *made at Fort Vancouver, on the Columbia River and vicinity, in 1832 and 1833.*

November.

Days.	Morn.	Noon.	Wind.	Weather.
1		52	w.	Clear.
2		52	N.W.	"
3	32	55	"	"
4	"	55	"	"
5	"	"	E.	"
6	"	"	"	"
7	"	"	"	"
8	"	"	N.W.	"
9	"	"	"	"
10	"	"	E.	"
11	"	"	"	"
12	"	"	"	"
13	"	"	"	"
14	"	"	"	"
15		"	S.E.	Rain.
16		58	N.W.	Clear.
17		50	E.	"
18		45	S.E.	Rain.
19		45	"	"
20		50	"	"
21		50	"	"
22		46	N.W.	Cloudy.
23		50	"	"
24		50	S.W.	Showery.
25		50	S.E.	Rain.
26		50	"	"
27	48	50	"	"
28	"	54	N.W.	Cloudy.
29	32	49	"	Clear.
30	32	49	"	"

(col "Not observed." in Morn. for 1–26)

December.

Days.	Morn.	Noon.	Wind.	Weather.
1	40	40	S.E.	Rain.
2	40	42	"	"
3	48	50	"	"
4	40	47	"	Pleasant.
5	41	48	"	Rain.
6	40	47	"	Pleasant.
7	32	40	"	"
8	32	40	N.W.	Cloudy.
9	38	44	S.E.	Pleasant.
10	37	43	"	Rain.
11	38	42	"	"
12	38	42	"	"
13	38	46	S.	Showery.
14	38	43	S.E.	Rain.
15	44	54	S.	"
16	50	48	N.W.	"
17	53	55	S.E.	"
18	52	51	"	"
19	44	49	"	"
20	45	48	"	"
21	42	46	S.	Showery.
22	40	41	"	Rain.
23	40	43	"	Showery.
24	41	44	"	"
25	39	44	"	"
26	40	46	S.E.	Rain & Shine.
27	40	45	"	"
28	41	43	"	Rain.
29	41	43	N.W.	Showery
30	36	42	"	Pleasant.
31	32	44	"	"

January.

Days.	Morn.	Noon.	Wind.	Weather.
1	52	40	N.W.	Cloudy.
2	35	40	"	"
3	38	45	"	"
4	38	42	"	Clear.
5	32	43	E.	"
6	32	39	"	"
7	32	39	"	"
8	28	35	"	"
9	25	34	"	"
10	32	32	"	"
11	32	40	"	"
12	25	37	"	"
13	18	33	"	"
14	17	32	"	"
15	17	33	"	"
16	20	33	"	"
17	20	28	"	"
18	26	39	S.E.	Hail.
19	31	40	"	Rain.
20	44	55	S.	Showery.
21	54	55	"	"
22	54	58	S.E.	Rain.
23	52	54	"	"
24	40	48	"	"
25	32	42	N.W.	Pleasant.
26	32	44	"	"
27	40	50	S.	"

February.

Days.	Morn.	Noon.	Wind.	Weather.
28	40	46	S.E.	Showery.
29	39	44	Varies.	"
30	39	45	"	"
31	40	47	"	Pleasant
1	40	47	Varies.	Showery.
2	40	46	S.E.	"
3	46	52	"	Pleasant.
4	46	50	"	Rainy.
5	45	51	"	"
6	47	51	"	"
7	43	47	N.W.	Pleasant.
8	43	47	"	"
9	40	44	N.E.	"
10	32	45	"	"
11	32	45	S.W.	"
12	38	46	"	Showery.
13	38	48	S.	"
14	40	50	"	Pleasant.
15	42	50	w.	Showery.
16	33	45	S.	Cloudy.
17	40	50	"	Rain.
18	41	50	S.E.	"
19	43	51	S.	Showery.
20	40	53	N W.	Pleasant.
21	42	50	"	"
22	37	45	"	"
23	32	44	"	"
24	32	44	"	"
25	32	45	"	"
26	32	50	w.	"
27	32	55	E.	"
28	37	55	S.E.	"

March.

Days.	Morn.	Noon.	Wind.	Weather.
1	40	50	S.E.	Rain.
2	33	55	N.W.	Clear.
3	"	55	"	"
4	"	57	"	"
5	"	57	"	"
6	"	58	"	"
7	"	59	"	"
8	"	60	"	"
9	"	60	"	"
10	"	55	S. to w.	Cloudy.
11	"	56	"	"
12	"	50	"	Rainy.
13	38	51	"	Cloudy
14	38	50	"	"
15	37	"	"	"
16	38	"	S.	Showery.
17	38	"	"	"
18	33	"	w.	Cloudy.
19	"	58	"	Pleasant.
20	"	51	S. to w.	"
21	40	55	"	"
22	33	50	S.E.	Rain
23	"	"	"	Pleasant.
24	"	"	"	"
25	"	"	S. to w.	Showery.
26	"	55	"	"
27	"	60	"	"
28	"	59	"	"
29	40	56	"	"
30	39	55	"	"
31	40	"	"	"

April.

Days.	Morn.	Noon.	Wind.	Weather.
1	32	50	S. to w.	Showery.
2	"	58	N.W.	Clear.
3	40	51	S.E.	Rain.
4	"	49	w.	Clear.
5	"	50	"	Showery.
6	"	45	"	Hail.
7	"	66	S. to w.	Rain.
8	"	51	"	Hail.
9	"	50	"	Rain & Shine.
10	"	50	"	"
11	"	54	"	"
12	32	60	E. to w.	Clear.
13	"	61	"	"
14	"	68	"	"
15	"	70	w	Cloudy.
16	38	63	"	Rain.
17	40	65	"	Cloudy.
18	40	60	"	"
19	32	55	S.	"
20	39	55	"	Rain.
21	40	63	"	Cloudy.

May.

Days.	Morn.	Noon.	Wind.	Weather.
1	38	50	S. to w.	Showery.
2	32	54	N.W.	Clear.
3	"	55	"	"
4			S.w.	Thun.show'rs.
5	39	"	S.E.	Cloudy.
6	40	"	"	Rain.
7	41	"	w.	Showery.
8	41	"	"	"
9	42	"	"	"
10	45	60	N.W.	Clear.
11	"	75	"	"
12	"	"	"	"
13	"	65	w.	Showery.
14	"	61	"	"
15	"	60	"	"
16	"	65	"	Cloudy.
17	"	61	"	"
18	"	62	"	Clear.
19	"	65	S.	"
20	"	67	S.w.	Showery.
21	"	70	w.	"
22	"	70	S. to w.	Cloudy.
23	"	67	"	"
24	54	65	"	Clear.
25	41	68	"	"
26	40	75	"	"
27	40	72	"	"
28	55	70	"	"
29	56	70	"	Cloudy.
30	60	71	S.E.	Rain.
31	"	"	"	Showery.

June.

Days.	Morn.	Noon.	Wind.	Weather.
1	50	70	S. to w.	Showery.
2	"	"	"	"
3	"	"	"	"
4	"	"	"	Cloudy.
5	"	80	"	Clear.
6	"	"	E. to w.	"
7	"	"	w.	Showery.
8	"	75	"	Cloudy.
9	"	76	"	Clear.
10	"	78	N.	"
11	"	92	"	"
12	55	95	"	"
13	"	88	"	"
14	"	88	"	"
15	"	72	w.	Cloudy.
16	"	55	S.	Thun. show'rs.
17	"	70	S. to w.	Cloudy.
18	"	"	"	"
19	50	75	N.E. to w.	Clear.
20	"	"	"	"
21	"	"	"	"
22	"	"	"	"
23	"	"	"	"
24	"	80	"	"
25	"	70	"	Cloudy.
26	"	"	"	"
27	45	"	N.W.	"
28	"	"	"	"
29	"	"	S.E. to w.	"
30	60	80	"	"

July.

Days.	Morn.	Noon.	Wind.	Weather.
1	60	80	N.W.	Pleasant.
2	55	85	"	Clear.
3	53	80	"	"
4	55	80	w.	"
5	53	84	E. to w.	"
6	46	78	"	"
7	59	79	S.E. to S.w.	Showery.
8	60	75	"	"
9	53	80	"	Cloudy.
10	60	81	"	"
11	53	74	N.W.	"
12	47	79	"	Clear.
13	52	95	"	"
14	56	91	"	"
15	47	84	w.	"
16	50	85	"	"
17	47	73	"	Thunder.
18	52	80	E. to w.	"
19	45	85	N.w.	Cloudy.
20	41	82	N.	Clear.
21	54	73	"	"
22	40	81	"	"
23	43	83	S.w.	"
24	54	78	"	"
25	48	76	N.W.	Cloudy.
26	44	82	E. to w.	Clear.

August.

Days.	Morn.	Noon.	Wind.	Weather.
27	45	85	"	"
28	48	80	"	"
29	50	81	"	"
30	55	82	N.E.	"
31	55	85	"	"
1	53	93	Northerly	Clear.
2	53	93	"	"
3	53	93	"	"
4	"	93	"	"
5	48	83	"	"
6	50	85	Southerly.	"
7	52	72	"	Cloudy.
8	58	72	S.w	"
9	60	69	"	"
10	55	75	w.	"
11	53	77	"	"
12	54	80	N.W.	"
13	46	80	N.E.	"
14	47	87	"	"
15	47	83	"	"
16	53	78	N.w.	Cloudy.
17	44	78	"	"
18	50	77	S.E.	"
19	53	72	w.	"
20	53	77	N.W.	Clear.
21	46	"	"	"
22	55	"	"	"
23	50	"	"	"
24	59	"	"	"
25	48	81	N.E.	"
26	52	95	E.	"
27	47	90	S.w.	Cloudy.
28	63	77	"	"
29	56	79	"	"
30	59	69	"	Showery.
31	52	67	"	"

September.

Days.	Morn.	Noon.	Wind.	Weather.
1	52	65	N.W.	Showery.
2	54	71	"	"
3	47	73	"	Cloudy.
4	44	81	"	"
5	54	76	"	"
6	43	79	N.	Clear.
7	44	76	"	"
8	47	85	"	"
9	55	88	"	"
10	53	80	S.	"
11	50	78	"	Cloudy.
12	51	69	S.w.	Rain.
13	48	67	"	Showery.
14	54	60	w.	"
15	50	65	Varies.	Cloudy.
16	51	69	"	"
17	48	67	"	"
18	54	71	"	"
19	48	67	N.E.	Clear.
20	48	72	"	"
21	55	74	Varies.	"
22	57	75	"	Rain.
23	53	78	"	Cloudy.
24	56	79	"	"
25	60	62	N.E.	"
26	55	58	S.E.	Rain.
27	50	70	"	Cloudy.
28	50	57	S.w.	Rain.
29	52	62	N.w	Cloudy.
30	51	63	"	"

October

Days.	Morn.	Noon.	Wind.	Weather.
1	50	56	S.E.	Cloudy.
2	55	66	"	Rain.
3	53	63	N.W.	Squally.
4	52	56	N.E.	Clear.
5	52	66	"	"
6	50	65	w.	Cloudy.
7	61	63	"	"
8	52	63	E.	"
9	52	62	S.E.	"
10	55	63	"	Rain.
11	55	64	w.	"
12	52	63	N.W.	Cloudy.
13	51	60	"	"
14	52	58	"	"
15	50	58	"	"
16	50	55	E.	"
17	50	65	"	"
18	50	57	"	Clear.
19	"	55	S.w.	Cloudy.
20	"	52	"	"
21	"	52	"	"
22	"	54	"	"
23	"	55	"	"
24	"	60	"	"
25	"	56	S.E.	Clear.
26	"	55	E.	"
27	"	51	S.w.	Rain.
28	"	50	S.E.	"
29	"	55	"	"
30	"	50	"	"
31	"	50	"	"

III. MISCELLANEOUS FACTS.

In answer to various inquiries addressed by the editor to **Mr. Ball,** after the perusal of the foregoing communication, he has been so obliging as to add the following notices which, we cannot doubt, will add to the interest of his valuable paper.

Events, Commencement and Motives of the Journey.

Mr. Ball left Baltimore, March 27, 1832, and passed by the rail road, and national road to Brownsville on the Monongahola, thence by steamboat to the Ohio, and then down that river, and up the Mississippi and Missouri, to Lexington, in the State of Missouri, where, he and his companions arrived April 29. He did not describe the countries, whose geological sections are so well exhibited on the rail roads and the rivers, because it has been done by others. Leisure, a strong desire to roam, especially to see the vast and untamed regions of the utmost west and the solemn ocean-barrier of the immense Pacific, rather than motives of personal advantage, induced him to unite himself to a party of adventurers, who were about to cross the Rocky Mountains.

On the 7th day of May, 1832, says Mr. Ball, we, the twelve who crossed the continent, with about as many more, who *started* with that intention, joined ourselves to a trading party of about seventy men, headed by a Mr. Wm. Sublette, and commenced our march, crossing the line of the State of Missouri on the 13th, as stated in my communication. The whole band of horses and mules used for the purpose of riding and packing goods, amounted to almost three hundred. We marched and encamped in the usual way of fur traders, always prepared to act on the defensive; and after being out a few days, subsisting entirely by the chase,—were, one night, on the mountains, fired upon by the Black Foot Indians, and lost some horses; and at another time, had a battle with Indians of the same tribe, when five trappers were killed. On the Lewis and Columbia, we subsisted chiefly on Salmon—at one time, we had nothing for four or five days, except for the two first days, some small fruit—but we had horses with us, and of course, ran no risk of starvation.

The difference of longitude between St. Louis and the mouth of the Columbia, is about 34°; therefore, by making an allowance of about 7° difference of latitude, with the diminished distance between the parallels of longitude, I estimated the direct distance to be about eighteen hundred miles. The entire distance which we travelled with horses at two thousand miles, while my companions considered it much greater; the distance up the Missouri and down the Columbia, travelled by water, at seven or eight hundred miles; therefore the whole distance travelled, from St. Louis, was about twenty eight hundred—one thousand more than the direct distance. The distance I travelled by land, was, in all, say five thousand, and by water, twenty thousand, equal to twenty five thousand, or the entire circumference of the globe.

Rocks, Springs and Physical features.

As to the rocks, you have, I presume, specimens from the Sandwich or Society Islands; for, although I have said that there is no appearance of craters on the continent: still the general aspect of the rock, is often precisely the same as in those Islands—black porous masses of a specific gravity little less than granite—is it not amygdaloid? The basalt on the Columbia more resembles the specimens of the Giant's Causeway, than the rock on the west of the Hudson, the Palisadoes, and that near your residence at New Haven. In fact, all the rocks show much stronger marks of ignition. I brought a few small specimens, which I wish you could see. I saw no *currents* of lava, or masses flowing through vallies, unless the columnar basalt, resting, sometimes on sand, along the Lewis and Columbia rivers, are to be considered such. I saw no pumice stone, but what I spoke of as cinders or scoriæ, would perhaps, be better described as resembling almost precisely over burnt brick or earthen ware. At the top of the deep ravines through which the creeks ran, the rocks sometimes presented that appearance, as though it *there* underwent the greatest heat. I do not recollect that I saw any dykes or walls of trap or lava or basalt, presenting an appearance as though intruded through other rock, or any volcanic craters or *balls* or lips of eruption-shapes or forms, except Mount Hood, &c. I earnestly wish it were in my power to describe the country so that you could *see* it, for it is well worth seeing.

The rock often had a vitrified appearance, and although not exactly tumefied, it presented pores of all dimensions, even to the capacity of twenty gallons; these cavities are of a kettle form—and the rock that was burnt differed as much from that which was not, as burnt brick or earthen from the clay from which they are made, or glass from the silex. Sometimes I thought the rock to be basalt, which, on the slightest examination, could be seen to be, at least in places, as evidently mica slate, or granite or sandstone, as though it had not equally strong marks of ignition. Did not the whole undergo this change from heat, when under water? May not a country undergo a baking or hardening, the gases escaping through crevices and fissures, without forming craters.

As to streams and springs, we often met with brooks of a size to carry a flour mill, coming out of the cavernous rock; they were of the usual temperature of the water at the same season in the rivers, and except along one creek, we saw but few springs, that were remarkably warm. On this they were very abundant, gushing out of the cavernous bluffs, at the temperature of 100°, and in sufficient quantity to warm the water of a creek forty yards wide, so as to render it unpleasant to drink—I saw no jetting springs, or those boiling from gas.

The whole country over which we travelled, for more than a thousand miles before reaching the ocean, presents these appearances of ignition, with the exception, perhaps, of one eighth part of the rocks. The soil was in most places barren, till you approach the ocean, for there is not a sufficient quantity of water retained near the surface to promote vegetation, the soil being porous, and the supply of rain is small.

Cultivation of Land—Departure.

In March of 1833, having no opportunity to leave the country, except by recrossing the mountains, and not knowing what might occur in the course of six months, I procured seeds, implements, &c. of the Hudson Bay Company, went up the Multnomah river about fifty miles from the fort, where some of the Canadian French, and half breeds had commenced farming, and with the help of one American and an Indian, enclosed some prairie ground, built a log house and raised a crop of wheat—and would have remained in that country could I have had a few good neighbors as associates, for I did not feel inclined to fall into the customs of the country and become identified with the natives. Therefore on application to the Company, about to send a ship to the Sandwich Islands, in the ensuing October, I obtained a passage—for the company were, in this, and in every thing, polite and accommodating. Of the twelve who reached the Columbia, one died, three re-crossed the mountains, the others, except myself, went to sea in the Pacific, or into the employment of the Company.

The North Western Coast.

On the 18th of Oct., 1833, we sailed from the Columbia river, for California. The coast is bold and the country immediately back consists principally of broken mountains, clothed with trees at some distance down the coast, but before you reach the Bay of St. Francisco, the country becomes prairie. So the continent below the latitude of 40° appears to be entirely prairie from the Pacific to Missouri, Arkansaw and Texas: with the usual exception of timber growing, occasionally, on the rivers and mountains. Mules have been bought

155

in Upper California and brought to the American market.

The country about the Bay of St. Francisco, is beautifully diversified with hills, mountains and plains, with occasionally a clump of trees; on the plains, graze immense herds of horses and cattle both wild and tame. The rock, as far as observed, was supposed to be Serpentine. The climate was delightful, for the range of the thermometer, during most of the month of Nov. was from 52° to 58°, and the sky serene—and it is said they never have frost, although in the latitude of St. Louis, Cincinnati and Washington. The temperature at sea till we reached the trade winds, was from 50° to 60°; then it gradually rose till, at the Sandwich Islands on the first of January 1834, its range was from 70° to 77°; I was informed that it sometimes rises as high as 85°. The greatest range is probably about 15°, the air being always tempered by the breezes from the sea, producing a delightful climate.

Features of Oahu.

As you approach the Island of Oahu, you behold high and precipitous mountains of curved, spiral and fantastic forms, rising to the height of from three to four thousand feet, and as you approach nearer, you will see rising from the plains along the coast, to the height of a few hundred feet, crater-formed hills, which although now clothed with grass, are of as perfect symmetry as they were when emitting flames. About one mile back of Honolulu, the principal town of these Islands, rises one of these craters, called the *Punch Bowl*; you at first ascend over a gradual slope where you see coral rocks partially burned, elevated some two or three hundred feet above their original place at the level of the ocean. Then the ascent is more abrupt, winding by a zigzag path, till one stands on a rim of rock, and before him sees a beautiful grass-clad basin, of about half a mile in circuit, surrounded by a similar rim, except at one place, where it is broken away to the depth of the basin.

Volcanic and Coral Rocks.

Not a fragment of rock was found at this or the Island of Tahiti, except what was volcanic or coral, and none is said to exist in those seas. Did the waves of the ocean once roll from America to China and New Holland, without an islet to interrupt their course, till the coral insect raised up its circular wall, from within which, the volcano burst forth? For, the low coral islands are generally of a crescent or circular form, and around the mountainous islands are found coral reefs. The Sandwich and Society Islands are all mountainous, each cluster containing about ten islands. In crossing the equator, and generally between the tropics, the same phenomena were observed on that side, as observed by Humboldt on this. The temperature was from 80° to 83°, the currents of the water and air were westward, but the upper strata of clouds show the wind above to be in the opposite direction. The temperature of the water was generally 81°.

Society Islands.

The approach to the Society Islands, presents a truly romantic appearance, and when we reached their reefs and sandy shores, shaded with cocoa trees and backed by varied and rich vegetation, we could feel no surprise at the delight of the seamen, so often described. Still, the number of the natives is said to have diminished one half in twenty five years, although the climate appears not unhealthy; but the generous natives of these numerous islands, pass away as do those of the American continent at the approach of Europeans.

Passage around Cape Horn—Arrival.

We passed Cape Horn the first of May; when above lat. 50°, we had frequent squalls of snow and hail, but it froze only once, and then when directly off the Cape, the water was at 43°, while the air was from that down to 32°, and extremely damp, the sun being, at noon, but 17° high in the north.

We hear much of the uniformity of the Trade winds, but in that ocean the winds above 30° of N. and S. lat., appear to blow almost as constantly from the west as the trades from the east. There is always a difficulty in getting from the Atlantic into the Pacific, but in returning, the wind, as uniformly, favors the navigator. That ocean, from its extent, gives the winds their natural play, let the reason of their courses be what it may. Stopping at Brazil, we reached Norfolk on the 16th of July last, and this place on the 22d, and observed, in this ocean, similar phenomena to those seen in the other.

THE

AMERICAN JOURNAL

OF

SCIENCE AND ARTS.

VOL. XXVIII.—JULY, 1835.

ART. XII.—*Geology and Meteorology west of the Rocky Mountains.*

(Communicated by Prof. Amos Eaton of the Rensselaer School.)

In exhibiting a transverse section across North America, at page 59 of 2d Ed. Geological Text Book, I was compelled to admit the word *unknown*, west of the Rocky Mountains. While I was preparing that work, John Ball, Esq., a graduate of Dartmouth College; Counsellor at Law, &c. was my pupil in Natural History. In less than twenty months from the time of his leaving this school, he furnished me with all that is necessary for filling up that blank in the profile.

I pledge myself for Mr Ball's accuracy, because *I know him*. He is most scrupulously exact in relating scientific truths, and a very accurate observer. I received his last letter, which he wrote to any part of this district, by the Fur Company, *via* Canada, dated March 3d, 1833, at Fort Vancouver, near the mouth of the Oregon, (Columbia river.)

The geology of the country west of the Rocky Mountains is remarkably simple and uniform. The general underlying rock is the Red sandstone, which some English geologists call saliferous rock, and which characterizes the red sandstone group of De La Beche. It is the same which contains the salt springs of the western part of the State of New York, and which underlies the basaltic rocks (greenstone trap) of Connecticut and Hudson rivers. It is the same which Dr. Edwin James describes, (See Long's Expedition) as the chief basis rock between the Rocky Mountains and the Mississippi. Therefore the geology of the east and west sides of the Rocky Mountains is remarkably alike. Mr. Ball says, " the Rocky Mountain rises up from the midst as it were of a horizontal sea of red sandstone; as if some tremendous force had driven it upwards, like an island forced up from the depths of the ocean."

Mr. B. agrees with Dr. James, in comparing the Rocky Mountains with Humboldt's description of the Andes; of which it is probably a continuation. It consists of slaty granite (gneiss) Hornblende rock, talcose slate, and some mica-slate. The talcose slate is probably a continuation of that which contains the gold of Mexico.

Mr. Ball considers almost the whole country as volcanic, if basaltic rocks resting on red sandstone are to be considered as volcanic. In numerous localities the red sandstone resembles the half-melted bricks which surround the flues in a kiln. The basalt (greenstone trap) has the appearance of scoriæ or smith's slag, at and near the base of basaltic columns. These columns are mostly regular polyhedra, often as perfectly pentahedral as those brought from the Giant's Causeway in Ireland.

The red sandstone often rises in peaks, like those on Connecticut River, between Northampton and Greenfield, several hundred feet in height; while channels of rivers open the rocks at their bases to a great depth. The grey puddingstone, which often caps the highest peaks, seems to defend it from the rapid disintegration to which the sandstone is subject. Many of these prominences are covered with eternal snow, never melting in the greatest heat of summer.

Near the west side of the Rocky Mountains, and along the upper branches of the Colorado, which falls into the Gulf of California; and the Lewis river, which unites with the Oregon, Mr. Ball found first graywacke and sparry lime rock. But he soon entered upon the red sandstone region; which continues, as the basis rock to the Pacific. After travelling about one hundred miles from the Rocky Mountains, the primitive boulders disappeared. The country is often very mountainous along the route to the Pacific; but the mountains are red sandstone, grey puddingstone, or basalt. Such is the simplicity and uniformity of the geology of the vast region west of the Rocky Mountains, that it can all be told in one sentence of six lines.

The most astonishing facts, communicated by Mr. Ball, relate to the Meteorology of that country. From the first of June 1832, to the first of November, (5 months) less than one inch of rain fell between the Rocky Mountains, and a strip of land from one hundred and fifty to two hundred miles in width bordering on the Pacific. Vegetation is exceedingly scanty thus far; and profuse beyond description as far as rains extend. For many hundred miles, the sky is always serene by night; and scarcely a cloud is seen by day. While crossing the barren plains, Mr. B. observed, that the flowers of plants greatly exceeded the herbage in size and brilliancy. All parts of the plants were much stinted in growth excepting the fructification. It seemed to him as if nature had manifested more solicitude for the reproduction of species there, than for their luxuriance.

The growth of all vegetables, along the two hundred mile border of the Pacific, is astonishingly profuse. The Deputy Governor of the English Fur Company, (Mc. Laughlin) raised twelve hundred bushels of wheat, a great quantity of barley, peas, potatoes, &c., last summer, (1832). He had purchased in California a considerable number of cattle, sheep, goats, swine, &c., which he had increased to four or five hundred. He lent Mr. B. oxen, plough, cows, axes, &c., and he commenced ploughing in January, in Lat. 45° 37′.—The vegetables of the preceding season were still standing in gardens untouched by frost. New grass had sprung up sufficiently for excellent pasture. Fruit trees were in full blossom.

The society of gentlemen at this place (Fort Vancouver, Lat. 45° 37′, Lon. 122° 37′) is good, but they have natives for wives. They are selected from a very friendly tribe of Indians, who are averse to war and exceedingly peaceable. These wives soon learn English cookery, and perform other domestic duties in good style. Mr. Ball devotes part of his time to teaching the women and children. As the Indians near Rocky Mountain stole his clothes, excepting what he wore out, he arrived at Vancouver in Buffalo skins. The ladies immediately furnished him in the best style of the place.

The meteorological observations at the end of this article exhibit the remarkable uniformity of temperature through the winter months.

Though the latitude is nearly that of Montreal, mowing and curing hay are unnecessary; for cattle graze on fresh growing grass through the winter. Cordier's theory of internal heat, particularly that part of it, which supposes some portions of the earth better conductors of caloric than others, would seem to derive some plausible support from that temperature which seems neither to be influenced by the sun's rays, nor by elevation.

I have made these selections, instead of publishing Mr. B.'s letter, because he wrote in a familiar style, without any view to its publication.

From June 12th to October 1, while travelling West from the Rocky Mountain across the Barrens, (says Mr. B.) we had scarcely any rain; and the heat ranged from 60° to 89°. In the fertile regions, the heat is generally much lower.

This meteorological table presents a subject for interesting enquiry. While the temperature was for some days from 12° to 15° below freezing, the most delicate fruit trees remained in full blossom, without being affected by frost. Is the earth absolutely warmed in a degree, uncommon in other countries, by internal heat? Is it to the same cause that we are to ascribe the rapid growth of vegetables, where the earth receives a due quantity of rain? Mr. Ball saw numerous warm springs issuing from beneath basaltic rocks along Lewis river, &c. The temperature of the water was generally about 100° Fah.

Troy, Sept. 6, 1833.   AMOS EATON.

157